LIFE THOUGHTS

FROM

PULPITS AND FROM POETS.

SELECTED BY

ALFRED I. HOLMES.

A SELECTION OF BEAUTIFUL THOUGHTS OF EMINENT CLERGYMEN, REPRESENTING ALL THE VARIOUS DENOMINATIONS; ALSO MANY BEAUTIFUL GEMS FROM THE POETS.

BROOKLYN, N. Y.:

PUBLISHED BY

THE AUTHOR, A. I. HOLMES,

180 NASSAU STREET.

1873.

Stereotyped at
THE WOMEN'S PRINTING HOUSE,
Eighth Street and Avenue A,
New York.

PREFACE.

WHO that is a lover of art would not be pleased to visit a gallery, where he could see displayed beautiful statuary, from the hands of eminent sculptors, or behold beautiful paintings from the most renowned masters of the art; oı who, being a lover of flowers, would not prize a walk through some magnificent garden, where there.is every variety and profusion of fruits and flowers, which have been cultured and arranged by eminent gardeners.

Now, what gems of painting or statuary are in the world of art, or what flowers are in nature, we believe these gems of thought, culled from the religious literary world, to be to the lover of religious literature.

The reader, as he peruses these pages, will recognize many illustrious names, standing out as luminous stars in American and English pulpits. Every thing of a sectarian character is omitted, and we believe that every thought can be appreciated by the Christian reader of any denomination. And the reader will find that these gems, emanating in many different minds, will be very diverse in their character: some well calculated to draw a tear, while others will most assuredly excite a smile.

Many of them cannot fail to interest and instruct the young, while others will drive away the melancholy and brighten the declining path of the aged. Like a man of *thoughts*, a book of thoughts ought to be a desirable companion, especially one which may contribute to arrest the careless and wandering, and to animate the sincere and virtuous. And we believe the reader who loves entertainment mingled with instruction, will peruse these pages with pleasure.

THE AUTHOR.

LIFE THOUGHTS.

A MOTHER sat by the window, sorrowing for her babe, and looking across the road into the burying-ground. Her boy, ten years old, came lovingly to her and said, —

"Mother, why do you cry? I have often seen you very tired of holding the baby; but now Jesus will hold her, and if he should get tired he will pass her all around among the angels."

Rev. F. G. Clark.

PASSED from our sight, within the veil,
 Still compassed by the Father's care;
Why should our hearts their loss bewail,
 And sorrow darken to despair?

They breathe the fragrance of the flowers
 From the fair groves of Eden shed—
Still ours, though gone before, still ours
 Are they we call the Early Dead.

W. H. Burleigh.

IN a glen of the Scotch Highlands lived a poor widow, whose only daughter had been decoyed to a large city, and into a life of profligacy and shame. The mother went after her, sought her out, and pleaded with her to come home. The daughter relented, and was returning home, when a new temptation assailed her, and she went back to her dark career of sin. The mother cast herself for help on the widow's God.

Late and lonely sat the poor widow one night, watching the flickering embers on the hearth, when suddenly she heard the door creak and the sound of a bare foot on the cabin floor. She turned to see, and lo! her daughter! As soon as the heart-breaking confession was over, the daughter inquired, "How came it, mother, that, at this late hour of the night, I found the latch of the door open?"—"*That latch*," replied the mother, "*has never been shut, day or night*, since you left me. I feared that, if you came and found it fastened, you might go away, and never return again."

Blessed mother! her heart kept its hold on the latch of that ever-open door. Oh! wanderer from God! oh! impenitent soul! Christ Jesus has set open a door into heaven for you when he shed his blood for your sins. That latch has never been shut against you, day or night, since you began to wander. The door is not only open, but entrance is easy.

Rev. Theo. L. Cuyler.

IN a wonderful panorama exhibited of the Pilgrim's Progress, I remember one scene. It was a rude, uncouth cross. It rather repelled than excited emotion, and I wondered as I saw the painting, why they should exhibit such a thing as that. All the others were beautiful: it was without form or comeliness. As we were gazing, a light was suddenly thrown upon it, a little film of gauze was raised, and, instead of this rude and rough picture, there was the most sublime, exalted conception of the Cross which I have ever seen in art. Now, what was there the second time that was not there the first? What was added? It was light—nothing but light. And if you do not understand the Bible, my dear brother, go home and ask God to throw light upon it.

Rev. Stephen H. Tyng, Jr.

I HAVE no faith in that woman who talks of grace and glory abroad and uses no soap at home. Let the buttons be on the shirts, let the children's socks be mended, let the roast mutton be done to a turn, let the house be as neat as a new pin, and the home be as happy as home can be; and then, when the cannon balls, and the marbles, and the shots, and even the grains of sand, are all in the box, even then there will be room for those little deeds of love and faith which, in my Master's name I seek of you who love his appearing. Serve God by doing common actions in a heavenly spirit, and then, if your daily calling only leaves you cracks and crevices of time, fill these up with holy service. To use the apostle's words, "As we have opportunity, let us do good unto all men."

Spurgeon.

HOW blest the sacred tie that binds,
In sweet communion, kindred minds!
How swift the heavenly course they run,
Whose hearts and faith and hopes are one!
Nor shall the glowing flame expire,
When dimly burns frail nature's fire;
Then shall they meet in realms above,
A heaven of joy, a heaven of love.

Mrs. Barbauld.

PHILOSOPHERS tell us that every uttered word produces a vibration in the atmosphere: an ingenious theory has therefore been broached that these vibrations never entirely cease! If this were true, we should still be moving among the inaudible words of all our progenitors. This seems fanciful in natural philosophy; but there is a sense in which every uttered word *lives for ever.* It lives in its influence on the speaker—in its influence on others. Paul's voice echoes still; millions of God's faithful messengers, being dead, yet speak!

Rev. Theo. L. Cuyler.

WE have seen a child weeping bitterly on his mother's knee, while the train was carrying him triumphantly on. "Poor child!" we thought, "why weepest thou? Thy mother's arms are around thee, thy mother's eye is fixed upon thee, and that bustle and rapidity, so strange and dreadful to thee, are but carrying thee faster to thy home." Thus man wails and cries, with God above, God around, God below, and God before him.

G. Gilfillan.

BY the thorn-road, and none other,
Is the mount of vision won;
Tread it without shrinking, brother!
Jesus trod it: press thou on!

S. Johnson.

WHILE I was in Europe, I stood in a grand cathedral, admiring the paintings and statuary, when a friend called my attention to the dome overhead. I looked upward to the ceiling far above us, but could see only a cloudlike hue. Soon, however, the confusion vanished, and angelic faces were looking down upon us from every part of the magnificent dome. It was a beautiful thought of the artist. And so the great cloud of witnesses gaze lovingly upon every worker for Christ. Sometimes I see only clouds about me; but they melt away, and I can behold the saints, the loved gone before me — with looks of encouragement and affection, filling the heavens around and above me.

Bishop Simpson.

RIGHT here at the foot of the cross, and here alone, can we find inspiration at once for the deepest piety and the purest philanthropy. See that degraded man: why do I love him? Because he is lovely? No; but because Christ died for him and for me. The golden chain which binds me to him passes through the heart of Christ. The broken links of brotherhood are welded together by being welded to Jesus.

Rev. C. D. Foss.

THERE is many and many a candle that will burn discreetly in a room where the air is still, which if you take it into the wind, flares and flutters and burns every way but the right way; and there are many Christians that are able to have the pure flame of Christian life burn steadily, if you only shield them, but that, if you move them about and bring them in conflict with each other in circumstances of temptation, show their weakness of Christian feeling.

Rev. H. W. Beecher.

GOD loves to hear his people sing in the night. At no time does God love his children's singing so well as when they give a serenade of praise under his window, when he has hidden his face from them, and will not appear to them at all. They are all in darkness; but they come under his window, and they begin to sing there. "Ah!" says God, "that is true faith, that can make them sing praises when I will not look at them; I know there is some faith in them, that makes them lift up their hearts, even when I seem to take away all my tender mercies and all my compassions." Sing, Christian! for singing pleases God. In heaven, we read, the angels are employed in singing: do you be employed in the same way; for by no better means can you gratify the Almighty One of Israel, who stoops from his high throne to observe the poor creature of a day.

Rev. C. H. Spurgeon.

IN terrible agony, a soldier lay dying in the hospital. A visitor asked him,—

"What Church are you of?"

"Of the Church of Christ," he replied.

"I mean of what persuasion are you?" then inquired the visitor.

"Persuasion!" said the dying man, as his eyes looked heavenward, beaming with love to the Saviour: "I am *persuaded* that neither death, nor life, nor angels, nor principalities, nor powers, nor things present, nor things to come, nor heighth, nor depth, nor any other creature, shall be able to separate *me* from the love of God which is in Christ Jesus."

I WAS looking the other day at a glass bee-hive, and it was very singular to observe the motions of the little creatures inside. Well, now, this world is nothing but a huge glass bee-hive. God looks down on you, and he sees you all. You go into your little cells in the streets of this large city; you go to your business, your pleasures, your devotions, and your sins; but remember, wherever you go, you can never get away from the Lord's observation.

Rev. S. H. Spurgeon.

IN the morning the thief was writhing upon the cross; in the evening he was exulting in glory! How close to each other are pardon and paradise, the cross and the crown, the battle and the prize, the wilderness and Canaan, the darkest midnight and the morning dawn, Calvary and heaven!

Rev. Newman Hall.

WHAT would in my boyhood have cost a small fortune, can now be had easily if a man will substitute pictures for tobacco. If a man, instead of tanning his mouth and smoking his head, would lay out for pictures what he expends for tobacco, it would make all the difference in his dwelling between walls handsomely decorated and pleasant, and walls without decoration, bald and cold.

Not that I would infringe upon your liberty of using tobacco. That is a precious liberty which I do not touch! I give you no advice. I merely say that the cost of annual tobacco would more than furnish, every year, a room in your house for your children. If you see more pictures, evanescent, in the indulgence of tobacco, and have more pleasure in them then you would in works of art, that is your liberty. Your children, perhaps, may have a right to say something, your companion perhaps may; but I say nothing.

Rev. H. W. Beecher.

A "CHANGEABLE SILK," as it is called, looks now brown and now green, because it is never quite green and never quite brown, but always composite of the two. And a changeable robe of religion looks now brilliant and now dingy, because it is never thoroughly humbled, and never thoroughly elate.

H. S. Carpenter.

SUPPOSE you destroy all the seeds and roots of weeds, etc., from your garden, and yet allow a man to walk along your garden fence, and cast weed-seed over on the clean soil: how long will your garden be kept free of weeds? So your heart may be made as clean as the blood of Christ can make it; and yet if you allow the devil, hell's seed-sower, to come up to the fence of your soul, he will seed it again with sin.

Rev. R. V. Lawrence.

YES, fair as the syren, but false as her song,
Are the world's painted shadows that lure us along;
Like the mist on the mountain, the foam on the deep,
Or the voices of friends that we greet in our sleep,
Are the pleasures of earth.

Mrs. Hale.

A MAN puts on a life-preserver in the billows, and so some souls put on faith. But there is many a one who no more thinks of carrying faith into his counting-house, than of wearing a life-preserver in his parlor.

H. S. Carpenter.

TRUE faith and reason are the soul's two eyes;
Faith evermore looks upward and descries
Objects remote; but reason can discover
Things only near, sees nothing that's above her.

Quarles.

SOME men choose home to spit their spleen and uncork the bottle of their discontent, which all day long they have been filling. Rather do this in the world where no one thinks enough of you to feel bad about it; but remember there is one at home who can be made to suffer as no one else in this wide world. If you have one smile, save it for your wife at home.

Rev. J. P. Newman.

THERE aie men that gather together their bags of gold and silver, and sit down and weigh and sound every ducat; and we call them misers. There are misers, also, of the soul, that ring their virtues, and generosities, and truth-speakings, and good deeds. And the most miserable of all miserable misers are these soul-misers, that are perpetually ringing the changes over their own little accumulations of virtue and attainment.

Rev. H. W. Beecher.

THE lungs can disuse some of their air-cells, until they collapse and close, and nevertheless, cherish life enough in the chest to withstay the contraction from a fatal reach. So the spirit can have some variety of religion without expanding to its full proportions.

H. S. Carpenter.

THERE are business men who are almost strangers in their own house. After an early breakfast, they are away, often without seeing a portion of the family; they "lunch down town," are home to tea, and out to some evening engagement, returning to find that most of the family are asleep. What do such men know of home? Not much but its bills. No family readlngs, no quiet gatherings around the lamp or drop-light, with song and story, and parting prayer. There is no charm, no sweet ness, no sanctity in such a home-life.

Rev. Dr. T. M. Eddy.

SOME fruit which you gather from your trees is of such a nature that if you were to try and eat it in the autumn, it would be very sour, and would make you very unwell; but just store it up a little, and see how luscious and juicy it becomes! It is a pity to destroy the fruit and pain yourself by premature use. It is just so with your troubles: they are all darkness now; do not meddle with them, leave them till God has ripened them and turned them into light.

Rev. S. H. Spurgeon.

THERE'S a bliss beyond all that the minstrel has told,
When two that are linked in one heavenly tie,
With heart never changing, and brow never cold,
Love on through all ills, and love on till they die.

Moore.

I WOULD rather have written that hymn of Wesley's,

"Jesus, lover of my soul,
Let me to thy bosom fly,"

than to have the fame of all the kings that ever sat on the earth. It is more glorious. It has more power in it. I would rather be the author of that hymn than to hold the wealth of the richest man in New York. He will die. He *is* dead, and does not know it. He will pass, after a little while, out of men's thoughts. What will there be to speak of him? What will he have done that will stop trouble or encourage hope? His money will go to his heirs and they will divide it. It is like a stream divided and growing narrower by division. And they will die, and it will go to their heirs. In three or four generations everything comes to the ground again for redistribution. But that hymn will go on singing until the last trump brings forth the angel band; and then, I think, it will mount up on some lip to the very presence of God. And I would rather have written such a hymn than to have heaped up all the treasures of the richest man on the globe. A man may be very useful and influential, and not be rich.

H. W. Beecher.

"GOD so loved the world that he gave His only begotten Son, that whosever believeth in Him should not perish, but have everlasting life." Precious words! which the Christian church has ever treasured as among the most costly gems in the casket intrusted to her care;—words to which we turn with more than ordinary delight, as a more lovely flower where all are beautiful; as a more brilliant star where all are bright;—words which the pious mother has often selected as the first to teach her lisping child for its guide in life, and which the aged saint has breathed as the best expression of his hope in death.

Rev. Newman Hall.

"HERE we rest," said the old Indian chief, long years ago. Having been pushed on and on by the white man: he went up to a large tree that he thought would stand, and inscribed on it hieroglyphics, and when asked what it meant, he said, "Alabama." What does Alabama mean? It means, "Here we rest." He crossed, as he supposed, the last stream, and the white man would disturb him no more. And so, when God's saints cross the river of death, though I think they will be very careful not to mar the tree of life, yet they will feel like inscribing on every tree their heavenly, immortal "Alabama"—here we rest forever.

Rev. H. Mattison.

THE most beautiful birth was the birth in the manger; the loveliest life was the life of the man of sorrows; and the most beautiful, sublimest death was the death upon blood-stained Calvary.

A. I. Holmes.

LIFE before God is transparent, like a well beneath the sky, not without depths of meaning, but with depths in which the stars can shine.

H. S. Carpenter.

FOR the structure that we raise,
Time is with materials filled;
Our to-days and yesterdays
Are the blocks with which we build.

Longfellow.

THE most foul things our sins have caused the earth to bring forth, are thorns and briers. Jesus wore them upon his pure and holy brow, that we might wear a crown of glory.

A. I. Holmes.

WHO wears the Christian name
Hath stamped upon his brow
His glory or his shame —
As he hath kept his vow,
And those bright garments of his second birth.

A. C. Coxe.

THERE are sometimes rare and beautiful wares brought into the market, that are invoiced at almost fabulous rates. Ignorant people wonder why they are priced so high. The simple reason is, that they cost so much to procure. That luxurious article, labelled "$1,000," was procured by the adventurous hunter, who, at the hazard of his neck, brought down the wild mountain goat, out of whose glossy hair the fabric was wrought. Yonder pearl, that flashes on the brow of the bride, is precious, because it was rescued from the great deep, at the risk of the pearl-fisher's life, as he was lifted into the boat, half dead, with the blood gushing from his nostrils! Yonder ermine, flung so carelessly over the proud beauty's shoulder, cost terrible battles with polar ice and hurricane! All choicest things are reckoned the dearest. So it is in heaven's inventories, too. The universe of God has never witnessed aught, to be reckoned in comparison with the redemption of a guilty world. That mighty ransom no such contemptible things as silver and gold could procure. Only by one price could the church of God be redeemed from hell, and that the precious blood of the Lamb; the Lamb without blemish or spot; the Lamb slain from the foundation of the world.

Rev. Theo. L. Cuyler.

A SAILOR boy on his first voyage to the tropics, is full of the prospect of crossing the equator. He expects to find there a black line drawn around the earth over land and ocean. He will know the exact moment when the ship's prow cuts clean through it. But, looking out for this great sight, he sees nothing except that the air grows milder, and the skies more genial, the sea becomes warm with perpetual summer, and along the coast he is charmed by the bloom of the fields and the singing of birds. But where is the line?" And what means this mildness in the air and ocean? "It means," some older shipmate tells him, "that you have already crossed the line. You have seen all that you will see of it." So a young seeker after Christ expects to know the very moment of his passing from death to life. But when some day, he asks, "Why do all things seem so new; Christ so gracious, and Christians so dear, and the Bible so full of meaning?"

it is, as some older brother perceives, because he has passed the great crisis. He saw no line. He remembers no sudden, wonderful change. He finds only that he has arrived, like Bunyan's Christian entering Beulah, at a region of sweetness and peace; that the time of the singing of birds is come, and the voice of the turtle is heard in the land.

Rev. G. B. Willcox.

AT Niagara—sublime beyond expression, yet even more beautiful than sublime—I was ravished with many visions of transporting loveliness; but one scene, beyond all others, will ever be impressed upon my memory. I saw a rainbow spanning the entire river, and hovering above the falls. One limit of it rested on British soil, the other on American. Just then the river divided, and the waters plunged, and foamed, and roared. But a little way beyond, both streams reunited, and flowed on in harmony toward the placid lake. Emblem, I thought, of our two nations. For a time it seemed as though they were divided, but they soon unite again; while ever over the angry roar of differing judgments, there is the pledge of heavenly peace and enduring love.

Rev. Newman Hall.

THE display of dress in many religious assemblies, is hardly less magnificent than that which one sees at the opera, or the dress rehearsal.

It is quite common to hear a congregation praised as being very "stylish." The lustre of silks, and the waving of plumes, and the glitter of tinsel, make the spectacle seem from the pulpit, on the Sabbath day, really a brilliant one. If the minister were as much given to the observation of millinery, as some of his fair parishioners are, his position would afford him a most eligible outlook. If he can only contrive to forget where he is, and what the errand is that has brought these people together, he may even take great pleasure in the fair vision.

Rev. W. Gladden.

IF such the sweetness of the streams,
What must the fountain be,
Where saints and angels draw their bliss
Immediately from thee!"

YOU know that the devil spins silk as well as hemp or flax; and when he wants to catch a trout that will not bite where it can see the line, he spins a line so small that it cannot be seen, and puts the bait upon it, and the fish is caught. And if there is ever an invisible line, with bait at the end of it, and with the devil at the end of the rod, it is when a man is going to make money for the sake of using it to do good with. If there is ever a time when Satan laughs, and says, "I have caught a gudgeon!" it is then.

If a man is ever drawn into the net of the evil

one, it is when he gives up his conscience, his moral sense, and his self-respeet, cutting his manliness through and through, that he may have the means of acting more manly. There are multitudes of instances in which every man, first or last, is brought under circumstances where he is tempted to succeed at the sacrifice of moral scruples, on the ground that, when he has gained success, he will be in a situation to act in accordance with his moral scruples again.

Rev. H. W. Beecher.

WHEN you want to manage men, do as bee-keepers do when they want to manage bees. Here are two men that have bees in a hive. One says, "I own these bees, and I am going to divide them, and move them." He prepares a place for them, and then goes to the hive, thrusts his hand rudely into the midst of them, and very soon he has bees all over him, and he moves *himself* very rapidly. That is just as I have seen men attempt to manage men. Another man gets a bowl of sugar and water, and washes his hands all over, and goes with the utmost quietness and serenity, and opens the hive, and puts his hand in gently, and the bees find everything sweet, and he can scoop them up as though they were so much flour, and put them in as many hives as he pleases (if he only takes care to put a queen-bee in each), and they will not sting him or fly away. And people say "Wonderful!

that man has a real magnetic power with bees." So he, has when he has sugar and water on his hands. Now, when you want to manage men, wash your hands with sugar and water.

Rev. H. W. Beecher.

MAN was made of social earth,
Child and brother from his birth.

Emerson.

GOD deals with a Christian disciple, we have sometimes thought, as they did with the Koh-i-noor diamond in the London Exhibition. They had it so adjusted that, at any approach of danger, by touching a spring they could bury it in a subterranean safe. When spiritual perils beset some child of God, — a jewel costlier far and dearer, — he drops him into a valley of humiliation, under the shadow of his wings, till these calamities be overpast.

Rev. G. B. Willcox.

HOW blest the righteous when he dies,
When sinks a weary soul to rest!
How mildly beam the closing eyes,
How gently heaves the expiring breast.

So fades a summer cloud away;
So sinks the gale when storms are o'er;
So gently shuts the eye of day;
So dies a wave along the shore.

Barbauld.

TWO spectators — one on this side of the grave, and the other beyond it — stand and look at death. One, as he looks from this side, sees only that part which relates to the physical condition. The other, looking through angelic eyes, beholds that part which relates to the spiritual being. They both look at one and the same thing, and one sees decay, while the other sees growth. One sees death, while the other sees life. One sees downfall, and the other sees uprising. One sees the end of this state, and the other sees the beginning of that state. One sees weakness, and the other sees strength. One sees dishonor, and the other sees honor. One sees mortality consummated, and the other sees immortality begun.

Rev. H. W. Beecher.

WHEN God lays a new-born babe in the arms of a wedded pair, he says to them, "Take this child and nurse it *for me*, and I will give you your wages." And the answer of Christian gratitude and faith should be, "O God! thou hast put thy noblest work into our hands. We accept the precious trust. We will try to stamp on this soft, plastic heart the impress of a godly example. We will shelter this young life under thy mercy-seat. We will bear with it as thou bearest with us. We will be truthful, that it may never learn falsehood. We will nurse this soul in its infancy with the 'sincere milk' of love, that in after years it may bear 'strong meat' for strong service of God and righteousness. O God! make our lives in harmony with thee, that this young life may reflect thine image in reflecting ours!"

Rev. Theo. L. Cuyler.

THE mistaken man who robs his overworked body and mind of any Sabbath commits a slow suicide; he who robs his immortal soul of the Sabbath is guilty of spiritual suicide. When Lord Castlereagh, the prime minister of England, broke himself down, and took his own life in a fit of mental aberration, Wilberforce said, "Poor Castlereagh! he never had any Sabbath!"

Rev. Theo. L. Cuyler.

CLING to the Crucified!
His death is life to thee;
Life for Eternity.
His pains thy pardon seal;
His stripes thy bruises heal;
His cross proclaims thy peace,
Bids every sorrow cease.
His blood is all to thee;
It purges thee from sin,
It sets thy spirit free,
It keeps thy conscience clean.
Cling to the Crucified!

Bonar.

USUALLY, men undertake to pray after a pattern; and the pattern usually fits them about as well as Goliath's armor would have fitted David. They undertake to pray more than they *can* pray. They multiply their petitions, because they have an impression that a prayer must be about so long. But your prayer should be just what you feel, just what you think, and just what you need, and it should stop the moment it ceases to be the real expression of your needs, and thoughts, and feelings.

Rev. H. W. Beecher.

WHERE is the lustre of the diamond, the beauty of the rose, the glory of the landscape, when the dark curtain of night is drawn over all? But the light of God's countenance, like the sun uprising and breaking forth from amidst dark clouds, bathes all objects in beauty.

Rev. Newman Hall.

OH! when those gates of pearl, those fountains, those golden streets and trees of life will become visible to the eye, what care we for a few days of sorrow on earth? When we gather at the throne, all shall be over; and then, oh! the songs of praise and the notes of joy that shall be uttered! Could I take away the veil this morning; could the invisible appear; could I see the forms of those that once stood beside me; could I behold those who have walked by my side; could we see the little ones that slipped out of our arms just when we listened with most pleasure to their prattling voices, what joy would fill our hearts! I may not see them now, but, thank God, I shall see them and be with them forever.

Bishop Simpson.

IN his Epistles, occurs the sentence of sentences, "God is love." Why is not this sentence sown in our gardens in living green; framed and hung on the walls of our nurseries; taught as the first sounds to little ones? Why not call God, Love? Why not change the name of our Deity? Why not instruct children to answer, when asked who made them, Love, the Father? Who redeems you? Love, the Son. Who sanctifies you? Love, the Holy Ghost?

George Gilfillan.

CALL it not dying, timid ones,
Who fear to cross the stream
That lands you on yon beauteous shore,
Where heavenly glories beam.

No: call it going home to God;
Call it a peaceful rest;
Call it departing from this earth
To live among the blest.

MANY a hero has bled to enslave mankind: Jesus died to set them free. Heroes have bled to impoverish men: Jesus died to enrich them. Heroes have bled to degrade men: Jesus died to ennoble and exalt them. Heroes have bled to dethrone competitors and rivals: Jesus died to en throne condemned and helpless rebels.

Rev. N. Vansant

HAVE you ever seen a great, honest, ignorant, awkward man carrying his first babe? He hardly dares to touch it. He balances it one way and another, looking at it wonderingly and almost idolatrously. And if it cries, almost as if it burnt him he lays it down, not knowlng how to manage or control it.

And if a man does not know how to carry such a babe, how can he know how to carry that babe which is himself; that young immortality which is in himself, and which it is his business to educate; that germ which is to take the stature and proportions of a son of God; that unknown something which is called the soul?

Rev. H. W. Beecher.

THE child stretches out its arms and calls to its father and mother for help. And the parents love its call. That voice of dependence, desire, confidence, is music to their hearts. No parent, however tender and wise, would wish his child never to ask anything from him. It would be very unnatural for a child to say, "My father has arranged all for me; he will do his best, and I need never tell him a trouble or a wish." Every true parent loves to hear his child asking comfort in trouble, protection in danger, and the supply of its wants. And God, who made a father's heart, represents Himself as our Father, and teaches us as children to "call upon Him in the day of trouble."

Rev. Newman Hall.

THE man who swears turns speech into a curse, and before his time rehearses the dialect of hell. He waits for no bait; but "bites at the devil's bare hook." The shrewd Quaker's advice to the profane youth, "Swear away, my young friend, till thee gets all that bad stuff *out of thee*," points to the real source of the vice; for it is out of an evil *heart* that proceed evil thoughts, false witness, and blasphemies.

We fear that the purest tongue will need much purifying before it is fit to join in the celestial praises of God's upper temple. For that worship let us attune our voices by ceaseless prayers, by words of love, by earnest vindications of the right, by habitual "speech seasoned with salt" of divine grace. The melody of heaven will spring from a *harmony of hearts;* each voice there will bear a part in the song of Moses and the Lamb.

Rev. Theo. L. Cuyler.

AND I regard a man and a woman that come together in the marriage state as coming together in the most sacred of all possible conjunctions before God; and when they lay the foundations of a household, they are silently laying the foundations of a more enduring influence than any other that can be established in society. And, as their children multiply and grow up, and exchange all the immunities of a refined, civilized, and Christian life, they become a power for good to those around about them. A Christian household in the midst of a community is frequently more potent than a Christian church. Oftentimes a church is an artificial institution, and has very little influence upon the neighborhood in which it is situated. You shall sometimes hear it said, "I like to go to church and sleep while the minister prays and preaches, and so pass away the time;" but nobody speaks so about the family: there is always freshness there; there is always vitality there; there is always something there that touches the taste and sanctifies it, and touches the heart and fills it. And the family is, I had almost said, God's mouthpiece, in this world, which speakes to ten thousand sympathies in us. A man that builds a household is not building up selfishness; he is building the mightiest influence in the world. It is not he alone who wields the sword that is a soldier; he that forges the sword on the anvil is also a soldier. The blacksmith says, "I cannot fight, but I can make something to fight with;" and he is a soldier. And a man that in the family is forging a bold-hearted boy, is putting a sword in the world that will be felt in the great battle of Armageddon. Do you think that when Luther's mother was working her boy out she was doing nothing? I tell you, all who are faithfully building up families in the world are building God's battering-rams against iniquity and for goodness.

Rev. H. W. Beecher.

OPPORTUNITIES, like eggs, must be hatched when they are fresh. The showers from heaven must be caught as they fall. Most men build shelving roofs to let them off. Sacred pleasures, like fruits, must be picked from the tree to get the genuine flavor. Stale juices are distasteful and unwholesome.

H. S. Carpenter.

THE only star that never sets,
Though all its sister fires may fly —
The only flower that never droops,
Though all its fair companions die —
Is fadeless hope.

Mrs. C. L. Rice.

YOU know, going into heaven will be like the ships going into harbor. There will be some tugged in almost by miracle, "saved so as by fire;" others will be going in just with a sheet or two of canvas — they will "scarcely be saved!" but there will be some who will go in with all their canvas up, and unto these "an abundant entrance shall be ministered into the kingdom of their God and Saviour."

Rev. C. H. Spurgeon.

SOMETIMES in their life my readers may have watched the growth of household flowers. They may have seen one of them neglected for two or three days, so that it drooped and faded like a dying bird. The long leaves were all trailing, pale, and withered. Then the water was renewed upon it, and the earth was stirred about the roots, and it was brought to an open window, in a sunny exposure, and the soft sweet light was poured upon it, and the fresh air breathed clear over it, and it revived. Is the life of plants a more sensitive and delicate thing than that of souls? Does it need more care? Alas, are there not to be found even refined and gentle mothers, who tend the flowering shrubs in their windows with more punctual, patient, fostering daily care, than they bestow upon those household plants that are blossoming for immortality?

Rev. H. T. Cheever.

GATHER ye rose-buds as ye may,
Old Time is still a-flying;
And this same flower that smiles to-day,
To-morrow will be dying.

Herrick.

WHEN I came down from my place in the country, I observed the trees along the Hudson River; and, seeing how succulent and green and plump they were, I said, "They must have had rain down here, anyhow." But it instantly occurred to me, that it was said in the Psalms that the righteous man should be like a tree planted by the rivers of water. There it was. The roots ran into the Hudson, and, although there was no rain, they did not want any rain.

Now, whether you have long roots, or grow by favoring streams, so that your roots have an everlasting supply, it is all the same. There be some long-rooted, or happy-rooted persons, that stand green through all the decline of spiritual concerns, to make the sadness more sad on the one side, and on the other side to make the cheer more cheerful.

Rev. H. W. Beecher.

JOHN BUNYAN tells us, that, as Christian was going through the valley, he found it a dreadful dark place, and terrible demons and goblins were all about him, and poor Christian thought he must perish for certain; but just when his doubts were the strongest, he heard a sweet voice; he listened to it, and he heard a man in front of him saying, "Yea, when I pass through the valley of the shadow of death, I will fear no evil." Now, that man did not know who was near him, but he was unwittingly singing to cheer a man behind. Christian, when you are in trouble, sing; you do not know who is near you.

Rev. C. H. Spurgeon.

I KNOW of a little girl in England, who loves to pray. But one night she was very tired and sleepy, and was getting into her little bed without saying her prayers. But her mamma told her to kneel down first to pray. So she folded her little hands, and said, "Please, God, remember what little Polly said last night; she's so tired to-night. Amen." I'm sure that the good Jesus hears even such a prayer as that.

Rev. Newman Hall

CHILDHOOD, sweet and sunny childhood,
With its careless, thoughtless air,
Like the verdant, tangled wildwood,
Wants the training hand of care.
Childhood is the vernal season;
Trim and train the tender shoot;
Love is, to the coming reason,
As the blossom to the fruit.

David Bates.

A CHRISTIAN is one who is positive. A Christian is a fruit-bearer. A moral man is a vine that does not bear fruit. But then it bears everything else, — good leaves, a good strong stem, a healthy root, everything that is good and nice in it, except the fruit. A Christian man is one that develops graces into positivity. He acts out of himself and upon others. A moral man is one that simply defends himself from the action of evil. A moral man is like an empty bottle, well corked, so that no defilement can get into it, so that it may be kept pure within. Pure*!* And what is the use of a bottle that is pure, if it is empty and corked up? A moral man, I repeat, is a negative. He does *not* swear, he does *not* steal, and he does *not* murder, and he does *not* get drunk; and his whole life is *not.* His language is, "Thou shalt *not,*" and "Thou shalt *not,*" and "Thou shalt *not!*" He is *not* all over, and nothing more! He is not positive. There is no avertness to him.

Rev. H. W. Beecher.

YOU have seen night wrapped in her sable mantle, woven with gems and stars; there they shine as ornaments worked by the needle of God, in that brilliant piece of tapestry, which is spread over our heads, like a tent for the inhabitants of the earth to dwell in. You have said, "Oh, how majestic! that star, that comet, that silver moon, how splendid! They are nothing but just a tiny portion of the skirts of God that drag in the dust. But what are the shoulders, what the girdle of divinity; what the bracelets of Godhead; what the crown that girdles his lofty brow, man cannot conceive. I could imagine that all the stars and constellations of stars, might be put together, and threaded into a string, made into a bracelet for the arm, or a ring for the finger of Jehovah; but I cannot conceive what God is himself. All I can ever learn, all that the thunder ever spake, all that the boisterous ocean ever could teach me, all that the heavens above, or the earth beneath, can ever open to my mind, is nothing but the "back parts" of God. I can never see, nor can I understand, what he is.

Rev. C. H. Spurgeon.

A BIRD upon the wing may carry a seed that shall add a new species to the vegetable family of a continent; and just so, a word, a thought, from a flying soul, may have results immeasurable, eternal.

Rev. H. T. Cheever.

THERE is a kind of painting called mosaic. It is composed of small pieces of stone or glass, almost immeasurably small. Each particle is almost worthless; you would crush it under your feet, pass it by unnoticed; but let the true artist construct that mosaic, let him take those infinitely small pieces, and place them in order, and what beautiful shading of outlines are given to it; how grand the conception! You can scarcely distinguish it from the finest painting by the pencil; and yet, multitudes of worthless pieces compose it. So I sometimes look upon humanity. In one sense we are insignificant. What

4

can we do, — so very feeble, inefficient, limited; what can we accomplish? And yet, when the great Artist of the universe takes us in our littleness, and places us in that mosaic which the universe shall yet gaze upon with wonder, oh! the great design of the painting shall appear in the ages, and, small as we are, we shall be part of God's great mosaic. In the redemption of humanity — the up-building of all that is glorious on earth — we may have some place, though small. And as the beautiful mosaic would be marred by the omission of the smallest particle, so, without us, that painting had been imperfect, but with us, it becomes complete.

Bishop Simpson.

AND that high suffering which we dread;
A higher joy discloses:
Men saw the thorns on Jesus' brow,
But angels saw the roses.

Mrs. J. W. Howe.

IT is said that migrating birds, that commonly in their vast journeyings keep very high in the air, require a wind that blows against them in order to make progress and keep their elevation, for it assists in raising them. So the soul of the Christian, winging its way through this world to a better, is aided rather than impeded in its spiritual migration, by the contrary winds of trial. Those storms that seemed against us, do only, when encountered in the right direction, assist to raise us, and keep us steadily soaring towards heaven.

Rev. H. T. Cheever.

BEHOLD that fair vase! See how beauteous it is. Think where it came from. The potter went to the field; tore away the turf; dug out some clay; carried it to the shop; wet it; worked it; put it in a wheel; turned it to the shape that suited him; put it in a glowing furnace; burned it there with various pigments; took it out; smeared it with paint; put it in the furnace again; took it out again; repainted it; put it in the furnace again; took it out again; with burnishing instruments rubbed off the external exudation; the bright colors appear; and it is finished. It is a fair vase; but what a process it has gone through to become such!

God is rearing something fairer than a vase—a beautiful temple, whose foundations are justice and liberty. It is rising up out of confusion and dirt; but it is God's hand that is building it; and he is used to working in such elements. He is accustomed to make noble men out of poor materials.

Rev. H. W. Beecher.

SUPPOSE you were rejoicing in the birth of a son to inherit your name and fortune, and some one were to say, "Wait! he is just born; do not yet regard him as your son." Would you not scorn such an objection? That infant may be very young, only a few minutes old: but he is as much your son as if he had been born years ago. And so, when a sinner repents and believes in Jesus, he is a child of God; and as such God loves him, embraces him, provides an inheritance for him, and if death should carry him hence, takes him at once to paradise.

Rev. Newman Hall.

WE can succeed only when we work in harmony with God's providences. Go on the bosom of that stream. It is easy to float down with the current, which God has made to flow from the mountain-top to the great ocean-bed; but let us reverse our course, and stem the current; then only shall we know its strength. The strongest arm is powerless before it, and the utmost effort impotent. So with us — we shall succeed if we work in harmony with God's plans: if we work in opposition, we shall be vainly striving against the current.

Bishop Simpson.

EACH day may be my last day. I can tell how many days I have lived; but I cannot tell how many days I have to live. Ordinary roads are provided with mile-stones, that inform the traveller how many miles more he must travel before his journey is finished. The highway to immortality presents the pilgrim with many a reminiscence of the distance he has come; but it tells him not the distance in advance.

The peasant can tell, as well as the astronomer, how often the sun will set ere the year closes; but what mortal has the sagacity and penetration to know when his own sun will set, and his earthly career have run out?

Rev. Samuel Dunn.

MEN never fall from a Christian life as a meteor falls through the sky, with a sudden flash. Men go down as stars do, gradually and quietly. The love of prayer becomes less. The neglect of prayer is occasional. The reading of God's word is causual. Nothing is extracted from it. Men read it because it is their duty to read it. It is not food to them. Still less is it fruit luscious to their taste. They backslide, step by step, falling upon lighter sins, as upon a boulder, and then upon more of them; till at last they slip, and spiritual death overtakes them.

Rev. H. W. Beecher.

OH! we learn many lessons when the head is low, that we do not learn in the heyday of prosperity and blessing. Just as it is in the natural world: you know when the sun is set, and the stars come out in their placid beauty,

> "Darkness shows us worlds of light
> We never saw by day,"

and we should never have known they were there if the darkness had not come. So in the night of God's providential dispensations, the stars of the great promises come shining out, broad and bright upon the soul; and we rejoice in their light and go on our way rejoicing.

Rev. W. M. Punshon.

OH! SWEET as vernal dews, that fill
The closing buds on Zion's hill,
When evening clouds draw thither;
So sweet, so heavenly, 'tis to see
The members of one family
Live peacefully together!

Knox.

AND was there not great significance in God's creating woman out of what he took from the side of man? This significance once struck the mind of a young lady, and she asked a surgeon why woman was made from the rib of man, in preference to any other bone. He gave the following gallant answer: "She was not taken from the head of man, lest she should rule over him; nor from his feet, lest he should trample upon her: but she was taken from his side, that she might be his equal; from under his arm, that he might protect her; from near his heart, that he might cherish and love her." In this record, then, let woman learn the relation that God instituted between her and man.

Let wives remember the design of God in relation to them is, that they should be helpmeets for their husbands; and oh! what a helper amid life's heavy toils, corroding cares, and ceaseless anxieties, is a true woman — a loving wife!

Rev. Geo. C. Baldwin.

DID you never hear, when the harpist was preparing for sweet melodies, how he took the chords that were out of tune, and commenced screwing them and fingering them, and how a wail went up from them, till, one by one, they had all been brought to the right key, and how then he swept his hands over them, and brought exquisite harmonies forth from them? The process of chording was one of hideous sounds; but the sounds that were produced after the instrument was put in order were sweet, and agreeable to the ear. And I believe that the proper condition of man is one in which his soul gives forth music, and an abundance of it.

Rev. H. W. Beecher.

ONLY those are crowned and sainted,
Who with grief have been acquainted.

Longfellow.

MOREOVER, it does not seem that this careful and laborious attention to dress would be the best possible preparation for the worship of God. I should think that one who had been prinking before the looking-glass for an hour or two on Sunday morning, studying the intricacies of modes and lingerie; vexed with pins, and ribbons, and dickies; tormented with grave apprehensions that something would seem to be in bad taste or in poor style,—such an one, I should think, would be wholly unprepared to find much profit in acts of devotion. If the church were only a lyceum, and there were no pretence of worship; if the object of coming together on the Sabbath were only to discuss important matters relating to this life,— there could not be a worse mistake than to spend the time preceding the meeting in such an employment. In no other way could the mind be more completely unfitted for serious and patient thought about any subject. But, since the chief object of these assemblages is to commune with the unseen God; to confess our sins before him, and to seek his forgiveness; to study his truth and learn his will,—it would seem that such a manner of preparation for the solemn service is both absurd and irreverent.

Rev. W. Gladden.

YONDER man is employed in in carrying sacks of flour every day. He carries so many hundredweight each time, and in the day it comes to tons; and so many tons in a day will come to an enormous mass in a year. Now, suppose, on the first of January, this man were to calculate the year's load, and say, "I have all that immense mass to carry; I cannot do it:" you would remind him that he has not to carry it all at once; he has all the work-days of the year to carry it in. So we put all our troubles together, and we cry, "How ever shall I get over them?" Well, they will only come one at a time, and as they come, the strength will come with them.

Rev. S. H. Spurgeon.

WHAT bliss is born of sorrow!
'Tis never sent in vain;
The heavenly Surgeon maims to save;
He gives no useless pain.

Ward.

TAKE a young face, and you do not by any means know, you are not at all sure, that it will be a likeness by and by, or that even one feature or expression will be found remaining. There may be so entire a change, both in the face and character, and in the face mainly *because* in the character, that the portrait of a few years further on, shall not have one trait in common with the portrait further back. But take an old face, and you have it to the end; there is no more change. Thus it is easier to paint an aged face than a young one, because the features are settled and unchangeable, sculptured, as it were, into marked and perceptible moulds and grooves of character and expression. Just so it is with the soul. The older each human being grows, the more likely it is that the character of the soul now is that which it will wear forever, and that if the likeness be taken now, it will be found to be a true likeness at the day of death.

Rev. H. T. Cheever.

WE find that the human mind is made to act with cheerfulness. I cannot, perhaps, exexactly define what cheerfulness is, but you know what it is. You know the difference between a rusty piece of iron and a piece of iron that is polished. Take a piece of iron before it has been polished, and hold it up: it reflects nothing. Now polish it, and hold it up: how brilliant it looks! How every man or child delights to look at it! Now, the difference between polished iron and iron that is unpolished, is the difference between cheerfulness and no cheerfulness. Cheerfulness in a man is that which, when people meet him, makes them happy. A cheerful doctor gives his medicine the moment he steps inside the room, half the time. And one of these sepulchral doctors, that carries death in his visage — I wonder that anybody gets well under his care. A clergyman, whose face glows with health, and courage, and hope, and cheer, has looked consolation into his friend before he has spoken a word. But one of these ministers, whose face is a perpetual interpretation of Watts' hymn, —

"Hark, from the tomb, a doleful sound" —

I marvel how he should be twice sent for, unless it

might be on the ground of the benefits of affliction. And in all the relations of life, the same is true. We find that in the mind there is a provision for cheerfulness. And cheerfulness gives pleasure.

Rev. H. W. Beecher.

WE speak much of Providence, and of the Almighty; we bow before an Infinite Power, and do homage to an Infinite Wisdom; but do we carry about in our breasts a perpetual sense of union and communion with the infinite Incarnate Love.

Rev. C. D. Foss.

HOW an old harper doats on his harp! How he fondles and caresses it, as a child resting on his bosom! His life is bound up in it. But see him tuning it: he grasps it firmly, strikes a chord with a sharp, quick blow, and while it quivers as if with pain, he leans over intently to catch the first note that rises. The note, as he feared, is false and harsh. He strains the chord with the torturing thumb-screw, and though it seems ready to snap with the tension, he strikes it again, bending down to listen softly as before, till at length you see a smile on his face, as the first true tone trembles upward. So it is, sorrowing Christian, that God is dealing with you; loving you better than any harper does his harp, he finds you a mass of jarring discords. He wrings your heart-strings with some torturing anguish; he bends over you tenderly, striking and listening, and, hearing only a harsh murmur, strikes you again, while his heart bleeds for you, anxiously waiting for that strain — "Not my will, but thine be done" — which is melody sweet to his ear as angels' songs. Nor will he cease to strike, until your

"heart in tune be found,
Like David's harp of solemn sound," —

not till your chastened soul shall blend with all the pure and infinite harmonies of his own being.

Rev. G. B. Willcox.

A PARENT'S love! it is a gleam
Of sacred light,
That makes the world an Eden seem:
Without its gentle, cheering beam,
All would be night.

Mrs. Gardner.

SOME of you have five or six children. There is one child of yours, perhaps, who is very tall, and handsome, and has, moreover, gifts of mind; you have another child who is the smallest of the family — perhaps has but little intellect and understanding. But which is the most your child? "The most?" you say; "both alike are my children; certainly as much one as the other." And so, dear friend, you may have very little learning, you may be very dark about divine things, you may but "see men as trees, walking," but you are as much the children of God as those who have grown to the stature of men in Christ Jesus.

Rev. C. H. Spurgeon.

IN a letter to a mechanic on the benefits of church-going, Timothy Titcomb uses the following words: "My first reason [for attending church] is, that unless a man puts himself into a fine shirt, polished boots, and good clothes once a week, and goes out into the public, he is almost certain to sink into semi-barbarism. You know that unless you do this on Sunday, you cannot do it at all; for you labor all the week. . . . A man needs to beautify himself with good clothes occasionally, to assure himself that he is not brother to the beast, by the side of which he labors during six days of every seven; and he needs particularly to feel that he has place and consideration in clean society."

Rev. W. Gladden.

SUNSHINE is blessed, but the earth withers in its constant clasp. Showers are refreshing, but the life of nature droops and shivers when it showers all the time. What the landscape asks is a sunshine refreshed by showers; a shower that remembers sunshine. And while the human soul is below the firmament of glory, it must have hopes and fears; it must be drenched and saturated with doubt, that fills its roadside pools, that it may bask in broadening beams of truth.

H. S. Carpenter.

MARK how yon clouds in darkness ride, —
They do not quench the orb they hide;
Still there it wheels, the tempest o'er,
In the bright sky to burn once more:
So, far above the clouds of time,
Faith can behold a world sublime;
Then, when the storms of life are past,
The light beyond shall break at last.

Sprague.

JESUS is never ashamed of His poor relations, nor treats them coldly because they need His help. The greater our distress, the more shall we prove his liberality and tender sympathy.

Rev. Newman Hall.

SHIPS on the sea were made to encounter winds and waves; so were souls in time. Ships must lie-to and tack in gales, and so must minds. It is more famous to outride them than to run before them.

H. S. Carpenter.

I WENT with a brother, one summer day, to extract crystals from a rock. He smote the rock vigorously with a sledge hammer, separating piece after piece from it, until at last the top of the crystal appeared; then one might see what he was after. It did not show upon the outside of the rock; but, when the crystal appeared, then it became evident that he was breaking the rock so as to extract the crystal. The rock was good for nothing; the crystal was everything.

The soul is man's crystal; the body is but the encasing rock that holds it; and God's providences are breaking and smiting, or cutting and chiselling it, to extract the perfect form of that precious crystal, which is worth more than its setting in the rock.

Rev. H. W. Beecher.

WHY do we mourn when another star
  Shines out from the glittering sky?
Do we weep when the voice of war,
  And the rage of conflict die?
Then why do our tears roll down,
  And our hearts be sorely riven,
For another gem in the Saviour's crown, —
  Another soul in heaven?

IF all men were equal in regard to wealth, there would be differences to-morrow. If all the money in the world were distributed in equal shares, one man would be extravagant, and another careful; one would be indolent, and another industrious; so that the next day some would be comparatively poor, and others rich. Until God makes all people's brains and bodily health just alike, there will always be men of low and men of high degree.

Rev. Newman Hall.

GOLD cannot buy happiness, and the parents who compel their daughters to marry for money, or station, commit a grievous sin against humanity and God. And the woman who marries a churl for his wealth will find that she has made a terrible bargain; that all the glitterings of heartless grandeur are but the phosphorescent gleamings of heart-wretchedness, that her life will be one of gilded misery, and her old age will be like a crag on the bleak side of a desert mountain, where cold moon-beams sometimes glitter, but no sunshine ever falls, no flowers bloom, no birds sing, but wild storms howl and hoarse thunders roar; and through the sweeping storm shall be heard the stern voice of the Great God, saying, "Your riches are corrupted, your garments are moth-eaten, your gold and silver are cankered, and the rust of them shall be a witness against you and eat your flesh as it were fire."

Rev. Geo. C. Baldwin.

IF men were wise in little things,
  Affecting less in all their dealings,
If hearts had fewer rusted strings,
  To isolate their kindly feelings;
If men, when wrong beats down the right,
  Would strike together and restore it;
    If right made might
    In every fight, —
  The world would be the better for it."

THERE is no long slumber between the race and the crown. The passage is short. To be dismissed from earth, from temptation, from passion, from the body, and from sin, is to be admitted into that greater but invisible world, upon the verge of which we are continually living. It is to emerge from time into eternity. It is to close the outward eye as needless, to lose sight of all its objects, and to open the inward eye upon the world of spirits. It is to say farewell to a group of weeping friends, and to bid welcome to the multitude of ransomed souls.

Rev. J. W. Alexander.

BUT let no man be too sure that "it is never too late to mend." There comes a time when it is too late to mend a coat, a hat, a pair of shoes; there comes a time when it is too late to mend a neglected and abused body and mind. Have we not seen many a man who, though still young, is, through dissipation, done for? His eye has lost its keenness of vision, his hand its steadiness and skill, his brain has almost ceased to be the organ of thought, the understanding is muddled, the memory is impaired; the case altogether is hopeless—it *is* too late to mend. Physically and mentally, therefore, a man may very easily and very rapidly get himself into an altogether irretrievable condition. And is there not the same awful possibility with regard to our moral nature? May it not come to pass that it shall be too late to mend this? May not a man go on in evil until all faculty of doing good is gone; until a paralysis from which there is no recovery (excepting through some miracle, which it is presumptuous and vain to look for) has seized the shrivelled, shrunken powers of conscience and of will, that might once have been used to such good purpose?

Rev. H. S. Brown.

O WONDROUS land!
Fairer than all our spirit's fairest dreaming;
"Eye hath not seen," no heart can understand
The things prepared, the cloudless radiance streaming.
How longingly we wait our Lord's command,
His opening hand!

O dear ones there,
Whose voices, hushed, have left our pathway lonely,
We come, erelong, your blessed hope to share;
We take the guiding Hand, we trust it only,
Seeing, by faith, beyond this clouded air
That land so fair!

ON earth I need the grasp of the hand of my friend to tell me he is there; it is the pressure on the hand that makes me feel he is there. Let Jesus make the same impression on my soul, as though his hand was put in mine, and I was leaning on his Almighty arm, just as consciously have I the presence and the support of the Almighty arm as if my eyes saw and my hands felt. Weak and feeble may be my heart when I come down to the cold waters of Jordan, but if he places the arms of his mercy about me, and puts his rod and staff in my hand, though there may be no outward symbol there, my soul does lean on the arm of the Almighty, and I go safely through.

Bishop Simpson.

YOUTH is not rich in time; it may be, poor;
Part with it as with money, sparing; pay
No moment, but in purchase of its worth;
And what its worth, ask deathbeds; they can tell.

Young.

TAKE the *moment* now passing; and how soon it is past! The instant which marks its presence rings the knell of its departure. It is no sooner present than gone. In the very act of looking at it, we lose it. While we seek to measure it, we exhaust it. Human thought, and perhaps even angelic, is not quick enough to catch it when on the wing. When past, it never returns. And yet of just this material life is made up.

Rev. S. T. Spear.

AS the lover of art, when passing through those galleries which are filled with the works of the great masters, frequently has his attention excited and his admiration called forth by the discovery of some new beauty springing forth from that force and freshness which ever mark the productions of genius, so the believer, as in meditation he passes through the gallery of Divine Revelation, frequently meets with pictures so full of grace, and pregnant with spiritual instruction, that with the poet he is compelled to exclaim, —

> "Father of mercies! in thy word
> What endless glory shines!
> For ever be Thy name adored
> For these celestial lines."

Balfern.

THE Past hath done its work! How well,
How ill, it matters not to say;
For lo! upon our ears doth swell
The summons of TO-DAY.

William H. Burleigh.

THERE are certain peculiarities of bad temper. It usually vents itself on the weak, and those that are not able to help themselves. Our peevishness generally works down to our inferiors and subordinates and dependents. It also is an infliction upon our friends; for we take it for granted that they love us well enough to bear it. We are often peevish and snappish toward them, when we would not be toward others. Toward superiors we are seldom liberal and free with our temper; but toward those that are below us in life we do not hold it back.

Many persons, it seems to me, reserve all their frets during the day ;- they almost do not dare to be cross in the presence of customers and superiors ; they bottle up their temper, and save it till they get home ; and then it is a household confection ! it is a luxury of the family !

Rev. H. W. Beecher.

MAN first learned song in paradise,
  From the bright angels o'er him singing ;
And in our home above the skies,
  Glad anthems are forever ringing.
God lends his ear, well pleased, to hear
  The songs that cheer his children's sorrow,
Till day shall break, and we shall wake
  Where love shall make unfading morrow.

Bethune.

'TIS greatly wise to talk with our past hours ;
  And ask them what report they bore to heav'n ;
And how they might have borne more welcome news.

Young.

THE material sun has spots upon its surface, and wonderful as it, is the radiance it emits from age to age ; still the telescope pointing toward it discerns spots of cloud ; but on the character of Son of God, who is the Sun of Rightousness, there is no spot. The holiest and the most sincere honor him most and worship him most ardently, and they who have sought to cast a stone upon it only illustrate in the fact the vileness of their own hearts.

Rev. R. S. Storrs, Jr.

ONE of the godliest and most effective merchants we know is a man who never cheats his soul of its closet devotions, and who gives a part of his Sabbath to his family, his Bible, and his meditations. He comes down from his Sabbath, on Monday morning, into the busy world, a refreshed, purified, and reinvigorated man.

Rev. Theo. L. Cuyler.

OF however much or however little importance it may be, I think there is nothing more beautiful to a right-minded and contemplative mind than a little child being taught by its mother to pray. There are sad scenes where a child is born into the world, and both father and mother are wistful for its good, but know not how to pray themselves, and some nurse, some dusky-faced Christian servant, is left to teach it how to say, "Our Father which art in heaven." One of the ways of making yourself all but divine to a child is to make your soul a ladder on which its little feet shall climb up to find the greater Father; for, in the order of nature, the child should think of God from the qualities which it sees in you. And reflexly, the child will bring down some of its little imaginings of God, and teach them to you. And the child that has been taught to pray by father and mother has repaid them a thousand-fold for all the care and attention that they have bestowed upon it.

Rev. H. W. Beecher

AS a rule, those who believe in God believe in His power. They believe that He could roll Jupiter one side, if Jupiter stood in the way of His plans. Nothing is too difficult for Him, and nothing can stand in His path. Believing this of God, suppose we believe Him to be our personal friend. Suppose we vividly think of Him as personal to us, and suppose we place Him in our thoughts, not away off beyond the reach of a telescope, but by our side, by night and day. Suppose we do not think of Him as hovering in the heavens, just beyond the stars, but close beside us wherever we are. Do we then belittle our thought of Deity? Do we detract from His greatness? Have we fallen into profanity?

Rev. Herman Bisbee.

BUT I think that children understand their prayers better than their parents do, often. The simplicity, the literalness, if I may so say, the nestling faith of the little child is the medium by which we are to be brought back to God in conversion. We are told by our blessed Master that, unless we become as little childdren, we shall not enter the kingdom of heaven. Those very things which make us superior to the child in a worldly point of view are a hinderance to our piety; and our children pray better than we do. We smile when a little child prays that God would give it an apple. The nurse comes to the admiring parent, and says, "What do you think the child said when I was putting it to bed?—It said, 'Pa, wont you mend my shoe?'—I said, 'You must not call God *pa.*'—'It said, 'Well, he is my Father, ain't he? and can't I call my father *pa*?'—'But,' I said, 'you must not ask God to mend your shoes.'—'Well,' it said, 'ma says I must ask him for everything.'" And they talk it over in the family, and think it singular that the child should look to God for everything; but in hundreds of instances, after men have gone through the storms of life, and found how weak is human strength, they come back, at an age of perhaps fifty or sixty years, to a simplicity in which, though they do not pray for an apple, or to have a shoe mended, they do pray in precisely the same spirit that the child does.

Rev. H. W. Beecher.

HAST thou a care, whose pressure dread
Expels sweet slumber from thy bed?
To thy Redeemer take that care,
And change anxiety to prayer.

Mrs. A. Julius.

A GLACIER in the Alps gleams in the light with its glistening pinnacles, a perfect miracle of beauty. And when the sun begins reducing it to ruins, toppling down this tower, lopping off that buttress, melting the whole into a shapeless mass, till finally it sinks and falls away, how sad a sight! what a magnificent structure demolished! But see the stream trickling out from under it. See it go bounding and laughing down the mountain-side to that far-off meadow. The sun was only turning the splendid, glittering, worthless ice-palace into the liquid wealth, that was to spread the fields with emerald and load them with vegetable gold. So God takes down the splendid fortune of many a Christian, and gives him for it the fertility of soul that brings forth some thirty, some sixty, some a hundred fold.

Rev. G. B. Willcox.

THE evening cloud, the morning dew,
The with'ring grass, the fading flower,
Of earthly hopes are emblems true —
The glory of a passing hour.

Pratt's Col.

"RESIST the devil and he will flee from you," and, should he return, the fact that you have resisted him before will make you all the more able to resist him again. Whether the particular devil that assails you be intemperance, or lust, or lying, or anger, or indolence, — resist; resist at first, and you will have less and less difficulty in all subsequent struggles with the adversary.

Rev. H. Stowell Brown.

IN God our might
We gird us for the coming fight;
And strong in him whose cause is ours,
In conflict with unholy powers,
We grasp the weapons he has given —
The light, and truth, and love of Heaven!

Whittier

AND who are *some* of these dead ones? They are our *kindred* gone — our children early called, our honored sires now taking their long, last sleep — once beings of great personal interest to us, loving us and loved by us. Can we, then, dismiss them from thought the moment we cease to see them? This would be alike unnatural and unreasonable. Some hypothesis, some theory, some opinion, some faith every one needs, with which to visit the great unknown whither the objects of his tenderest love have gone. The absence of all thought is hardly possible. The broken ties of earth and the bleeding hearts of time force meditation into the soul. The very effort to drive it away will be sure to keep it there. The partialities of human friendship venture upon the prophetic office and write an oracle over the dead. The fond mother sees her smiling infant in the skies.

Rev. S. T. Spear.

ALL things that are planted, and are to be preserved, must have roots; and into those roots the life retreats in safety for the winter. But if the seed-time, and summer, and harvest, are neglected, and the roots not formed, then nothing can live through the season of death that is approaching. So the soul must have its roots in Christ; for the winter is coming, when all that the soul can do will be just to retreat to Christ; just to take refuge in him just, as it were, to lie buried with him for the resurrection.

Rev. H. T. Cheever

THERE is a lesson in each flower,
A story in each stream and bower;
On every herb on which you tread
Are written words, which, rightly read,
Will lead you from earth's fragrant sod
To hope, and holiness, and God.

Cunningham.

THE *hour* that is passing will soon be in its sepulchre. Three hundred and sixty ticks of one's watch or clock will write its doom and place it with the hours "beyond the flood." The clock strikes ten. It is just an hour since the same clock struck nine. How soon that hour is gone! Thus hours proceed. To improve them when present, and give them a tongue when past, "is wise in man." Where are our departed hours? They are gone.

We shall see them no more, and act in them no more. Their record is written, and their review is waiting for the scenes of the final judgment.

Rev. S. T. Spear.

THERE is many a man who at home is so good that you could not persuade the mother or the child that he was not a saint. They look upon him as being like an angel, and they love him, and daily twine about him as a clasping vine covers the trellis. In the family the social instincts take the predominance in him, and there he has a character that is sweet and lovely. But go over on the street where Shylock does business, and see how different this man is there. His social faculties no longer are in the ascendant, and another set of powers take the control of his mind, and he begins to exhibit the wolf, the fox, the tiger, the lion, and the alligator in him — for man is a compound of every animal on the globe; and when his animal propensities take the lead, he is quick, sharp, and selfish; and persons who know him say, "That man's shadow will corrode gold, he is such a despicable stingy wretch! and do you say there is more that is good than that is bad in that man? Away with your nonsense! Why, he has a grip like a vice in his hand! He stamps his image and superscription on every piece of money that he touches! And you call him good, do you?" The man *is* ugly in that character; but you did not see enough of him. You did not see him at home in his family. You denounce him as an old hypocrite; but he is no more a hypocrite than you are. You do a great many things on Sunday that you do not think you are bound to do on Monday. You have two characters. You drill differently at different times. There is the company drill, the battalion drill, and the corps drill; and men's faculties sometimes drill in companies, sometimes in battalions, and sometimes in corps. There are different orders, different leaders, and different words of command.

Rev. H. W. Beecher.

THE spider's most attenuated thread
Is cord, is cable, to man's tender tie
On earthly bliss; it breaks at every breeze.

Young.

A VERY little girl, in England, was asked by her mother if she knew how Christ could save her. "O yes!" she replied; "I will tell you. One day I was naughty, and went up into the nursery. Presently I heard nurse coming upstairs to have me punished. I looked around to see what I could do, and I saw your wide dress hanging on the chair. I ran to it, and covered myself all over, so that nurse could not see even my foot. Now, just so, when God comes to punish me for my sins, I run to Jesus, and he covers me all over, so that God cannot see even my feet."

 Rev. F. G. Clark.

EACH care, each ill of mortal birth,
  Is sent in pitying love,
To lift the ling'ring heart from earth,
  And speed its flight above.
And every pang that rings the breast,
  And every joy that dies,
Tell us to seek a purer rest,
  And trust to holier ties.

Montgomery.

DEATH'S but a path that must be trod,
  If man would ever pass to God.

Parnell.

WHEN you go to the brink of the waters that you are about to cross, hold up the cross, and by magic power they shall cleave asunder, as did ancient Jordan before the ark of the covenant, and you shall pass over dry-shod, and in peace. When your feet are toiling up the slope, and you arrive at the gate of heaven, hold up the cross; the angels shall know it, and the everlasting doors shall unbar themselves that you may enter in. When you pass through the ranks of applauding seraphim, that you may pay your first homage to the throne, present the cross, and lower it before the face of the Master, and He, for whose sake you have borne it, will take it from you, and replace it with a crown.

Rev. William Morley Punshon.

THE first death was probably thought a sleep; as the first sleep, according to Milton, was mistaken for death. I stand by the side of an infant, and behold it in quiet slumber. What on earth can be more lovely? The eyes are closed; the senses are locked up; the great external world is shut out. All is stillness and repose. We look and wonder, but feel no pain, because we expect a resurrection from this slumber. In like manner I stand by the couch when a beloved friend has closed his eyes. The doors of sense are shut; the outer world is excluded; but the greater, lovelier, more awful inner world is there. The marble brow, the serene, unmoving features, the settled smile of lips which were late so eloquent; all speak of deep slumber. But Christianity tells me to dismiss my fears, for Jesus comes to awake him out of sleep.

Rev. J. W. Alexander.

THE man who passes through Western valleys, will occasionally find a little rivulet murmuring. It scatters verdure along its dewy course; the flowers bloom more brightly, and the grass looks more green. But he says, "It is a little thing, and I will dry it up." Let him make a circuit of the mighty basin, and the result of this drying-up process of the little rivulets will be, that the great Father of Waters will disappear, and no longer roll its mighty tribute back to the bosom of old ocean. It is not a safe way to deal with God and ourselves to belittle each particular duty, and at the same time think we can be religious in general, without attending to the details.

Bishop Ames.

HE who dwells in a valley, can drink of the stream, though its source be inaccessible in the mountain clefts.

So a soul may taste the flow of spiritual life, though it be, at the same time, utterly unable to trace a course of theology. Theology climbs the mountain, or clambers and slips. Religion dwells by the stream. A man must return from his theology, in order to reach his religion; and then he will find that his religion is his supply of theology.

H. S. Carpenter.

IF solid happiness we prize,
Within our breasts this jewel lies,
And they are fools who roam.

Cotton.

YOUR child is falling from a window. By the action of a natural law, he will be killed. But he cries out for help, "Father! Father!" Hearing his call in this his "day of trouble," you rush forth, and catch him in your arms. Your child is saved. Natural law would have killed him, but you interposed, and without a miracle saved him. And cannot the great Father of all do what an earthly parent

Joes? And if, in the day of adversity, we, while falling, cry to Him for succor, can He not deliver us?

Rev. Newman Hall.

TO what voices do the dead not listen? Music can charm the serpent, but it cannot awaken the dead. The voice of an orator can rouse a nation to frenzy, but let him try his eloquence on the dead, and a hollow echo will rebuke his folly. The thunder in the heavens can appall a city, but there is one spot in it where it excites no alarm, and that spot is the tomb.

"The lark's shrill clarion, or the echoing horn,
No more shall rouse them from their narrow bed."

There is but one voice which the dead will hear. It is that voice which shall utter the words, "Awake, and sing, ye that dwell in dust; for thy dew is as the dew of herbs; and the earth shall cast out the dead.'

G. Gilfillan.

THE air is full of farewells to the dying,
And mournings for the dead:
The heart of Rachel, for her children crying,
Will not be comforted.

Longfellow.

THE rules for securing success in secular affairs, will apply to the advancement of the soul in grace. The real currency in commerce is metallic, the broad earth over. And the gold and silver which make up the basis of personal wealth, are the product of the mines; each glittering coin the result of the miner's hard toil with sieve, or with mattock. Now, the currency of God's kingdom is *truth*, and the Bible is the ore-bed. To every one of you this mine is open. He must be a blind, or a careless miner, who does not come out of this inexhaustible ore-bed, with some new and massive "nugget," as the result of every hour's research.

Rev. Theo. L. Cuyler.

ANOTHER fault of morals in business, is taking advantage of mistakes. For example, change is being made for, and the man gives you back not only all you gave him, but a little more, as well as the article you have taken. You pocket the money, and say, "I am not bound to do business for him and myself too. It is his lookout. I am not responsible for his blunders." Now I want to know if that is honest? And yet are there not some men here who have done it, and know it, and have never made reparation? I know men, who, I suppose, you could not bribe to join a band of counterfeiters, and make plates, and produce bogus money, and circulate it, but who, if they are riding down town at night, and have a bad bill put on them, say, "I cannot afford to have it lie on my hands," and shove it along, having no conscience in the matter. How many men are there that, when they get hold of a bad bill, do not have a sort of impulse to get rid of it, without stopping to consider what the moral character of such an act is?

Because you have a bad bill put on you is no reason why you should put it on somebody else. And though a man does not make bad bills, if he lets one go out of his hands deliberately, he is a counterfeiter in the sight of God. Some men say, "I was very uncertain about it; some days I thought it was counterfeit, and other days I thought it was not; and on one of those days when I thought it was not counterfeit, I passed it!" Now, if it was a mere question of a dollar, of five dollars, or of ten dollars, it might be a matter of amusement; but it is a question of manhood. Back of all that money, is your truth, your fidelity, your morality, your honor, and trustworthiness; and that ought to be a matter above dollars and cents to you. If you take in a counterfeit bill, do not wait to let the devil tempt you twice; burn it. That ends it.

Rev. H. W. Beecher.

IT would be well to have it understood that these *Golden Bitters*, *Santa Cruz Bitters*, *Plantation Bitters*, and numerous other preparations of the same class, whose names are paraded on every picturesque rock along our great thoroughfares by pandering scoundrels, are rum, *rum*, RUM, with a little something added to disguise it. To advertise these things is to encourage intemperance; and to suffer them to go unexposed, is to leave the community the prey of a subtle and most damaging evil. All these promises of rejuvenation, all these pretences of ability to revitalize worn-out men, are miserable shams. All these preparations for men and women, that claim the power to do such wonderful things, are scarcely disguised abominations of intemperance, are fit only for deception, and are a shame and disgrace to any respectable store, or respectable family. And it is high time that this outrageous hypocrisy, under the color of medicine, should be exposed, and trod into the ditch, from which it came, and to which it belongs.

Rev. H. W. Beecher.

A SHIP is sinking, and the crew are in danger of being swallowed up by the waves. At the peril of their lives, a hardy crew push out in the life-boat. Battling with the breakers, they at length reach the wreck, and offer to save all on board. They say, "Our boat is large enough for you all; it is strongly built, and well able to reach the shore; we can soon pull you through the surf; we will not deceive you; we promise to save you all, if you will leave your sinking ship, and trust yourselves to our care." Some of the crew believe, enter the life-boat, and are saved. But some are drunken, distrust the boatman, or think it safer to stay on the wreck. Though these perished, it might be said that those brave boatmen were the saviors of all the crew, because able and willing to save them, but especially the saviors of those whom they actually brought on shore. Even so the life-boat of the gospel comes out to those who are perishing in the waves of sin; large enough, strong enough for all!

Rev. Newman Hall.

HOW terrible is the mistake those parents are making, who are constantly cherishing the selfishness of their daughters, by administering to their vanity, by loading them with finery, and exempting them from duties which they ought to discharge. How many a mother makes herself a slave, in order to make her daughter a lady; wears out her own energies, in order that her daughter may loll away her time in laziness, and waste her sympathies over the sickly sentimentalism of a shilling novel! And what a lady such a girl makes! A man who has regard for his future peace and prosperity, had better marry a great doll, on whose India-rubber face the red and white paint legitimately belong, than marry her; for what can humanity expect of a selfish wife — a cold-hearted, selfish mother?

Rev. Geo. C. Baldwin.

IF there is any day of the year on which you ought to clear your table of all intoxicating drinks, it is the first day of January. It is the worst day in the year for a man to begin a bad habit on. And it is an unkindness for you to put them there on that day; for you know that, when young men come into your house, and the sideboard is there, and wines are proffered to them, it will be an exception for one of them to have the moral firmness to say, "I never take them." You know that there are scores and scores of young men that will drink against their wish and against their judgment, because they are ashamed to make themselves an exception to those with whom they are in company. You know that, by their sympathies and kinder feelings, they will be dragged into a compliance that is bad for them. And, allow me to speak the truth, it is disgraceful to you. You have no business to spread a snare on your table, for the young and unwary, catching them at unawares.

Rev. H. W. Beecher.

THAT sex which almost alone was friendly to the Saviour, which anointed His feet with ointment, and followed Him with tears to His cross, which prepared sweet spices for His burial, and was the first to hail His resurrection, has, in turn, been especially befriended by His gospel. It has raised her from the degrading condition as a slave, or her still more degrading condition as a mere instrument of passion, to be a refined and purifying influence in society, and to lend to home the dignity and the grace of the mother, wife, sister, and daughter.

Rev. E. H. Chapin.

THOUGH fools spurn Hymen's gentle powers,
We, who improve his golden hours,
By sweet experience know,
That marriage, rightly understood,
Gives to the tender and the good,
A paradise below.

Cotton.

NO grander scene occurred in the life of our Washington, than the following: Immediately after organizing the government, he hastened to Fredericksburg, to visit his aged mother, who was sinking under disease. He said to her, "The people have elected me President, but before I go to fulfil the mission, it was my duty to come and bid you adieu; as soon as business will allow, I will hasten to you." She interrupted him, and said, "You will see me no more; my disease is fast approaching my vitals. I hope I am prepared for a better world; but go, George; fulfil the high destiny heaven has assigned you; go, my son, may heaven and a mother's blessing attend you." The President bowed his noble head and wept. The brow, around which Fame wreathed the purest laurel virtue ever gave to man, relaxed from its lofty bearing. That face, which could have awed a Roman Senate in its Fabian day, was bathed in tears. He never saw her more; but what an example has he left to the young men of America!

Rev. Geo. C. Baldwin.

LIKE the little child which strays from its watchful and tender parent, during the hours of play, but hastens back at the approach of alarm, so the believer, overtaken by calamity, awakes from his dream, and endeavors to retrace his steps to the neglected mercy-seat. But ah! in how many cases does he here learn his lamentable distance from God; and how mournfully he is made to cry, "Oh, that I knew where I might find Him!"

Rev. J. W. Alexander.

"THE path of sorrow, and that path alone,
Leads to the land where sorrow is unknown:
No traveller ere reached that blessed abode,
Who found not thorns and briars on the road."

THESE pulsations are virtually a clock, located in the framework of our being. Their number is fixed in the arithmetic of God. As life proceeds, the number lessens, and continues to lessen, till the last feeble, final beat is passing, and the soul spreading her pinions for another scene. The heart has paused! The man is dead! Time with him is no more! Millions upon millions of these pulses once were future; but now not one is future. They are all gone; and nothing but a miracle by the hand of God, can reproduce a single one of them. Every pulse marks a minute portion of time *gone.* Every pulse shortens the series; every pulse is an approach to the last one. Thus life glides, and thus its vital current flows. Arouse thyself, O sleeper! and rebuke thyself, vain presumer! ere all these pulses gone shall proclaim that thou art gone! "What thy hand findeth to do, that do with all thy might." Waste no time; for surely you have none that you can afford to waste.

Rev. S. T. Spear.

DO not all the graves compose this one melancholy chorus, and say, "Yet there is room — room for thee, thou maiden, adorned with virtue and loveliness; room for thee, thou aged man; room for thee, thou saint, as surely as there was room for thy Saviour; room for thee, thou sinner, as surely as thy kindred before thee, have laid themselves and their iniquities down in the dust; room for all, for all must in us at last lie down.

G. Gilfillan.

"EARTH to earth, and dust to dust!"
Here the evil and the just,
Here the youthful and the old,
Here the fearful and the bold,
Here the matron and the maid,
In one silent bed are laid;
Here the vassal and the king,
Side by side lie withering;
Here the sword and sceptre rust;
"Earth to earth, and dust to dust!"

Croly.

WHO, by searching, can find out God, and who can find out the Almighty to perfection? As well attempt to pronounce on the merits of the whole Astor Library, when you had read the first line in the first book you took down in the alcove, as attempt to pronounce authoritatively on the attributes and acts of the infinite Jehovah, from what you have seen afar off in His creation, or experienced during the few brief summers and winters of His overruling providence.

Rev. R. L. Cuyler.

SLEEP is the gift of God. We think that we lay our heads upon our pillows, and compose our bodies in a peaceful posture, and that, therefore, we naturally and necessarily sleep. But it is not so. Sleep is the gift of God; and not a man would close his eyes, did not God put His fingers on his eyelids; did not the Almighty send a soft and balmy influence over his frame which lulled his thoughts into quiescence, making him into that blissful state of rest which we call sleep. True, there be some drugs and narcotics, whereby men can poison themselves well-nigh to death, and then call it sleep; but the sleep of the healthy body is the gift of God. He bestows it; He rocks the cradle for us every night; He draws the curtain of darkness; He bids the sun shut up his burning eyes, and then He comes and says, "Sleep, sleep, my child! I give thee sleep."

Rev. C. H. Spurgeon

A SABLE night returns a shining morrow,
And days of joy ensue sad nights of sorrow·
The way to bliss lies not on beds of down;
And he that has no cross, deserves no crown.

Francis Quarles.

IT is a remarkable fact, that the one who loves his mother, who honors his mother, is never a bad man; she is never a bad woman. Tell me how a young woman treats her mother, and I will tell you what her general character is. Tell me how a young man treats his mother, and I will tell you what his prospects are for time, and a vast eternity. Men who have stood highest in the world's regard, have been thus distinguished. Olympia, the mother of Alexander, was a severe woman. Alexander's deputy, Antipata, once wrote letters of complaint against her to the Emperor. He replied, "Knowest thou not that one tear of my mother, will blot out a thousand letters of thine?"

Rev. Geo. C. Baldwin.

WHAT matter though the scorn of fools be given,
If the path followed, leads us on to heaven?

Mrs. Hale.

OH, that we could enter on each day's duties, and close each day's work, as if we had possibly seen our last sunrise, or last sunset. That were not a frame of mind inconsistent with earthly enjoyment. No! How bright the sky; how sweet the song of birds; how beautiful the wayside flowers; how full of pleasure everything to that sun-burned man, who expects, in a few more hours, and after long years of exile, to find himself at home.

THOSE islands which so beautifully adorn the Pacific, and which, but for sin, would seem so many Edens, were reared up from the bed of the ocean, by the little coral insect, which deposits one grain of sand at a time, till the whole of those piles are reared up. Just so with human exertions. The greatest results of the mind are produced by small, but continued efforts.

Rev. John Todd.

THE wise, the just, the pious, and the brave,
Live in their death, and flourish in the grave.

Joseph Green.

"O MOTHER! sweetest name on earth,
We lisp it on the knee, —
And idolize its sacred worth,
In manhood's ministry.
And if I e'er in heaven appear, —
A mother's holy prayer,
A mother's hand and gentle tear,
That pointed to a Saviour here,
Shall lead the wanderer there."

I HAVE on earth, to lay up a good store for the world to come. I must examine my heavenly ledger daily. I must look into my bank account, not weekly, monthly, or quarterly, as the man of worldly business does, but daily. Once a year to take stock of grace, will not suffice for me who am trafficking for eternity. This I must do every day. Before I close my eyes each night in sleep, I must have my accounts audited and accepted up to the last moment, in due preparation for the general audit.

Rev. Samuel Dunn.

HEAVEN'S great harbor of refuge is All-prayer; thousands of weather-beaten vessels have found a haven there, and the moment a storm comes on, it is wise for us to make for it with all sail.

Rev. C. H. Spurgeon.

LET Niagara's restless, rolling flood, with its thundering plunge into the deep below, be our preacher. See that stupendous waterfall, forever painting Nature's bow upon its own spray; see those impetuous Rapids, sweeping toward you, and then sweeping by you; see that deep, majestic current, that no earthly power can stay; mark the admiring thousands who have looked and wondered on these shores; and here behold in one of Nature's grandest objects an impressive emblem of life. Life is a stream, a rapid stream. Onward! onward! is its unchanging law. Everything that falls upon its bosom is borne onward with it. Not a drop of this stream ever rises to the clouds to descend, and pass again along the same channel. No tides and no vapors, no sun-beams and no gales, can change the position of the passing moment. Once, and but once, does it float down the stream of life. Once we have it, and then we have it no more. No man ever twice awoke to precisely the same life. Our position to-day in life's stream is not what it was yesterday. The rushing torrent is ever bearing us onward, and soon will empty us with all the contents of moral being into the great ocean of the eternal future. A moment's wise thoughtfulness as we thus move may save us an eternity of agony.

Rev. S. T. Spear.

THE dead,
 The only beautiful, who change no more;
The only blest, the dwellers on the shore
Of spring fulfilled. The dead! whom call we so?
They that breathe purer air, that feel, that know,
Things wrapt from us.

Mrs. Hemans.

A CHRISTIAN grave-yard is a holy spot. Why should it be a gloomy mansion? Nay, the graves of the just are blessed, for death is not the victor there, but life; death is but the minister of life. A Christian grave-yard is a cradle, where, in the quiet motions of the globe, Jesus rocks his sleeping children. By-and-by he will wake them from their slumber, and in the arms of angels they shall be translated to the skies.

Rev. H. T. Cheever

I SHALL never forget the impression made upon me, during the first year of my ministry, by a mechanic whom I had visited, and on whom I urged the paramount duty of family prayer. One day he entered my study, bursting into tears as he said: "You remember that girl, sir; she was my only child. She died suddenly this morning; she has gone, I hope, to God. But if so, she can tell him, what now breaks my heart, that she never heard a prayer in her father's house, or from her father's lips! Oh that she were with me but for one day again!"

Norman M'Leod.

IT is the misery of the wicked that he is an instrument out of tune; and the discordant strings are so many nerves, vital and sentient, and carrying anguish to the centre of feeling. But when the harp is new-strung; when the hand of grace moves over the harmonious chords; when the consciousness of the sanctified heart testifies that unity and love are at least preluding the choral joys of heaven, it is a breath of Heaven's health.

Rev. J. W. Alexander.

MY life is like the summer rose
  That opens to the morning sky,
But ere the shades of evening close
  Is scattered on the ground — to die!
My life is like the autumn leaf
  That trembles in the moon's pale ray:
Its hold is frail, its date is brief,
  Restless, and soon to pass away!

R. H. Wilde.

OH! if we could throw out of our hearts this feeling of unkindness toward men, we would see the heavens opened oftener. If we would turn away from hatred, strife, or variance against men, then we should have sympathy in the courts above, and would rejoice in the presence of God. There must be this world-wide philanthropy in our hearts before we are prepared to see God in his glory. And now I say to you, young women and young men — I speak to you, ye men of business — if there be, this morning, in your heart an angry feeling toward any human being, exterminate it if you hope to see the heavens opened and Jesus standing at the right hand of the throne of God. The dying saint cannot hate; the living saint can no more hate than the dying one; and if on a dying bed, you must not only forgive all, but love all, living and breathing in life; you must have the same benevolence if you would stand by the portals of glory.

Bishop Simpson.

"MAMMA, who made all those beautiful stars in the sky?"

The mother replied, "Our heavenly Father, my child."

"Then, mamma, I'll send him a kiss," Mary answered; and, suiting the action to the words, she kissed her hand, and threw it upward toward the sky.

Was not the offering accepted by the loving Father, who has said to all who *do not* trust and obey him, "Kiss the Son, lest he be angry, and ye perish by the way, when his wrath is kindled but a little?"

LET never day nor night unhallowed pass,
But still remember what the Lord hath done.

Shakspeare.

LIKE every social body, they are subject to tides of fashion. You know that there is a fashion of bonnets, a fashion of coats, a fashion of pleasures and amusements, and a fashion of eating and drinking, and there is a fashion of remedies. Doctors have fashions. And just now the tide sets very strongly in the direction of alcoholic stimulants — particularly of Bourbon whisky. Everybody has, first or last, one of three complaints. Everything is either neuralgia, or the heart complaint, or dyspepsia, with the doctors; and Bourbon whisky seems to be the great wholesome stimulant. The minister, whose nervous system is deranged by too close application to his professional duties, drinks Bourbon whisky -- the doctor told him to. The merchant, who has overtaxed his powers of body and mind by confining himself night and day to his business, drinks Bourbon whisky — his physician told him to. The lawyer, whose brain is perpetually at work, and intensely at work, drinks Buorbon whisky — his doctor told him to. Everybody that feels bad is drinking Bourbon whisky, under medical prescription! I do not say that it is not a good remedy. I have no question that it is, when properly prescribed, in special instances, as is quinine, or any other tonic or stimulant. But the indiscriminate and almost universal prescription of it I know cannot be right. I think that matter has gone full as far as fashion will justify, and that physicians should begin to hold back, and to discriminate, and to make fewer cases in which this all-healing remedy is applicable. Otherwise, under the cover of a medical prescription, we are going to have a deluge of whisky on the land again. For as soon as it is found out that the physician prescribes whisky for everything, men will not go to him any more, but will buy it in large quantities and at wholesale rates, and administer it themselves!

Rev. H. W. Beecher.

YOU come to an empty bird's-nest, and pick up the down that clings to it, or a stray plume that dropped; but, finding no other trace of the birdling, you say, it has flown away. And you come to a child's empty cradle, or a household tree, that stands grim and bare now, or shudders and moans in the breeze; and you say, that bird has learned to fly; it vanishes from its nest just as it was plumed of wing and clear of note.

H. S. Carpenter.

I DARE do all that may become a man;
Who dares do more is none.

Shakspeare.

A MERCHANT had become a member of his Church under the following circumstances: He had been for some time convinced of sin, and anxiously seeking in various methods to find peace with God. But all was in vain. He still carried about with him a heavy burden of remorse and fear. One day, passing a canal bridge on the public road leading to his office in the City of London, he saw a crowd, and going up to ascertain the cause of the gathering, he saw a blind man seated by the wayside, reading aloud from a copy of the Bible, specially printed for the blind in raised type. As the gentleman came up, the reader had reached the bottom of the page; and as he was finding his place on the other side, he mechanically repeated over and over the last clause he had read — "Neither is there salvation in any other; for there is none other name — none other name — none other name"— The gentleman passed on; but the words still rang in his ears, and in his heart too—"*None other name —none other name.*" They whispered to him during the hours of business, and they were his companions on his walk home. As he lay down to rest, like vesper bells from some ancient village church, they rang their plaintive chime — "None other name — none other name." And then the great truth flashed on him, and he saw that he had been seeking peace in his own efforts, rather than by simple reliance on the Saviour.

Rev. Newman Hall.

ONE of our most eloquent senators once said, that an Englishman's cottage was his castle. The winds may whistle through every crevice, and the rains penetrate through every cranny, but into that cottage the monarch of England dare not enter against the cotter's will. That is just the state of the case between Christ and the human soul. He has such a respect for the will of that immortal tenant that he has placed within us, that he will never force an entrance. He will do everything else; he will knock at the door—

"He now stands knocking at the door
  Of every sinner's heart;
The worst need keep him out no more,
  Or force him to depart."

But he will not force an entrance.

Rev. W. M. Punshon.

O GOD! how beautiful the thought,
How merciful the blest decree,
That grace can e'er be found, when sought.
And naught shut out the soul from thee!

Eliza Cook.

OH, I am weary of earth," said the child,
As it gazed with a tearful eye
On the snow-white dove that it held in its hand,
"For whatever I love will die."

Montgomery.

JUST like the guide who has engaged to show the traveller through the dark and tangled mazes of a strange country. The traveller may become alarmed and say, "I hear the howling of wild beasts off there, or the roar of the dreadful cataract off yonder, and I am afraid; I do not see the way out of this dreadful place." The guide says, "That is my business; don't you see this light? I have a lamp; follow me; I have engaged to guide you; keep to me, and I will bring you out."

So the Saviour said to those disciples, as he says to all Christians everywhere and in all time: "I am the way." Oh! how much trouble, anxiety, perplexity, and fear we might be saved if we just did our duty faithfully, and inquired what was the will of the Master—what would he have us do?—and leave the result to him!

Bishop Kingsley.

DEPRIVE us of the Bible! As well forbid us to gaze on the jewelled sky, or to be fanned by the winged and searching air. Deprive us of the Bible! Call it sin for us to look at the sun, and to bask in the blaze of his enlivening beams. The very same hand which launched yon orb upon his ocean of light, and bade him shine upon the evil and upon the good, has sent this orb into the world, and has sent it on purpose that it may be a lamp to all our feet and a lantern to all our paths.

Rev. W. M. Punshon.

WHEN I have seen a happy father and mother looking on the prizes their children brought home from school, or enjoying the home that filial love had provided for their old age, then have I seen how God rewards parental patience and fidelity. When I have seen pious parents beholding their children as they stood up before the alter to profess Christ in the freshness of a youthful consecration, then have I said to myself, "God is paying those parents their *wages*." They once dropped the seed with faith and tears; now, their sheaf is large and golden. God rewards a mother's fidelity and a father's godly example with accumulating interest through all eternity.

Alas! I have seen other "wages" too, paid dearly for, by parental impiety or neglect of duty. Eli's sin was repaid in Eli's sorrow. I have seen a frivolous, prayerless mother paid in the wages of a broken heart. And when to many a father's door a drunken son has been brought home from a Sabbath-breaking debauch, it was only the wages of his own sin which a just God was paying him. The "wages of sin is death" — and of no sin more surely than parental. It is death to peace of mind — death to domestic happiness — death to the neglected or misguided souls of their offspring.

Rev. Theo. L. Cuyler.

THE mother, in her office, holds the key
Of the soul; and she it is who stamps the coin
Of character, and makes the being who would be a savage
But for her gentle cares, a Christian man.

Anonymous.

TAKE this child and nurse it for ME, and I will give thee thy wages — is the inscription which God's hand writes on every cradle. "When I dressed my child each morning, I prayed that Jesus would clothe it with purity," said a godly mother to one who inquired her secret of good training. "When I wash it, I pray that his blood will cleanse its young soul from evil; when I feed it, I pray that its heart may be nourished with truth and may grow into likeness with the youthful Jesus of Nazareth." Here was religious training *from the cradle.* It began with the dawn, and its course was like the sun, grow ing more full-orbed in beauty until the "perfect day." That mother received her golden wages in the early conversion, usefulness, and honor of all her children. "Go thou and do likewise."

Rev. Theo. L. Cuyler.

OF all the joys that brighten suffering earth,
What joy is welcomed like a new-born child?
What life so wretched, but that at its birth
Some heart rejoiced, some lip in gladness smiled?

Mrs. Norton.

OH! how are our souls dissatisfied when we listen to a sermon destitute of Christ. There are some preachers who can manage to deliver a sermon, and leave out Christ's name altogether. Surely, the true believer will stand like Mary Magdalene over the sermon, and say, "They have taken away my Lord and I know not where they have laid him." Take away Christ from the sermon, and you have taken away its essence.

Rev. C. H. Spurgeon

I HAVE fancied many a time that I have seen Jesus with his eye upon the suffering poor — looking down upon the poor woman, who plies her needle while others sleep and while she needs sleep — and, for every tear and every sigh, Jesus says, "I am adorning this mansion a little more; I am putting something in order that will make that woman a little more happy and joyful when she enters her eternal rest; for all things shall work together for good to them that love God."

Bishop Kingsley.

LOST time is not like a lost note capable of recovery; once gone, it is forever gone. Each day, like every child of sorrow, has enough of its own, and needs not that a portion of its predecessor's responsibilities be added to its own account of responsibility. Every day, as it opens, must find me, and when it closes, must leave me, prepared, by the grace of God, for my last day. Short reckonings here are absolutely necessary to safety. What a day or an hour may bring forth who can tell? One day's accounts, if unsatisfactory, if unsettled, may lose me an eternity of bliss! If I sleep in guilt, I may wake up in hell!

Rev. Samuel Dunn.

THE heart, by a law of its constitution, must have something to which it can attach itself. Its emblems are the summer tendril and the clasping ivy. It was never formed for the hermitage or the monastery — and you must do violence to all its excellent charities, before it will entirely denude itself of all objects of solicitude and love.

Rev. W. M. Punshon.

I'LL tread a righteous path; a good report
Makes men live long, although their life is short.

Watkins.

THERE is no house on the shores of time, which the waves will not wash away; there is no path here which the foot of disappointment will not tread; there is no sanctuary here which sorrow will not invade. There is a home provided for the soul, but you can reach it only by living for God: to none others than those who thus live will its doors be opened.

Rev. John Todd.

DO you ask me for pleasure?
Then lean on His breast,
For there the sin-laden
And weary find rest.
In the valley of death
You will triumphing cry, —
"If this be called dying,
'Tis pleasant to die!"

R. M. McCheyne.

TWO years ago, a mariner, who had been on a whaling voyage to the Pacific, entered New Bedford. He left his wife and a little boy behind, and had been gone three years. As the ship came near, he became so excited that when the orders were given he could not obey, having lost control of himself. By and by he saw people in the distance, and asked the privilege of looking through the glass. Up yonder on the hill, back of them all, he saw a woman, by whose side there stood a boy, and she had a glass, in the use of which she appeared to be very much interested. I need not describe the scene of their coming together. They met; but after a few weeks he had to take another voyage, and run the risk of shipwreck and of never returning. But when we meet, we shall not part again.

"There all the ship's company meet
That sailed with the Master beneath;
With shoutings each other they greet
And triumph o'er sorrow and death.
The voyage of life is at end,
The mortal affliction is past;
The age that in heaven they spend
For ever and ever shall last."

Rev. H. Mattison.

HAVE you ever visited a factory just before the dinner hour? The whizzing of wheels, the rattling of shuttles, the rumble of heavy machinery,—these sounds, with the rapid motion of everything around, have overwhelmed you. You were wearied with the intense activity; but suddenly, on the ringing of a bell, the engine has stoped, and all was still. How delightful and emphatic that silence!

Such is the Sabbath rest in the great factory of human toil. Over-taxed toiler, thou mayst pause! The busy wheel may stand still. The anxious brain may be tranquil. Exhausted nature may recruit her powers. Households may gather together. The husband, with his wife, may leisurely enjoy the gifts of God. The father may gather his little ones around his knee. It is a holiday — God's gift to man.

Rev. Newman Hall.

DID you ever come near a magnetic apparatus or an electric machine? I remember the feelings I had when I was a boy, at the first touch of the wire. I did not know what strange thing it was; I was fearful to go near, and had trembling sensations as I approached the magnetic apparatus. And yet, just as others took hold of the wires and felt the electric sensations, so I felt them. The law of the Spirit of God is uniform. The same electricity that thrills you thrills me; the same magnetism that touches me can touch you.

I have been to the cross; my brethern and sisters have been to the cross; and when by faith they have taken hold, oh, the divine power that has come! oh, the thrill of glory that has gone through the soul! oh, the chains that have fallen off! The dungeon flamed with light and the soul was filled with glory and with God.

Bishop Simpson.

ACCOUNT for it as we can, we know that a community entirely composed of men, would be a community of sheer barbarians. In a large degree, woman has subdued this rough speech, and checked this fierce selfishness, and converted man from an Arab or a sea-king, to the methods and amenities of a gentleman.

Rev. E. H. Chapin.

WHEN a Christian is well grafted into Christ, he will bear a great variety of fruits. Paul tells us that the choicest yields of the Spirit are "love, joy, peace, long-suffering, gentleness, goodness, meekness, temperance, and faith." A healthy Christian will yield all these in full measure. Others will excel in some special grace. We know of certain church-members who are so completely under the cold shade of the world, that the half-dozen sour dwarfish apples they yield are not worth any man's gathering. We know, too, of others so ladened that you cannot touch the outermost limb without shaking down a golden pippin, or a Seckel, or a jargonelle. Such spiritual trees make a church-orchard beautiful. They are a joy to the pastor who walks through them. Every stooping bough and every purple cluster that hangs along the walls bespeaks the goodness of the soil, the moisture of the Spirit's dews, and the abundance of God's sunshine.

Rev. Theo. L. Cuyler.

YOUNG man, have you a mother? I charge you before God, to love, to honor, to cherish, to obey her! Little dream you of the tide of love that swells in her heart towards you; little do you know how much she has done for you! or how much she will do for you! Though all others forsake you, she will not! The greater your danger, the sterner your trials, the darker your misfortunes, the heavier your sorrow, the closer will she press her throbbing heart to yours—the closer entwine its mighty tendrels about you! Not many years hence you will see her in her coffin, and then you will know what it is to lose your earliest, truest, best friend. Study, then, by acts of kindness, by words of affection, and above all, by virtuous, God-fearing Jesus-loving lives, to gladden her heart and throw sunshine on her path to the grave! and then a dying mother's blessing will be yours, and the holy benediction of your mother's God will be upon you for evermore! Such is the advice and pledge of the Holy Bible! Such is the advice of all the wise and good.

Rev. Geo. C. Baldwin.

THERE is an inner life, which, though unseen, is loftier, vaster, and more eventful. The history of the man, is the history of his immortal part. While men look on the panorama of sensible things, the poverty, the pleasures, the journeys, the expeditions, the wars, the disasters, the triumphs of our race; eyes are gazing upon us from the spiritual world, intent upon those great realities which escape us in the pilgrimage of the spirit; the shade and texture of the reason; the dangers, and crosses, and wounds of the moral part; the new birth of the soul; the mysterious assaults of principalities and powers; the sublime conflict with evil; the armor, the triumph, and the salvation.

Rev. J. W. Alexander.

A THOUSAND savage beasts of prey
Around the forest roam;
But Judah's Lion guards the way,
And guides the traveller home."

IS it the declared will of God that in all things Christ should "have the pre-eminence." God is very jealous for the honor of his Son. It is quite possible for us to fix our thoughts too exclusively on the first Person of the Trinity, but hardly on the second. "He that hath seen the Son hath seen the Father."

Rev. C. D. Foss.

ALL the operations of the divine life are very different things in practice from what they are in theory. It is just as it is in agriculture. A man to be a practical farmer must be a working man. It is one thing to have romantic ideas of green glades, and longings after a quiet farm in the country, and to be turning over books of landscape-gardening, and studying the chemistry of soils and manures, and quite another thing to go into the fields and ditch, and dig, and plough, and harrow. It is one thing to manage a farm by proxy, and have all your work done by others, and quite another thing to take hold with the oxen, and clear up wild lands, and break the fallow ground, and plant corn and potatoes with your own hands.

Now, although the managing of a farm can be done by proxy, if a man has wealth enough, yet there is no such possibility in the Christian life. Here you have to keep your own vineyard, and to work you own farm. A man cannot dig in his own heart with hired laborers; he can do nothing there at second-hand. The digging and the ditching, the ploughing and harrowing, he must do himself. If it could be done by others, there is many a Christian merchant, who would pay a thousand dollars a year salary to any man who would farm his heart for him, and get the work done, while he could be all the while accumulating money. There are many persons, both poor and rich, who would give all that they are worth, if they could get some trusty agent to farm out their hearts for them, with the assurance of keeping them in good order and fruitful.

Rev. H. T. Cheever.

ONE who ponders for but a moment upon the *number* of beings in death will be struck with the *numerical* vastness of the problem, where are the great nations of antiquity, long since swept from the earth? Where are the aborigines that once wandered on this soil, hunted in its forests, fished in its streams, saw God in the clouds and heard him in the winds? Where are the sainted heroes who floated in the "May Flower," bowed on its deck, and made Plymouth Rock immortal? Where are the Fathers of Revolutionary toil and glory? Where are the great men of history, and the uncounted millions who have lived and died unknown to fame? Whither has gone and where has terminated this stupendous flow of mind, that for so many centuries has been pouring over the cascade of death? Who that claims to be a man can look into the great mausoleum of a buried race with not a thought in his mind, or a feeling in his heart, or a word on his lips? Who can survey the amazing spectacle in cold and sullen silence? It is not wonderful that poetry should burn at this altar, and with death for her theme breathe the most exciting inspirations of song. It is not wonderful that philosophy has in every age thoughtfully trod the banks of that mighty sea we must all sail so soon.

Rev. Samuel T. Spear.

GO to the ant, thou sluggard, learn to live,
And by her weary ways reform thine own.

Smart.

ALL the presses that to-day are rattling in the land, scattering their leaves of blessing and of hope or of sorrow, rattled in the brain of Faust long before they worked in the eyes of men. Fulton's head was the first engine-house whence rolled out the engines that to-day a e tugging and lifting and pulling at the burdens of mankind; and the wires of national intelligence that whispered in the ear of the New-England mother the last words of her dying boy on the fields of Gettysburg, before his lips were sealed, were once coiled up in the narrow study of Morse. The suspension-bridge is but a crystallized idea. John C. Fremont carried in the fluids of his thought the victorious fleet long before Commodore Foote floated into the Mississippi. Ericsson walked up and down Pennsylvania with the Monitor in his massive brain, full-rigged, and with cannon and crew, long before she sailed in the waters below. Power's Greek Slave stood patient and voiceless, yet pleading, in the temple of his thought long before it quickened the cold marble into life; and the Heart of the Andes is but one canvas on the soul of Church, indicating what is within. The chisel of the sculptor and the brush of the painter are but the magic wand with which Genius crystallizes her inspired ideas.

Rev. C. H. Fowler.

WHEN you select articles of dress, you hold them up from the sombre dusk, or the unnatural glare of the wareroom, into that temperate and every-day light, in which they are to be worn. So to select the color and the texture of a principle, one must consider how it will make up, and how it will wear in the scenes which await it.

H. S. Carpenter.

A MAN who wanted to know where a certain city in Europe is, if he did not know the geography of Europe, would not know anything about it; and how can I know where heaven is till I understand the map of the universe? If an angel should come down here, and tell me, I should not know what he meant. We must die to understand that. But that there is a heaven is a glorious and important truth.

Rev. H. Mattison.

I WENT to Boston, a year ago last June, to a great convention there. I had never been in New England. I went to No. 5 Cornhill, and saw one hundred ministers, but there was not one among them all that knew me. I went elbowing my way among them, and got a new idea. I thought, if there will be no recognition of friends in heaven, what a lonesome place it will be for a poor man who gets there! At length, I found a man who exclaimed, "Why, Brother Mattison, is it you!" "Is this Brother Mattison?" said another, and so the introduction went around. It was a Book-Room heaven in a short time. I expect it will be so when we join our sainted friends in heaven; I expect that we shall know each other there.

Rev. H. Mattison.

IF the victorious "Kearsage" were to spring a-leak from striking on a sunken rock, what matters it that the captain should take to studying his charts, or the pilot to noting his compass, or the sailing-master to make up the log, or the marines to their accustomed drill? These are all proper occupations at the proper time. But they don't save the ship! How can they escape, if they neglect to stop that leak? Oh! unforgiven, unconverted reader, what shall it profit thee to enjoy all art, and all polite letters, and revel amid wealth uncounted, if at last thou awake amid the agonies of the lost.

Rev. Theo. L. Cuyler.

NEVER did angels taste above
Redeeming grace and dying love."

A WEARY traveller, parched with thirst, toils along a dusty road. To beguile the tedium of his journey he may whittle out a toy, repeat passages of poetry, or follow a close course of reasoning; yet all the while his husky throat clamors for water; he cannot forget it; and ever and anon, in the pauses of other occupation, it is the absorbing matter of reflection. So prayer is a quenchless thirst for the living waters of salvation, fixed in the soul forever, but entirely compatible with the employment of body or mind in other things for a season.

Rev. J. Mudge.

GIVE us Christ always, Christ ever. The monotony of Christ is sweet variety, and even the unity of Christ hath in it all the elements of harmony. Christ on the cross and on the throne, in the manger and in the tomb — Christ everywhere is sweet to us. We love his name, we adore his person, we delight to hear of his works.

Rev. C. H. Spurgeon.

DID you ever see orchestras getting ready to play? They take a tuning-fork that is at the concert-pitch, and strike it, and get the note exactly, and chord the instruments, one after another taking the pitch, and all of them at last coming into harmony. It makes no difference if they played only two hours ago, they are obliged, at every performance, to repeat the same operation; and frequently it has to be repeated two or three times, if the performance is long.

Now, no man can chord his heart so that it will go without tuning from one day to another. Every day we must take the Word of God as the concert-pitch, and tune our hearts up to that; and we must do it not only every day, but many times a day. We must do it so often that we shall have something more than a vague conception of Christ.

Rev. H. W. Beecher.

THEN in life's goblet freely press
The leaves that give it bitterness;
Nor prize the colored waters less,
For in thy darkness and distress,
New light and strength they give.

Longfellow.

SUPPOSE he had told us of the wonders of heaven, we might have thought, after all, that the words had an oriental exuberance, that it could hardly be really all that; but when I see the Lord willing to die to purchase heaven for such a poor sinner as I consciously am, then I know how vast, how lovely, how lustrous and full of wonder it is. If he had broken bits from the pavement of heaven, and brought them to me; if he had plucked amaranthine flowers from the gardens of Paradise, and brought them down; if he had shown me in a mirror all the wonder and mystery of that heavenly estate, he could never have portrayed to me as he does, when he is willing to die to buy it for me, that, by the purchase of his blood, heaven may become my immortal inheritance. He appeals to my moral nature in its aspiration after eternal life, by the power of the Holy Ghost, and so he shall conquer the world. Dying, he shall subdue it to himself, and lifted up upon the cross, he shall call all nations, kindreds, and tribes around him till they accept him as their Redeemer, till they bow to him as their Ruler, till they worship him as their God.

Rev. R. S. Storrs, Jr.

A DEATH, not such as we may hope for, surrounded only by those who love us, whose gentle offices and tender tones half disguise the fierceness of the last enemy, but death embittered by the crushing grief in the garden, and the mock kiss of the traitor, and the cowardly desertion of the disciples, and the ruffian insults of the court, and the cruel torture of the scourge, and the bitter taunts of the Scribes, and the writhing agony of the cross, and the midnight horrors of a mental woe, which wrung from the sufferer the appalling cry, "My God, my God, why hast thou forsaken me?"

Rev. Newman Hall.

WHEN I stand before the throne
Dressed in beauty not my own;
When I see thee as thou art,
Love thee with unsinning heart,
Then, Lord, shall I fully know —
Not till then — how much I owe.

Rev. R. M. McCheyne.

I CANNOT see here without helping out my sight, first with glasses, then with a microscope, for the minute creations of the Deity, and then with the telescope, to bring distant objects near; but when God raises me from the dead, who can tell but I will be able to adjust my eye to make it telescopic and microscopic, and thus make it serve all the ends that God can make an optical instrument serve in the land of mortals. O brethren! it doth not yet appear what we shall be in the world to which we go. Who can doubt that heaven will be of surpassing beauty and magnificence?

Rev. H. Mattison.

HOW will my last day on earth find me? Struggling in vain, for more of this mortal life, or anticipating, with seraph glow, my entrance upon life eternal? Unwilling to quit the tenement of clay, or ready to depart and to be with Christ? It will be the one or the other. Its issues are awe-ful to contemplate. The die will then be cast. My condition will then be one of infinite joy, or of infinite woe. I shall then curse the day that I was born, or I shall bound and leap with exultation that ever life, that shadow of life eternal, was given to me! Which will it be when my last day terminates?

Rev. Samuel Dunn.

HUMBLE we must be, if to heaven we go;
High is the roof there, but the gate is low.

Bailey.

ONE of the obvious evils of the practice of elaborate dressing for church is the waste of holy time. Some of the good women whom we see at church every Sabbath, must have spent two or three hours in the work of preparation. The task of putting on so much finery is no slight one. And it is not seldom the case, we suspect, that individuals stay at home on the Sabbath because so large a part of the morning is occupied in sleep, or in the cares of the house, that there is not time enough left to dress for church. If the toilet were a little simpler, less time would be required to make it, and the hours thus saved, might be profitably spent in reading, or in restful thought. Many persons complain that the Sabbath is to them the busiest day of the week. Is not the work of the toilet one very large part of their labor?

Rev. W. Gladden.

THERE are regions beyond the most distant nebulous outskirts of matter; but no regions beyond the divine goodness. We may conceive of tracts where there are no worlds, but not of any where there is no God of mercy.

Rev. J. W. Alexander.

THE wife of Tigranes was among the captives on a certain public day when Cyrus, the conqueror of Asia, was reviewing his troops. While the captives pressed forward to see the conqueror, Tigranes presented himself before Cyrus and offered a thousand talents for the redemption of his wife. Among the observations afterwards made respecting the appearance and glory of the conqueror, this noble lady was asked what she thought of Cyrus. She had not seen him. On what, then, was your attention fixed? On the man who offered a thousand talents for my redemption. And on whom should the attention of Christians be chiefly fixed, but on him who gave, not a thousand talents, but his own most precious life, for their redemption.

Rev. E. D. Griffin.

BURDENED with guilt, wouldst thou be blest?
Trust not the world, it gives no rest;
Christ brings relief to hearts opprest:
Oh! weary sinner, come!

Come, leave thy burden at the cross:
Count all thy gains but worthless dross;
His grace o'erpays all earthly loss,
Oh! needy sinner, come!

Come hither! bring thy boding fears,
Thy aching heart, thy streaming tears;
'Tis Mercy's voice salutes thine ears,
Ho! every sinner come!

THERE is a third mistake, or sin we had better name it. It is the sin of him who brings all the work of the week and all his plans for business into the house of God. How much better is such an one than those sacrilegious hucksters and brokers who once set up their bird-stalls and exchange-tables in Jerusalem's sacred temple? For this man brings his counting-room or his shop to church in his heart. He makes bargains or computes the rise in gold during the prayer, sells stocks or buys produce all through the sermon, and goes home with new plans for the Monday's toil and traffic. "You are the first minister," said a friend once to his pastor, "who ever has preached me out of my flour-store." We honored the frankness of his confession; but are there not hundreds of human *bodies* in our churches on every Sabbath, whose *souls* are in flour-stores or brokers' offices, or warehouses, or in barns and harvest-fields? Whom do these worship, God or Mammon? Jesus Christ tells them that they cannot worship both at the same time.

Rev. Theo. L. Cuyler.

SUPPOSE the stars blotted out in darkness, suppose the angels dead; imagine the glorified spirits above are all gone, and you are left alone, the last man, and there is God looking at you. What an idea it would be for you to think of—that there was only you to be looked at! how steadily he could observe you! how well he would discern you! But mark you, God does really look at you this night as much, as entirely, as absolutely without division of sight, as if you were the only being his hand had ever made. Can you grasp that? God sees you, with all his eyes, with the whole of his sight—you—you—you—you are the particular object of his attention this very moment. God's eyes are looking down upon you; remember that!

Rev. C. H. Spurgeon.

BUT enough we know to assure us, not only that God's angels are fighting, and that too on the right side, but that they are our comrades-in-arms, if we be soldiers of Jesus Christ, contending for the right, the good, and the true. We may not know the manner or the measure of their co-operation in the secret conflicts of the Christian with the guerrilla bands of the world, the flesh, and the devil, that sweep across his soul at times, nor the part they take in the grand encounters of the church with the "abominable army" of the great rebel. But the fact stands out too vividly to be evaded, that they are not idle spectators of the holy war.

Rev. F. N. Zabriskie.

HE is the freeman whom the truth makes free,
And all are slaves besides.

Cowper.

WHEN this passing world is done,
When has sunk yon glaring sun,
When we stand with Christ in glory,
Looking o'er life's finished story,
Then, Lord, shall I fully know —
Not till then — how much I owe.

Rev. R. M. McCheyne.

WE have slept soundly all night, happily unconscious of existence, with its toil and its care; and now the *day* has dawned. The monarch thereof is painting the eastern sky with golden colors. We awake with a species of surprise, having for several hours been absent from ourselves. We rush to the duties of the day; soon it is mid-day; and soon the shades of evening again mantle the earth. Another morn appears, and then another; and at length the last morn is on the wing. Thus our days fly, and thus they will, till all have flown. Soon these lapsing days will place us all in the great yesterday of the infinite past. Solemn preachers are they to the living; solemn monitors to the sinful, and monitors to the good.

Rev. S. T. Spear.

THE more you live with Christ the better you will love him. There are some people in the world of so unlovable a nature, that to see them once in seven years is quite enough if you wish to love them; the less you know of them perhaps the better. But of Jesus Christ it can be said, the longer you live with him the better you will love him.

Rev. C. H. Spurgeon.

MANY a young woman, who cannot do a sum in the simplest mathematics, who knows no more of history than she does of sciences, is as ignorant of literature as she is of the stars; cannot parse a sentence, any more than she could unravel an eastern hieroglyphic: has not even the ability to write a decent love-letter — is sent to dancing schools, where her feet are educated, while her head and her heart are left untaught, and uncared for. How much the blame of this rests upon misguided parents, and a false public taste, God only knows; but these are mournful facts, over which every lover of humanity must weep.

Rev. Geo. C. Baldwin.

"WHAT is woman, what her smile,
Her look of love, her eyes of light,
What is she, if she in her heart deride
The blessed Saviour? Love may write his
Name upon her marble brow,
Or linger in her curls of jet,
The light spring flower may scarcely bend
Beneath her step; and yet, and yet,
Without this choicest grace,
She is a lighter thing than vanity."

THE Creator of this great universe must be good. Books of evidence, begone! One sunset, one moonlight hour, one solemn meditation of the night, one conversation at evening with a kindred heart, is worth you all! Such scenes, such moments, dissolve the most massive doubts easily and speedily as the evening air sucks down the mimic mountains of vapor which lie along the verge of heaven.

G. Gilfillan.

OTHER things stop; but time never halts a moment. The miracle of Joshua is not repeated; the sun and moon no longer stand still; the shadow has never gone back upon the dial-plate.

Time has not lost a second. He led us through the spring, treading on flowers; he led us through the harvests of the summer, and the orchards of the autumn. He has shaken down the last leaf, and darkened the forests with mourning. December is the sexton of the year, and gathers all the glories of the field into the sepulchre.

Rev. Theo. L. Cuyler.

IF God hath made the world so fair,
Where sin and death abound,
How beautiful beyond compare
Will Paradise be found?

Montgomery.

A DEITY believed, is joy begun;
A Deity adored, is joy advanced;
A Deity beloved, is joy matured.
Each branch of piety delight inspires.

Young.

DO your tenants say, "I should have known that he had become a Christian by the way he collects his rents?" Do your business associates and your neighbors say, "How much more fair and just he is in his dealings than he used to be?" Is your nature, that was once as hard as a granite rock, now soft and mossy on the surface, so that vegetation might almost grow upon it? It is your *life* that is to determine whether you have the spirit of

Christ, and if you have not the spirit of Christ you are none of his.

Rev. H. W. Beecher.

THE Christian's soul plumes her immortal wings in anticipation of that pure and happy realm of rest in "our Father's kingdom." When the heart's bitter sorrows are over here; when all of the tears have been shed on earth; when the breast has swelled enough with wrongs, injury, and grief; when the mockery of human happiness has disclosed its Dead Sea fruit of dust and ashes to our souls, then, then shall we leave the sin-stained earth forever; then shall our spirits—like the white-winged doves of Eden—soar up into celestial airs; glide with the music of Paradise around its *welcomed* entrance into the home of heaven, OUR HOME, where the lost and loved of earth will meet us. There no cheek will blanch to receive the pure kisses of the redeemed; there no heart will shrink with wounded feelings from the stranger and unknown; there all will be one family for evermore in that serene and matchless place, where "angels' feet make music over all the starry floor."

S. T. Matthews.

THERE is not a daisy that was not organized to be a daisy, but I should like to see one that did not have the sun to help it up from the seed; there is not an aster that was not organized to be an aster, but where is there one that grew independent of the sun! What the sun is to flowers, that the Holy Ghost must be to our hearts, if we would be Christians. If there is a man who can be a Christian without the help of God, he has a heart such as I never knew a person to have.

Rev. H. W. Beecher.

TELL me, my sacred soul,
O tell me, Hope and Faith,
Is there no resting-place
From sorrow, sin, and death?
Is there no happy spot
Where mortals may be blest,
Where grief may find a balm
And weariness a rest?
Faith, Hope, and Love, best boons to mortals given,
Waved their bright wings, and whispered "Yes in heaven."

Anonymous.

IF you want to drive a wedge into a lock, you do not want a hole as big as the butt-end of the wedge. Let there be a hole just large enough to get the sharp end in, and that is sufficient. When the little end is once entered, then, with rap upon rap, the wedge will make way for itself, and at last the lock will split open.

And when a man wants to be rent asunder, he does not need to begin with anything but a little lie, about as thin as a sheet of paper. If there is only a place just large enough to get temptations in, you may be sure that battering will open a passage-way for all the rest. And so men are deceived. It is a small sin is it? — smaller than the sharp side of an axe? But is it not large enough for a cutting-edge? The smaller it is, the worse it is. If temptations presented themselves blunt-end first, every man would be shocked by them; but they do not. The danger of temptation is that it comes fair-looking and disguised.

Rev. H. W. Beecher.

SINCE I have been trying to talk here this morning, young men have been thinking where they spent last evening, and where they are going to spend to-morrow evening. Young ladies have been planning how they shall array themselves, and what will be the next articles of apparel they are to purchase. They are not thinking of Jesus. How shall the word of life reach their hearts?

Bishop Simpson.

SUPPOSE I should attempt to persuade a nation that our Indian corn was excellent for food, by offering them the cob and husk without the grain. I might insist as strongly as I pleased that it was full of nutriment; but after they had partaken of the cob and husk, supposing them to be the corn, they would declare corn to be innutritious. Now, what an ear of corn is without the grain, that Christianity is without kind, genial, sympathetic love. Christianity with this love left out is nothing but cob and husk. When the corn is growing, the cob serves a good purpose as a centre for the grain to form itself upon, and the husk is a grand wrapper for protecting it from the weather while it is yet tender. I do not, therefore, speak against the cob or the husk. I regard them as important inside and outside influences, provided for the ripening of the corn. I do not speak against churches, and "means of grace," and religious institutions, but I do say that churches, and means of grace, and religious institutions, which do not produce love, are mere cob and husk. True Christian love is the grain. That is to be the bread of life. It is that which is to transform man, and lead him in his treatment of his fellow-men, to imitate him who bowed his majesty, and laid his head in the grave, giving his life to show his love for us, and to rescue us from eternal death.

Rev. H. W. Beecher.

YET even night hath its songs. Have you never stood by the seaside at night, and heard the pebbles sing, and the waves chant God's glories? Or have you never risen from your couch, and thrown up the window of your chamber and listened there? Listened to what? Silence — save now and then, a murmuring sound, which seems sweet music then. And have you not fancied that you heard the harp of God playing in the heavens? Did you not conceive that yon stars, that those eyes of God, looking down on you, were also mouths of song— that every star was singing God's glory, singing as it shone, its mighty Maker, and his lawful well-deserved praise? Night hath its songs.

Rev. C. H. Spurgeon.

WHY does a man wish to be a child again? Because he has got no Father in the future; he has got no home beyond, and he goes back again to the home he once had, when he was tolerably innocent, and nearer heaven than he has ever since been. Ah! of all the sadnesses that can come upon a man in this world, is to be constantly travelling, travelling, travelling on, with no home in prospect! A soul without a home! a soul without a home! Three is no sadness in this world, nothing on this side of hell that I know of like that. And yet that is just why many people long to be children again, because they do not know what is before them in the future.

Rev. W. M. Punshon.

IT is the neglected wheel that capsizes the vehicle, and maims for life the passengers. It is the neglected leak that sinks the ship. It is the neglected field that yields briars instead of bread. It is the neglected spark kindling near the magazine whose tremendous explosion sends its hundreds of mangled wretches into eternity. The neglect of an officer to throw up a rocket on a certain night caused the fall of Antwerp, and postponed the deliverance of Holland for twenty or more years. The neglect of a sentinel to give an alarm hindered the fall of Sebastopol, and resulted in the loss of many thousand lives.

And, my friend, it will be the stupendous aggregation of all your fatal neglects — of all the neglected Sabbaths, joined to the neglected offers of grace, and added to the neglected duties, and multiplied by the neglected drawings of God's Spirit — that will sink you (if you die impenitent) into perdition.

Rev. Theo. L. Cuyler.

ON some very cold morning of February a man wakes up in his house, and says, "Every window here is curtained with ice. Frost is on every pane, and obstructs the light. And now, I am not going to take a step in my daily duties, nor have a morsel of breakfast, till every particle of this ice is removed." So he begins to scrape the glass; and before he has finished cleaning the second pane, the frost is formed on the first one that he scraped, as much as it was when he began. He makes very slow progress. And if I were in his presence, I would say, "My friend, build a big fire in the stove, and that will get your breakfast; and while it is getting your breakfast, the heat that it will diffuse throughout the room will melt the ice, and the light will be let in through the windows in the most legitimate way."

Now, there are thousands and thousands of chrystallized skepticisms and difficulties that attach to a man's understanding because there is not any fire in the heart; because that very moral state which solves difficulties is wanting in him. And if he would have his difficulties solved, he must believe in the Lord Jesus Christ. The way to solve difficulties is to be in full communion with God.

Rev. H. W. Beecher.

A MAN might say, "That star is a little thing, it is a single beam of light, and does so little toward dispelling the darkness, we may safely blot it from the firmament;" and yet, if you repeat that blotting-out process in detail, you will clothe the heavens in sackcloth and plunge the earth in eternal night. That is not a safe way to deal with moral and religious interests, nor, indeed, with other matters.

Bishop Ames.

I LOOK out of my window at a tree covered with foliage. I see the leaves waving in the wind; silver-bordered with sunshine, some of them; dark with shadows, some of them. Altogether, the mass of foliage pleases me. The general contour is pleasing. I go out and pluck a branch, and, as I hold it in my hand, the branch pleases me.

And I pluck a leaf, and the leaf pleases me. And so I find that I not only admire the tree as a whole, but that I admire the branches of the tree: I admire each and every leaf of the tree. So God loves the whole mass of men, and yet loves each separate individual comprising the mass. He is the near and dear friend of each person. He is a personal God, walking before, and holding the hand of each.

Rev. Herman Bisbee.

IN Greenwood's bowers,
Among the flowers,
With angels watching overhead
Resting lowly,
Calm and holy,
Sleep our precious dead.

And heavenly keepers
Guard those sleepers
Until the resurrection morn,
When forms of brightness,
In God's own likeness,
Shall rise with beauty heaven-born.

AND he who clothes the lilies with their lovely dress, taking the seed at first rotting in the earth in Spring, and carrying the germ of life up by his power into the light of day, and there causing the rays of the sun, and all the influences of the elements, to weave for them a Summer array, with which the impearled golden robes of Solomon in his greatest graudeur were not to be compared in glory. He who clothes the lilies with such loveliness, will much more take care of the germ laid with our mortal frame in the earth, will raise it into the light and air of heaven, and there will swallow up mortality of life, giving to every believer in the Lord an array, perhaps incomparably more glorious than even the vesture of the angels.

Rev. H. T. Cheever.

THOUGH earth may be dark
And life may be drear,
There's light in the sky;
Our home is not here.

We look far above,
Our home is on high,
Beyond the dark clouds
There's light in the sky.

The sun ever shines,
Clouds ever obscure,
But far up above
The sunlight is pure.

So trouble and grief
May cloud our way here
'Tis only above them
The sunlight is clear.

OUR fallen being has two motions, like the globe; one upon its own axis, and the other in its orbit. While intent solely on present enjoyment, absorbed in the plans of to-day, and careless of the future, man whirls with his carnal mind upon the apis of self, regardless of that swift, stupendous, controlling motion in the orbit, which is sweeping him from God.

Rev. H. T. Cheever.

SUPPOSE you have a ship about to sail with a valuable cargo for a distant port; but the tide must be favorable before that ship can start. Hour after hour passes, and then at length you see by the change in the current, and the swinging round of the ship at anchor, that the tide has turned. Now, then, you at once weigh anchor and sail! What would you say if some one objected and said, "No; wait! the tide has only *just* turned!" So, when the tide of a sinner's affections, which was flowing downwards, begins to flow upwards, that sinner is at once on his way to paradise; the change is complete; the tide is as fair now as it ever will be; why, then, wait? That vessel is on its way to glory!

Rev. Newman Hall.

CHILD Christians there are, whose heads are reckoned white with age on earth;—but they are called flaxen-haired on high. We call them wrinkled here, but *there* they call them dimpled.

They seem to us to be very dull and still, but the hand almighty rocks their cradles when they cry.

H. W. Carpenter.

IF always on the thorns my feet must tread,
And heavy clouds hang darkly o'er my head;
If all the sunshine from my life depart,
And cold, gray ashes lie upon my heart;
If all my hopes, like swift-winged birds must fly,
And every flower of promise droop and die;
If always through a mist of gathering tears
My eyes watch sadly for the coming years;
O Father, when Death's river I've crossed o'er,
And my feet stand on the *farther* shore,
Shall not thy seal upon my forehead be,
"Perfect through suffering," purified by thee?

Myrta May.

THE Church of Christ was designed to represent him on earth, and to minister to all the moral needs of the human race. Her work, then, is not done when she sends out preachers and teachers; when she exhibits sacraments and liturgies; when she puts up churches at home and mission stations abroad. She must grope her way into the alleys and courts and purlieus of the city, and up the broken staircase, and into the bare room, and beside the loathsome sufferer. She must go down into the pit with the miner, into the forecastle with the sailor, into the tent with the soldier, into the shop with the mechanic, into the factory with the operative, into the field with the farmer, into the counting-room with the merchant. Like the air, the church must press equally on all the surfaces of the shore-line of society; like the sea, flow into every nook of humanity; and like the sun, on things foul and low as well as fair and high — for she was organized, commissioned, and equipped for the moral renovation of the world.

Bishop Simpson.

BE not sorrowful or fearful at the thought of death. There are many Christians troubling themselves and saying, "Am I ready to die?" That is not the question. Are you ready to live? Have you Christ in you, the hope of glory? If Christ be in you, he will take care of you. Live for Jesus, and all will be well in the dying hour. Whether you die at home or abroad is a very little matter; whether you die in the midst of friends or of enemies is of small account. Live for Jesus and he will never forget you. If you live for the world, it may forsake you; if you live for wealth, it may leave you, and you may die in poverty; if you live for fame, men may turn against you; if you live for pleasure, your ability to enjoy it may pass away, and your senses grow dim; if you live for the mazy dance, your feet may be unable to move. You may love the sound of the viol, but the ear can no longer hear; if you live for the beautiful, your sense of sight may pass away; if you live for your children, they may be smitten down and leave you desolate, or, what is far worse, they may almost forsake you, and leave you worse than childless in the midst of a cold and unfeeling world; if you would live for any form of earth, you may be forsaken; but, oh! live for Jesus, and he will never forsake you.

Bishop Simpson.

HOW sweet, when the turmoil of life shall distress me,
When heart-weary, soul-weary, friendless, alone —
When sorrow's dark waves compass round and oppress me,
As weak with despair and affliction I've grown.
And when the keen blasts of adversity chill me,
When 'mid the wild tempest I tremble and quake,
O then with what rapture the whisper shall thrill me,
"Fear not, for thy Saviour will *never* forsake."

Though friends may prove false, and though foes may surround me,
The tongue that *now* praises soon *censure* and *blame*,
Though life's fiery trials may gather around me,
Still, still I'll not shrink while that promise I claim.
My spirit may droop, and my sad heart may quiver,
When strongest temptations my pathway o'ertake,

Still I *know* that bright angels are guarding me ever,
  I *know* there is *One* who will never forsake.

And when in death's twilight my life star is fading,
  When down to the chill river's brink I shall come,
When the dark angel's pinions my dim eyes are shad
      ing,
  Ere I pass o'er that tide to my glorious home,
Then, while the last ray of my spirit is beaming,
  And lingers a while its last earth look to take,
While I see in the distance the golden harps gleam-
      ing,
  O whisper *onee* more, "I will never forsake."

Josephine White.

HABITS are soon assumed, but when we strive
  To strip them off, 'tis being flayed alive.

Cowper.

YOUNG man, you think that you can never become so lost to the right and the true. Alas! so once thought nine-tenths of the very men who now hold that a good bargain justifies any conduct. Remember that avarice is a root full of life, and that it will grow unless eradicated at once. I beg you, therefore, to place a just estimate on money, and nothing more; and when the tempter shows you how it can be gotten by lying, cheating, or perfidy, look him steadily in the eye, and ask, "*How much must I give for it?*" How much of my manhood, my self-respect? How many scorpion stings must I arm my conscience with? How many thorns must I plant in my dying pillow? How many of the attributes of God must I array against myself? How much moral blindness must I bring upon myself?

Rev. G. C. Baldwin.

I WOULD give more for one poor woman, whose poverty only makes her laugh and sing; who is contented with her humble lot; who bears her burdens with cheerfulness; who is patient when troubles come upon her; who loves every one, and who, with a kind and genial spirit, goes about doing good, than for all the dissertations on the doctrines of Christianity that could be written, as a means of preventing infidelity. I have seen one such woman, who was worth more than the whole church to which she belonged and its minister put together; and I was the minister, and my church was the church! She lived over a cooper-shop. The floor of her apartment was so rude and open that you could sit there and see what the men were doing below. She had a sort of a fiend for a husband — a rough, brutal shipmaster. She was universally called "Mother." She literally, night and day, went about doing good. I do not suppose all the ministers in the town where she lived carried consolation to so many hearts as she did. If a person was sick or dying, the people in the neighborhood did not think of sending for any one else half so soon as for her. I tell you, there was not much chance for an infidel to make headway there. If I wanted to convince a man of the reality of Christianity, I said nothing about historic evidence: I said, "Don't you believe Mother —— is a Christian?" and that would silence him. Where there is a whole church made up of such Christians as she was, infidelity cannot thrive. You need not be afraid of its making its way into such a church. The word of God stands sure under such circumstances, so that nothing can successfully rise against it.

Rev. H. W. Beecher.

WE should display the best traits of character at home. It is the place where the real character is displayed. This world is a masquerade. When in society, the best of men are conscious of restraint. They measure their words, guard their actions, watch their spirit. Without intentional hypocrisy, they do not always act out themselves. The proud assume an air of humility; the ambitious appear contented; the passionate seem calm; the petulant patient, the selfish liberal, the austere gentle and yielding. But at home the true man is seen, and the woman too. The motive for disguise has ceased to operate; then the "holy are holy and the filthy are filthy." The polished man in society is at home the uncouth husband and the rough father; the sweet and elegant lady in society is the brawling wife and scolding mother in the midst of her family; the amiable brother and gentle sister abroad are at home disagreeable and unkind to each other. But there are those who appear to best advantage at home. Careless about the empty plaudits of others, they are happiest when surrounded by those they love best. *Then* they shine as stars of the first magnitude, while in the promiscuous assemblage their calm, steady light is lost in the dazzle of fashion.

Rev. J. P. Newman.

IF a child is in a foreign land, and he receives intelligence that some relative has died and left him great treasures, how he hies back to his native country! And what does he care for the danger, or sickness, or discomfort of the voyage? He is on his way home, and the more he is withstood, the more he presses forward. We are on our journey home. Our Father's house awaits our coming. Its honors, amenities, and dear delights are ours. And not one thing withstands us that we may not overcome.

Rev. H. W. Beecher.

IT takes us much time to create light: we must form companies and erect machineries before we can turn the night of our great cities into a partial day; but to-morrow morning, however black the previous night may have been, the great Father of

Lights will illuminate our whole nation in a few minutes, and make each wave of the sea and each dew-drop of the lawn to gleam with silvery sheen. God has but to bid the sun accomplish his course, and the world is lit up and the shadows flee away. How perfectly the work is done! The illumination is unrivalled in lavish glory. All our means of enlightenment are poor when compared with the sunlight; and so scant that we must needs measure its cubic feet, and dole it out for gold, while the Lord pours his infinitely superior illumination in measureless oceans over hill and dale, field and city, gladdening the cottage as well as the palace, and burnishing the beetle's wing as well as the eagle's pinion. Even thus our heavenly Father can readily enough turn the deepest sorrows of his people into the sublimest joys, and he needs not to vex the sons of men with labor in order to achieve his purpose of pity; his own right hand, his own gracious spirit, can pour forth a fulness of consolation in a moment.

Rev. S. H. Spurgeon.

YOU may have noticed a school of fish playing close to the shore, till suddenly, when the shallows perplexed and frightened them, they turned as by one impulse and glided swiftly out into the depths. That was the thought of death to them. What to us is a solid bank, is to them a mist, a void, a breathless nothingness, a chasmal end. So to those who live an earthly and sensuous life, God's beach of all immensity, God's bank of everlasting truth, is but the touch of doom — the article of death. They know no God there. They flee shuddering away, and die at last.

H. S. Carpenter.

THERE is weeping on earth for the lost!
  There is bowing in grief to the ground!
But rejoicing and praise 'mid the sanctified host,
  For a spirit in Paradise found!
Though brightness hath passed from the earth,
  Yet a star is new-born in the sky,
And a soul hath gone home to the land of its birth,
  Where are pleasures and fulness of joy!
And a new harp is strung, and a new song is given
To the breezes that float o'er the gardens of heaven.

W. H. Burleigh.

THAT which produces faith comes from abroad, though faith itself be an act of the mind. I believe there is such a land as Spain, though I have never seen it; but geographers write of it, historians tell of it, and travellers have described it, and the telegraphic reports bring me tidings from it. I believe there is such a country; but the tidings from without must come to me as the foundation of my faith. The realm of faith lies outside of my senses and my observation. "Faith cometh by hearing:" it is that which lies away from me. It may be the visible that I have not seen, or it may be the invisible; it may be the past of thousands of years ago or the past of yesterday; it may be the future of ages to come, or the future of to-morrow. All these alike are the subjects of faith.

Bishop Simpson.

THE human mind is a kingdom of powers or faculties which are very different one from another, but which may be made perfectly to harmonize. When they are influenced aright, they, like the instruments of a band of music, blend and enrich each other; but when they disagree, they clash, and, as with an ill-assorted orchestra, though each instrument be good, the whole effect is discordant and detestable.

Rev. H. W. Beecher.

A JUST God: look that out in the Gospel dictionary, and you will find it means a Saviour. Heaven is no longer a fortress to be besieged, a city to be taken, a high, impregnable elevation to be scaled; it is the grand metropolis of the universe, to which the King, in his bounty, has thrown up a royal high-road for his people, even through the blood of his Son.

Rev. W. M. Punshon.

MANY a man has his convictions without ever knowing what they are, as we pass famous places on the road and afterward inquire for them.

Has them in his low spirits. Has them in his softened feelings. Has them in his unusual stirs. Has them in his dreams; and lets them pass as strange sentiments while he waits for them to come.

H. S. Carpenter.

AS exercise quickens the pulse and diffuses a healthful glow over the physical system, so acts of religious duty increase our Christian vitality, and develop within us that fervency of spirit which enables us to serve God all the more acceptably in proportion to our usefulness to our fellow-men. Mere theory in religion, however orthodox, avails little without corresponding practice. Hence, many in the Church become weak and effeminate. What they need is to exercise themselves into godliness, and to bring forth the fruits of holy living.

Rev. D. P. Kidder.

I GRANT that you may take Christian duties in detail, and make them look contemptible. I grant that there are some Christians who beggar their souls, and rob themselves of all spiritual comfort by this process. As an old pastor, I have found them in the church over which I have had to watch: they were good, upright, moral men. When I have sought to bring them to the prayer-meeting, they had not time to go there, but they "loved the church." When I wanted a teacher in the Sabbath-school, they could not serve me, but they "loved the church." When I wanted aid to plant missions, they could not help me, but they hoped that Christianity would conquer the world. It is an easy matter for Christians to destroy all their vitality and religious power by neglecting certain religious duties.

Bishop Ames.

WHILE the storm was fiercely blowing,
While the sea was wildly flowing,
Angry wind and angry billow
Only rocked the Saviour's pillow :
Jesus slept.

But when sudden grief was rending
Human hearts, in sorrow bending ;
When he saw the sisters weeping
Where the brother's form was sleeping,
"Jesus wept."

GO to that fifth floor, and look upon that poor wretch, hungry, thin, cadaverous, a mere skeleton, hardly able to raise himself from the floor, but on the wall yonder is spread out a canvas. He rests a little, and then, staggering, he goes to his work and adds a few more strokes of the brush, and then he rests a little. So the hours pass, till by and by the painting is finished. The artist is dead, and France to-day would not take a thousand millions for that representation of the struggle for their nationality.

Just in the next room is another pauper, as ragged, as hungry, as helpless. He dies, and they

> "Hurl his bones over the stones,
> As a pauper whom nobody owns."

He had no idea, no purpose, no aim. This man has a gift of inspiration: he takes hold of some infinite thing, and God swings him into the eyes of men, and makes him equal to the demand. The other is without it, dies like a sheep, and is forgotten. So God will take us if we will enter into this work that is before us; he will breathe upon us, and multiply our strength, and send us out to certain and inevitable victory.

Rev. C. H. Fowler.

IF we look into the deep interior wants of human nature, we find there a craving for repose, and that natural craving is met by God's merciful provision of the Sabbath. The Creator made it, — not for Jews alone, or for Christians, but "for man." To his tired and care-ridden children our Heavenly Father seems to say, at the end of every week of toil, "Come ye into a retired place for a little, and rest a while." To the industrious mechanic he says, "Lay aside your tools, and rest; let the body be relieved of its load, and let the soul go out and feed in my spiritual pastures." To the overwrought student, and the professional thinker, the kind injunction is, "Put away your books and your pen, and rest awhile." The tasked brain requires repose. The soul needs the elevation and the sanctifying influence which worship and close contact with God are sure to bring. Every man, woman, and child requires a Sabbath, and would require it even if there was no eternity to prepare for.

Rev. Theo. L. Cuyler.

WHEN Wesley begun, he commenced without means, but he said, "This ought to be done." He laid the foundation, and God helped him to raise the superstructure. Many of you, doubtless, have heard the incident related of him when endeavoring to found an orphan-school at Newcastle-upon-Tyne. He had his plans arranged and his workmen engaged, and he was going to leave. They desired one hundred pounds for materials to commence the work, but Wesley had not the money. His plans were all laid and the time fixed for leaving, but where would the money come from? Just as he was about to leave, a Quaker called upon him and said, "John, I had a strange dream about thee last night; I thought I saw thee with a parcel of little lambs in a storm, and thee was trying to shelter them and had no place. I woke up and thought of thy orphan-house, and here is my check for one hundred pounds." This was just the sum that was wanted. God intended that the poor children should be taken care of; so that he put into Wesley's mind the purpose to go forward, and placed in the old

Quaker's pocket the money and the heart to give it. God works by diverse agencies: we little know what he is doing in the world. He is putting a thought into this heart and a thought into that heart. His work is like a grand mosaic picture. Here and there are stones of different colors and shadings, and they are scattered all over the earth. There is no picture about it, but God's Spirit takes hold of the colors and the shadings, and works, by and by, a beautiful picture. God saw it all, but we could not see it. Faith takes hold of it, saying, "It is God's will it should be done." All the great works of earth have been done by faith. The churches planted, the institutions raised, the great universities founded, the lights that shine in the world and are drawing men toward Christ, are the works of faith.

Bishop Simpson.

A BOY slips from a load of hay, and the father springs down and seizes the wheel without thinking, and his son is pulled out, yet it was four times as much as he could lift at any other time. Somehow, in nature God does so multiply us that when we undertake it seems that nothing is impossible. Yonder in the valley of Switzerland the peasantry are out for a holiday. They are playing simple, rustic games, and the children on the bank are swinging themselves. The eagle soars above them, circling round and round, till by and by it darts like an arrow, seizes the little one, and flies away to its eyry yonder on the mountain. They all look and wonder and cry; but the mother, somehow, darts on up the mountain, on above the hunter's path, up above the track of the wild chamois, setting in the very clouds and storms, where eternal winter sits and shivers. She seizes and rescues her little one. There is the opening opportunity blest by the benediction of Him who makes all men stick to the work that is put upon them.

Just yonder, in a burning building, right up under the trembling rafters, is a child asleep. The father (you may have seen him) rushes up through sill and sash and blinds, until he swings himself into the window and rescues the little one. Tell me whence that numbness of nerve that did not heed the red hot bar, and whence that superhuman strength that carried him to that dizzy height? It was a bare purpose, supported and sustained by Him who has said, "My strength is sufficient for thee." So when God opens a door for us, he would have us go in and enter upon the work.

Rev. C. H. Fowler.

WE honor the kindly spirit which, on the birthday of the year, prepares a liberal entertainment. We honor the hospitality which flings wide the door to all who wish to come in and enjoy it. But the well-furnished markets and groceries of every town have an ample store of "creature-comforts," without drawing upon the liquor-cellars and wine-vaults. There are many drinks both palatable and proper that never cause redness of the eyes, or thickness of speech, or delirium of the brain. Under their influence, young men do not reel on the sidewalks, or mistake the door-plates of their friends, or venture on silly impertinences toward the ladies who entertain them. Under their influence *nobody's* son is carried home drunk to shame and rend a parent's heart.

Rev. Theo. L. Cuyler.

MAN first learned song in Paradise,
From the bright angels o'er him singing;
And in our home above the skies,
Glad anthems are forever ringing.
God lends his ear, well pleased, to hear
The songs that cheer his children's sorrow,
Till day shall break, and we shall wake
Where love shall make unfading morrow.

Bethune.

"THE poor ye have with you always," said the Master. "Not if we can help it, Lord," cry out the worshippers in a thousand gorgeous temples. "We intend to keep the poor by themselves. We don't think they would feel at home in our gay assemblies; and we have no thought of laying aside any of our magnificence for the sake of doing them good."

Rev. W. Gladden.

OFTEN have the two or three praying passengers in a ship been regarded with ridicule when they daily met for supplication beneath blue skies, when the ship was wafted by a favorable breeze; and often, when the clouds have gathered, and the wind has risen, and the waves have mounted high, and the vessel has been in peril — often have those who ridiculed been then the loudest in their appeals for mercy. And often those who in health have argued against prayer, in sickness and the prospect of death have called earnestly on God.

Rev. Newman Hall.

THE steps of Faith
Fall on the seeming void, and find
The rock beneath.

Whittier.

GOD had one son without sin, but he never had a son without chastisment. He who always did his Father's will, yet had to suffer. Courage, my heart, courage! for if Jesus suffered — if that pang which tears thy heart first was felt by him, thou mayest be of good cheer indeed.

S. H. Spurgeon.

A FRIEND who is with me has been telling me of a class of little boys he teaches at Philadelphia, on Sunday nights. One evening a newspaper boy met him in the street, and said, "O captain,

I'm mighty glad to see ye. There's poor Billy; he's so badly, and so wants to see ye." My friend went with the little boy, and found Billy lying on some rags in the corner of a wretched room, very, very ill. Billy was so delighted when the captain went in! The room was dark; and Billy, with a feeble voice, said, "I'se here, captain — I'm mighty glad to see ye." My friend was filled with pity for him, and asked if he could send him a nurse, or some medicine, or some nice food. "No, captain; it wasn't that I wanted ye for. I wanted to ax ye two questions. The first is, did you tell us the other night as how Jesus Christ died for every feller?" — "Yes, I did; for Jesus Christ tasted death for every man." Billy then said, "I thought so. Now I've another question. Did you tell us as how Jesus Christ saves every feller that axes him?" — "Yes," said my friend; "for every one that asketh receiveth." Billy replied with a very feeble but happy voice, "Then I know that he saves me, because I axes him." My friend paused to wipe away the tears that gushed from his eyes, and then bent down to speak to the boy. But Billy's head had dropped back on his pillow of rags, and his happy spirit had gone to Jesus.

Rev. Newman Hall.

YOU can take a dead leaf, or a dead log, or a dead body, and trace its dissolution. You can burn it; then science will tell you how much gas was given to the air, how much earthly matter to the sod. The soul leaves no ruins and no ashes. Death is not, therefore, the soul's decay, but the soul's departure.

H. S. Carpenter.

WITH Faith our guide,
White-robed and innocent, to lead the way,
Why fear to plunge in Jordan's rolling tide,
And find the ocean of eternal day?

Anonymous

HOW many now hymning their praises in heaven, or still watering their couch with tears on earth, will alike testify, that until God smote the earthly idol, or broke the human staff, or dried up the creature spring, Jesus was to them as an unknown Saviour and Friend.

Rev. O. Winslow, D. D.

THE deepest affection in the believing heart will always be the love of Jesus. The love of home, the love of friends, the love of letters, the love of rest, the love of travel, and all else, are contracted by the side of this master passion. "A little deeper," said one of the veterans of the first Napoleon's old guard, when they were probing in his bosom for a bullet that had mortally wounded him, and he thought they were getting somewhere in the region of the heart, — "A little deeper and you will find the Emperor." Engraven in the Christian's heart, deeper than all other love of home or friends, with an ineffaceable impression, that nothing can erase, you find the loved name of Jesus.

Rev. W. M. Punshon.

THE path of sorrow, and that path alone,
Leads to the land where sorrow is unknown;
No traveller ever reaches that blessed abode
Who found not thorns and briers on the road.

Cowper.

A DAY is coming when we shall be compelled to leave the homes of earth, however endeared. We must embrace for the last time the friends united to us as our own souls. Though we have travelled along the road many a year together, we must now separate, and go on alone. They may accompany us to the river side, but we must cross it by ourselves. What cheering voice will then greet us? What kind roof will receive us then? What loving friend will welcome us then.

Rev. Newman Hall.

GOD wrote the law of the Sabbath on man's nature. No law of health is more clear and imperative. The body demands a respite from toil through full four and twenty hours in every seven days; even the beast of the field mutely asks for the fourth commandment. The very *proportion* of time that is required for Sabbath relief has been fixed by that All-wise Creator who made the Sabbath for his earthly children. That time cannot be safely altered by a moment. In the mad era of her revolution, in fidel France decreed that one day in ten should be a legal day of exemption from work. But medical men pronounced that the change was hurtful, and that the allotted time for rest was insufficient. God was wiser than infidelity or mammon.

Rev. Theo. L. Cuyler.

EACH cloud that dims thy upward way
Shall more endear the glorious day
That gilds the land of love!

Bowring.

I NOTICED in a shop window last week, a little invention of singular interest. A small metal wire, with a circular disk at each end, was suspended by a thread, and continued without ceasing to oscillate between two small galvanic batteries, first touching one and then the other. A little card informed me that this piece of metal had continued to move to and fro between those two batteries for more than thirty years, and had during that time passed over six thousand miles. The whole affair was so inclosed within a glass case that nothing was likely to disturb it, and so it kept the even tenor of its way with a history which could be summed up in two lines of plainest prose. To and fro, to and fro, for thirty years, and that was its whole monotonous history. Men's quiet lives are much after the same order: they have gone to business on Monday morning and home at night, the same on Tuesday and all the days of the year; no dire struggles, no fierce temptations, no gracious victories, no divine experiences of heavenly love; their whole inner life meagre of interest, because so free from every trial. But look at the man who is subject to trials, temporal and spiritual, and acquainted with difficulties of every sort! He is like yon mass of iron on the prow of a gallant bark which has crossed the Pacific, and bathed itself in the Atlantic; storms have dashed upon it, a myriad of waves have broken over it; it has seen the terrors of all the seas, and gleamed in the sunlight of both hemispheres. It has served its age most gloriously, and when old and worn with rust, a world of interest surrounds it.

Rev. S. H. Spurgeon.

HEARERS who sit under the ministrations of the truth without the Spirit, may be likened to a man standing upon the brow of a hill which commands the prospect of an extensive landscape. The varied beauties of flood and of field are before him; nature is clad in her richest livery; there is every variety calculated to interest and to inspire; rugged rocks frown as if they would keep sentinel over the sleeping valley; the earth yields her increase, the crystal streamlet leaps merrily along, impressions of the beautiful are everywhere visible. There is just one drawback to the picture, and that one drawback is, that the man who stands upon the summit of the hill is blind. That is precisely the state of the case in reference to truth in the Bible. It is there in all its grandeur, but the man has no eyes to see it.

W. M. Punshon.

WHO can look on the earth,
And view the varied beauty, and the bloom
That lingers still, with Eden loveliness,
Upon the mountain top and on the plain,
And say, There is no God?

David Bates.

I STOOD by the bedside of a dying Christian mother. There sat her three little daughters and the husband weeping. They all knew she would die. She had given each of them a little memento and her word of blessing. They had promised to meet her in heaven. She sunk away; her eyes became elevated, and she ceased to breathe or to stir. After a little time she started, looked around the room, and with an expression of evident surprise, said, "I have come back again; I was almost there; I thought I should see Jesus in a moment. Oh! what brightness! Oh! what beauty I saw!" And then she began to speak of some who had gone before, and began to look to see if she could find them.

She said, smilingly, "It did not seem like dying; it seemed to me like going away from this poor sick body to be forever with Jesus."

Bishop Kingsley.

EVERY man ought to strive to draw lessons from what he sees and hears. Like the bee gathering honey from the flowers, we should gather wisdom from all which the mind can light on. And God has made the world so that this is possible. One who observes thoughtfully will find emblems all around him. Just as a mirror gives back your image, so all material things, the cloud and tree and leaf, the floating atom and the revolving world, give back a spiritual meaning, and speak to us in parables. The sun — it is an emblem of the great Son of Righteousness. The rock — it is the emblem of God's eternity. The withered leaf — it is an emblem of human hope when sin has blighted it. The dying year — it speaks as a premonitor of departing life. The ripe harvest — it is a waving parable to teach men that what a man sows, that shall he also reap, and that rich beyond thought is the final reward of him who sows seed for the harvest of heaven.

Rev. E. H. Gillett.

HAVE you heard any unbeliever on his dying bed send out for his fellow-doubters or fellow-deniers, to listen to his final confession of lies, or to pillow his head in the sinking moment? Have you seen them gathering around their comrade, and trying to pluck the dart from the stricken deer? On the other hand, how often have we stood by the bed of death, when the tranquil believer has said, "See in what peace a Christian can die!"

Rev. J. W. Alexander.

THE bodily man — at first infantile, then youthful, then fully developed, then feeble and bending under the weight of years — presents a spectacle which, though familiar, is nevertheless to the eye of contemplation most impressive. We are never children but once, and never men but once. We quit each stage of life to meet it no more forever. That which time develops and matures, time as certainly destroys. It ripens and blasts with equal power. Man's body is in fact a clock. Looking upon its dial-plate, he can tell the time of day in the journey of life. Those gray hairs point to the evening. Those feeble steps suggest a sunset. That constantly increasing descent from the altitude of bodily perfection warns the traveller that the grave will soon conceal him from mortal sight.

Rev. S. T. Spear.

A CHAMOIS-hunter of Chamouni, crossing the Mer de Glace, endeavored to leap across one of the enormous crevasses or fissures by which the ice-ocean is in many places rent. He missed his footing and fell in, but was able, by extending his arms, to moderate the speed of his descent, and thus reached the bottom, a hundred yards below, without fracture of limb. But his situation seemed hopeless. He could not scale the slippery walls of his crystal prison, and in a few hours at most he must be frozen to death. A stream of water was rushing below the ice, downward towards the valley. He followed this, the only possible path. Sometimes he had to bend low in the narrow tunnel; sometimes he waded, sometimes he floated down. At length he reached a vaulted chamber, from which was no visible outlet. The water which filled it darkly heaved. Retreat was impossible; delay was death. So, commending himself to the help of God, he plunged down into the centre of the gurgling pool. Then followed a moment or two of darkness, tumult, and terror; then he was thrown up amidst the flowers, and the hay-fields, and the merry songs of the vale of Chamouni.

Whether fact or fable, this narrative will illustrate our theme. Our path may be often dark and dangerous. Escape may seem impossible. Death may put on its most appalling form. But, uttering our watchword, "Jehovah Jireh," let us still advance. Even if we see no light beyond, let us plunge into the darkness. It will be darkness for a moment only. Then we shall be ushered into that world of light and bliss, where we shall prove, in the fullest sense, that eye hath not seen, nor ear heard, nor hath it entered into the heart to conceive, the things which God had provided for those who love him.

"When life sinks apace, and death is in view,
The word of His grace shall comfort us through;
No fearing or doubting, with Christ by our side,
We hope to die shouting, "The Lord will provide!"

Rev. Newman Hall.

FAITH builds a bridge across the gulf of death,
To break the shock blind nature cannot shun
And lands thought smoothly on the further shore.

Young.

"WHILE He affords His aid,
I cannot yield to fear:
Though I should walk through Death's dark shade,
My Shepherd's with me there."

WHY did our Father cause flowers to bloom over so large a portion of the earth? They are not food, they give no shelter, they furnish no clothing, they are of no absolute use, in the common meaning of the term. Wherefore, then, did the earth by his command bring forth flowers? To beautify it, to enliven it, to fling a gladness and brightness over the world! What flowers are to the earth, acts of kindness, of courtesy, of hospitality, are to men. How often a gentle tone, a kind look, an act of unostentatious politeness, a generous hospitality, has filled a careworn soul with peace, a stricken heart with joy, a smitten spirit with gladness!

Rev. Geo. C. Baldwin.

FOR nothing more destroys the happiness around about men than a bad temper. It is in the power of one person in a family to keep that family in smoke all the day long.

Rev. H. W. Beecher.

A MAN that begins to drink to relieve disagreeable sensation, or because he wants to take into his stomach something that is warming and exhilarating, is putting a serpent into his bosom. Coiled and frozen, it may be; but he does not know how soon it will thaw out, and lift itself up and strike him dead. It is not safe to form the habit of using intoxicating drinks. If it were necessary, it still would be dangerous; but, since it is utterly un necessary, yea, since it is positively unwholesome, what motive should impel a young man to form such a habit? What should impel a young man to form a habit against his own interest? What should impel a young man to form a habit that threatens at every moment to lance him with a poison lance?

Rev. H. W. Beecher.

IF a stone be thrown into a lake, you cannot tell where the wave will first strike, but it will strike somewhere, and wherever it strikes, you that threw the pebble, threw the wave. The master of the bad character is the owner of the evil. The evil may have spread till it is growing up in China, while the man himself may be in England or America; but it is all the same as if we were there on the spot, to see and know its progress. It as surely comes back to him, as lies come home to roost.

Rev. H. T. Cheever

TO be good is to be happy; angels
Are happier than men, because they're better.

Rowe.

IF a hundred persons are shut up in a dungeon, and a messenger announces good news to every one of them, would it not seem a strange mockery to ninety of them if freedom were possible only to ten?

Indeed, unless there is a Christ for *every one*, the gospel cannot be good news to any one.

Rev. Newman Hall.

A SECOND duty I commend to you is to dwell on the love of Jesus so constantly as to keep you thankful and cheerful. A fretful, scolding, morose "servant of Christ" is a disgrace to the name. When you encounter one cross, set over against it ten blessings. The more grateful you are, the more you have to be thankful for. In the English collieries the same buckets that come down full go up again to be filled afresh; and, as God's bounties descend tc your soul, let there be a continual uprising of youı gratitude to him. Send up the line of buckets to be filled with new mercies. A servant of Jesus ough to be the happiest creature on the globe.

Rev. Theo. L. Cuyler.

THERE are angel guards above us,
Who joy to makes us glad;
And a Father who doth love us:
Then why should we be sad?

O ye in grief repining,
And ye with sorrow bowed!
"There is a silver lining
To every sable cloud."

Annie E. Howe.

FLOWERS, what are they? They are but the thoughts of God solidified; God's beautiful thoughts put into shape. Storms, what are they? They are God's terrible thoughts, written out that man may read them. Thunders, what are they? They are God's powerful emotions, just opened out that men may hear them. The world is just the materializing of God's thoughts; for the world is a thought in God's eye. He made it first from a thought that came from his own mighty mind; and everything in the majestic temple that he has made has a meaning.

Rev. C. H. Spurgeon.

IN many of the large stores in our great cities you may see a patent elevator, designed to convey the inmates of the store and others from one floor to another. Step upon the platform—it is motionless; now take hold of a designated chain or rope, and pull. At once you find yourself gradually rising, until you have reached one floor and another, and you ascend at length to the highest part of the building. So, my friends, God has provided the means of salvation to your very hand. Even now each one of you stands upon the broad platform of redemption; but it is motionless, and must remain motionless, so far as you are concerned, until you set in operation those hidden forces by which it alone could be moved. Oh! unlock those folded arms. Oh! reach forth that hand of faith and grasp the golden chain of mercy which God lets down from heaven. Now pull that golden chain by prayer and Christian effort, and you shall find yourself surely and sweetly rising toward God and toward heaven.

Rev. N. Vansant.

WHAT the child habitually sees, it will catch and imitate. Character and example teach powerfully, before language is either uttered or understood. Before the child has learned its A B C, or the name of God, it has begun to learn and imitate the character of its parents, and the language of the heart. If they themselves are the children of God, endeavoring in love, in faith, in prayer, in hope, to commit their little one to Him, and train it for Him, then they are sowing seed for a harvest of blessedness and glory. But if they themselves are neglectful of God and eternity, and living only for this world, they are teaching their child, even before it can understand or lisp a syllable, the language and the life of irreligion.

Rev. H. T. Cheever.

WHAT is this world, this great world of ours, but "love" spelled out large? The stars, if we could read them rightly, spell "love." If we could interpret the language of the floods, we should hear them whispering "love." And could we gather together all flowers, and distil their essence, and get an extract from them, we should find that its smell was "love." Every thing in this world telleth of love. But would you know the heights and depths and lengths and breadths of the love of God which passeth knowledge, come hither to the cross.

Rev. C. H. Spurgeon.

IN the Scriptures many impressive images are drawn from the leaves, grass, and flowers, those striking monitors of human mortality. "Man," says the prophet Isaiah, "fades as a leaf;" "his glorious beauty is a fading flower;" he is "as an oak whose leaf fadeth, and as a garden that hath no water." In one of his most moving complaints, Job likens himself to "a leaf driven to and fro." And the

Psalmist says, "As for man, his days are as grass; as a flower of the field so he flourisheth; for the wind passeth over it and it is gone; and the place thereof shall know it no more." These are a few of the simple pathetic allusions of the Hebrew poets to the flower-like frailty of our race, and they are the impressive, sublime voice of inspiration. They are most truthful images from natural objects, forcibly illustrating our weakness and the common doom.

G. P. Disosway.

LEAVES have their time to fall,
And flowers to wither at the north wind's breath,
And stars to set—but all,
Thou hast all seasons for thine own, O Death!

Hemans.

A MAN whose heart is not in communion with God, can no more read the higher lessons of nature, than a man by the roadside can tell what message is flitting through the air, by gazing on the parallel wires of a telegraph. He must put himself in connection with the communicating mind.

Rev. H. T. Cheever.

HAPPY the home where prayer is heard,
And praise is wont to rise;
Where parents love the sacred word,
And live but for the skies.

Anonymous.

I AM waiting by the river,
And my heart has waited long;
Now I think I hear the chorus
Of the angels' welcome song.
Oh, I see the dawn is breaking
On the hill-tops of the blest,
"Where the wicked cease from troubling,
And the weary be at rest."

Far away beyond the shadows
Of this weary vale of tears,
There the tide of bliss is sweeping
Through the bright and changeless years.
Oh, I long to be with Jesus,
In the mansions of the blest,
"Where the wicked cease from troubling,
And the weary be at rest."

They are launching on the river,
From the calm and quiet shore,
And they soon will bear my spirit
Where the weary sigh no more;
For the tide is swiftly flowing,
And I long to greet the blest,
"Where the wicked cease from troubling,
And the weary be at rest."

By Wm. O. Cushing.

WHEN a man, driving from the meadow, sits and sings cheerily upon his vast load of fragrant hay, how every one, looking upon him, thinks of his happiness and content! But, by and by, at an unlucky jog, down goes the wheel, and over goes the load, and the man is at the bottom, with all the hay on him. And now he cannot halloo so that you can hear him. And if somebody does not extricate him, he will be smothered.

Just in that way rich men are in danger of being smothered. The whole wain of your prosperity may capsize, and the superincumbent mass may hide you from the air and sun of a true life.

Rev. H. W. Beecher.

MY crown is in my heart, not on my head,
Not decked with diamonds and Indian stones,
Not to be seen; my crown is called content;
A crown it is that seldom kings enjoy.

Shakspeare.

THINK gently of the erring! Oh! do not thou forget,
However darkly stained by sin, he is thy brother yet;
Heir of the self-same heritage, child of the self-same God!
He hath but stumbled in the path thou hast in weakness trod.

Julia A. Fletcher.

A DROP of ardent spirits will kindle into rage the fire that burns in the veins of a man given over to intemperance, but all the vats of a distillery will not satisfy nor quench it; it grows continually stronger, and demands more and more. So it is with all our passions, which, the more we obey and yield to them, the stronger they grow; and the stronger they grow, the more easily they are excited, but the more impossible to be restrained. And precisely so is it with the blessed desire of a regenerated soul after holiness. The stronger *that* grows, the more easily it is excited, but the less easily satisfied, until, indeed, God himself satisfies it with his own likeness and infinite fulness in heaven.

Rev. H. T. Cheever.

MUCH better faith was that of a little boy in one of the schools at Edinburgh, who had attended the prayer-meetings, and at last said to his teacher, who conducted the prayer-meeting, "Teacher, I wish my sister could be got to read the Bible; she never reads it."—"Why, Johnny, should your sister read the Bible?"—"Because, if she should once read it, I am sure it would do her good, and she would be converted and be saved."—"Do you think so, Johnny?" — "Yes, I do, sir, and I wish the next time there's a prayer-meeting you would ask the people to pray for my sister, that she may begin to read the Bible."—"Well, well, it shall be done, John." So the teacher gave out that a little boy was very anxious that prayers should be offered that his sister should begin to read the Bible. John was observed to get up and go out. The teacher thought it very unkind of the boy to disturb the people in a crowded room and go out, like that, and so the next day when the lad came, he said, "John, I thought that was very rude of you to get up in the prayer-meeting and go out. You ought not to have done it." — "Oh, sir," said the boy, "I did not mean to be rude, but I thought I should just like to go home and see my sister reading her Bible for the first time." That is how we ought to believe, and wait with expectation to see the answer to prayer. The girl was reading the Bible when the boy went home. God had been pleased to hear the prayer; and if we could but trust God after that fashion, we should often see similar things accomplished.

Rev. S. H. Spurgeon.

WE put it to every man's sentiment that there is connected with places made memorable in history, peculiar associations and peculiar feelings. Nay more, we come to the holier feelings of our nature. Bereaved mother, thou who hast laid away in the grave the little one who was dear to thee, and hast in the drawers of thine own apartment the little trinkets, toys, and garments which that little one wore, dost thou think there is nothing peculiar in them? Wouldst thou have careless hands toss them about, and speak as though they were of no worth, and pass them away for the veriest trifles as incumbrances? Proud and presumptuous son or daughter, who has followed a revered mother to the grave! hast thou not some little relic, some parting gift, it may be a lock of hair, thou hast laid by, — that wealth could not buy from thee? and is there no holy association in it? Oh! shame to the man who can so far violate the noblest feelings of man's nature as to call every thing on this earth common! And now let me ask, if these places are sacred, is not the place where God comes sacred? If the place where the Father of his Country lived and died has a sacredness, I ask you, proud, scornful man, not to stand uncovered in the temple consecrated to the holy God, and speak not lightly thy irreverent words. In temples where God manifests himself, and where souls are born to glory, there is a sacredness.

Rev. Dr. Cummings.

WHAT was there to begin with, when God made the world? There was nothing; but nothing could not stand in God's way — it was at least passive. But, my brethren, in our hearts, while there was nothing that could help God, there was much that could and did oppose him. Our stubborn wills, our deep prejudices, our ingrained love of iniquity, — all these, great God, opposed thee, and aimed at thwarting thy designs. There was darkness in the first creation, but that darkness could not obstruct the incoming of light. "Light be!" was the eternal fiat, and light was. But, O great God! how often has thy voice spoken to us, and our darkness has refused thy light! We loved darkness rather than light, because our deeds were evil; and it was only when thou didst put on the garments of thine omnipotence, and come forth in the glory of thy strength, that at the last our soul yielded to thy light, and the abysmal darkness of our natural depravity made way for thy celestial radiance. Yes, great God! it was great to make a world, but greater to create a new creature in Christ Jesus.

Rev. C. H. Spurgeon.

OH! spread thy wings, my soul, and fly
Through realms of space, and find a spot
Where living souls shall never die,
Nor weep no more, or sorrow not.

Go speed thy way to yonder sun,
Which sheds on all its friendly light.
Is peace found here? is joy begun?
Will this dispel my sorrow's night?

Go ask those distant stars of heaven,
For ages rolling in their spheres —
Is it to you this power is given,
To give me life through endless years?

Go on ! survey the watery deep,
  And ask the aspiring waters where
Within its bounds, the soul can sleep,
  And sweetly rest from sin and care.

Return ! return again to earth,
  And find some quiet, secluded spot,
Where peace and joy can yet have birth,
  To die no more, or languish not.

Ah, house of clay ! for thee I've found
  A place to hold thy coffined clay.
'Tis solemn, cold, low in the ground,
  Where thou must lie till the last day.

But *I*, the *soul*, shall haste away
  And roam through spirit-fields above.
And live through an eternal day ;
  Forever in my Saviour's love.

A. I. Holmes.

WHEN one in danger is snatched as a brand from the burning, it makes all the ranks of heaven shout. It is a little like this world after all, for God has made heavenly and earthly things after the same pattern. Here, for example, is a family out in a wild region of country. They have a number of children, and among them there is one little boy more wayward than the rest. He is told by his careful mother " not to go out of that gate ;" but he wanders, and further and further, until by and by he is missed at home. His mother sends the older children out to call him, but they cannot find him. Time wears away, and she becomes alarmed. She goes out, and with such a voice as only a mother possesses she calls her child. There is no answer; she sends to the field for her husband and the elder children; night comes on; they come and send for the neighbors, who light their torches, form themselves into a sort of cordon, and go forth after the little wanderer. They sweep the woods; the stars come out, the night deepens, the morning dawns, and still the child is not found. There sits the poor mother at home, with her face buried in her hands, and those hands all wet with her weeping. The next day, about three o'clock (I am only telling you a true story), a man picks up a little shoe out of the mud in a swamp. Here is the track, and on and on he goes, till he comes to the little fellow sitting down in a puddle of water, with his hair and clothes nearly torn from his body. Looking up, he says, "Good man, won't you take away these woods and let me see my mother?" That man puts the found lamb on his shoulders and brings it back. How careful they are in breaking the news! They first communicate it to the children and father, and then delicately to the mother. "The child is found." Will you tell me, when that little fellow comes home with his hair almost torn out of his head, does she go to the other children, to Johnny, Willie, and Mary, who had remained at home, and throw her arms about them? No: she forgets them, and does not remember any child in the world, for the time being, but the one who was lost. It is upon him she pours her kisses and drops her scalding tears. It will take her nearly a lifetime to persuade herself that she does not love him better than the rest, just because he had been in such danger.

Rev. Dr. Nadal.

RELIGION.

IN sorrow, joy,
In conflict, peace,
And comfort in affliction's hour,
Its trust in him
Whose strength can bring
Freedom from the tempter's power;
And like the sun,
In the horizon,
As it drives away the shades of night;
So the grave shall be
From darkness free,
Illumined with a glorious light;
And on the other side
Of the swelling tide,
The pearly gates shall open wide;
And we shall be,
Like him we see,
Happy through all eternity.

A. I. Holmes

WHY should I be enamoured of virtue, if I am to be banished from God's presence? Do not tell me of the warnings, for it is only prophesying to me beforehand what I am to meet. Do not tell me of the promises; you only mock my misery. I do not want the gates of pearl shown to me from afar, if I cannot enter. I do not want the Son of God revealed to me in his glory and in his love, if I am to be banished from his presence for evermore because I have sinned. First of all, atonement and forgiveness for the past, and then everything else; but until then, nothing. So Christ comes to bring atonement, and offer us a ground of justification and forgiveness, and he does it in his death.

Rev. R. S. Storrs, Jr.

WHAT would be thought of a man who was ashamed to own his country, nor would take up even speech in her defence among strangers, in a foreign land? It is when broad seas part us from our native shores, that the love of country burns strongest. Her songs sound sweetest in the exile's ear. Those faults of hers we lay bare at home, we conceal abroad; and, like dutiful sons, try to cast a mantle on her shame—hiding it from the eyes of aliens. We are not ashamed of our country; yet, alas! how many seem ashamed of their religion and their God?

Thomas Guthrie, D. D.

THIS world's a dream, an empty show; there is nothing lasting beneath the stars; everything of seeming joy soon palls upon the mind. Take to study, and ransack all the learned tomes, and your mind will soon be satiated with knowledge. Take to travel, and behold the fairest realms, climb the summits of the Alps, or traverse the valleys with all their picturesque beauty, and you will soon say, "I have exhausted all; I know it; I am weary of it." Follow what pursuit you will, like Solomon, you may get to yourself gardens and palaces, singing men and singing women; or, you may, if your folly be great enough, give yourself to wine; or, if you will, addict yourself to commerce; but of the whole you will say ere long, "Vanity of vanities, all is vanity." The world is but a mirage; it melts, it disappears as the traveller passes on, and mocks his thirst with the deceptive image of the true. But, beloved, the spiritual life is not so. There is a freshness, a vivacity, a force, an energy, a power about it that never grows stale. He that prayed yesterday with joy, shall pray in fifty years' time, if he be on earth, with the self-same delight. He that loves his Maker, and feels his heart beat high at the mention of the name of Jesus, shall find as much transport in that name, if he lives to the age of Methuselah, as he doth now. Year by year its sweets grow sweeter, its lights grow brighter, its novelties grow fresher, its joys more joyous, and its exhilarations more intense.

Rev. C. H. Spurgeon.

I LOATHE to hear a believer say, "Well, if I am but just saved, that is enough for me; if I may just get in behind the door in heaven, I shall be content." So you will, my dear brother, but you ought not to talk in that way. Your business is to show forth as much of Christ to his Glory as you possibly can. What! are you so selfish that if you can creep into heaven that will content you? I would like to carry my Master a whole casket of jewels in my bosom; I would fain say to him, "Here am I and the children whom thou hast given me." I would desire to die with the sweet satisfaction, "I have finished my course, I have kept the faith; henceforth there is laid up for me a crown of life that fadeth not away."

Rev. C. H. Spurgeon.

A TREASURE! So men speak of the child who, like a beautiful flower with a worm at its root, may droop and die; of fame won on a stage, where the spectators who applaud to-night may hiss to-morrow; of riches that, like scared wild-fowl on the reedy margin of a lake, take to themselves wings and fly away. But how much worthier the name the Friend who never leaves us; health that sickens not, and life that dies not; love that never cools, and glory that never fades; a peace that troubles may disturb, but do not destroy—being to it but the raging tempest that shakes the arms of a tree which it cannot uproot; the swelling, foaming, angry billows that toss the bark, which, securely anchored, they cannot part from its moorings nor dash on the surf beaten shore!

Thomas Guthrie, D. D.

"WHAT is he worth?" is probably the most frequent interrogatory that one of our countrymen is prone to make in regard to any other. No inquiry in relation to personal appearance, or place of residence, to mental qualities or moral character, is quite so current as the hourly question, "How much is he worth?"

If it were used in its full significance, this would be the most pregnant, the most just, and the most comprehensive question that could be propounded in regard to any immortal being. When asked in the ordinary way it simply means, How large are his estates? how much gold has he in his bank-vaults? And the ordinary answer would be, "The man is worth an hundred thousand, or a half-million." Then we can only say that he will have an hundred thousand, or half a million of dollars to account for at the bar of God. Then will he be either the happy reaper of immortal joys when every well-employed dollar shall nod like a golden ear in the full sheaf of his heavenly harvest; or else must he meet a half-million of scorpions to torment his soul through his dreary eternity of despair. Is a man worth uncounted thousands in bullion or bank-stock, in real estate or rare commodities? Then he ought to be worth a vast deal to the community in which he lives, and to the church of Jesus Christ. He ought to be worth—bread to the hungry—schooling to the ignorant—libraries to those whose souls are larger than their purse—Bibles to the unevangelized—and mission-schools to the heathen children at our doors. He ought to be rich towards God in the large and liberal employment of his high stewardship.

Rev. T. L. Cuyler.

THERE'S a beautiful land by the spoiler untrod,
  Unpolluted by sorrow or care;
It is lighted alone by the presence of God,
  Whose throne and whose temple are there:
Its crystalline streams, with a murmurous flow,
  Meander through valleys of green,
And its mountains of jasper are bright in the glow
  Of a splendor no mortal hath seen.

And throngs of glad singers, with jubilant breath,
  Make the air with their melodies rife;
And One, known on earth as the Angel of Death,
  Shines here as the Angel of Life!
An infinite tenderness beams from his eyes,
  On his brow is an infinite calm,
And his voice, as it thrills through the depths of the skies,
  Is as sweet as the seraphim's psalm.

Through the amaranth groves of the beautiful land
Walk the souls who were faithful in this;
And their foreheads, star-crowned, by the zephyrs are fanned
That evermore murmur of bliss;
They taste the rich fruitage that hangs from the trees,
And breathe the sweet odors of flowers,
More fragrant than ever were kissed by the breeze
In Araby's loveliest bowers.

Old prophets, whose words were a spirit of flame,
Blazing out o'er the darkness of time;
And martyrs, whose courage no torture could tame,
Nor turn from their purpose sublime;
And saints and confessors, a numberless throng,
Who were loyal to truth and to right,
And left, as they walked through the darkness of wrong,
Their foot-prints encircled with light,

And the dear little children, who went to their rest,
Ere their lives had been sullied by sin,
While the Angel of Morning still tarried, a guest,
Their spirits' pure temple within, —
All are there, all are there, in the Beautiful land,
The land by the spoiler untrod,
And their foreheads, star-crowned, by the breezes are fanned,
That blow from the gardens of God!

My soul hath looked in through the gateway of dreams,
On the city all paven with gold,
And heard the sweet flow of its murmurous streams,
As through the green valleys they rolled;
And though it still waits on this desolate strand,
A pilgrim and stranger on earth,
Yet it knew, in that glimpse of the beautiful land,
That it gazed on the home of its birth!

William H. Burleigh.

IN the New Testament the Lord Jesus explains this phrase of being in himself in another way. He represents us as being in him as the branch is in the vine. Now, the branch derives all its nourishment, its sap, its vitality, its fruit-bearing power, from the stem with which it is united. It would be of no use that the branch should be placed close to the trunk; it would be of no service even to strap it side by side with the stem; it must be actually in it by a vital union. There must be sap-streams flowing at the proper season into it, life-floods gushing into it from the parent stem; and even so there is a mysterious union between Christ and his people, not to be explained but to be enjoyed, not to be defined but to be experienced, in which the very life of Christ flows into us, and we by the virtue that cometh out of him into us, become like unto him, and bring forth clusters of good fruit unto his honor and unto God's glory. I trust you know what this means, beloved, many of you. May you live in the possession of it daily! May you be one with Jesus, knit to him, united to him, never to be separated forever. As the limb is in the body, even so may you constantly be one with Jesus.

Rev. C. H. Spurgeon.

NOAH'S Ark was a type of Christ. The animals that were preserved from the deluge passed through the door into the ark, the Lord shut them in, and high above the foaming billows they floated in perfect safety. We are in Christ in the same sense. He is the ark of God provided against the day of judgment. We by faith believe him to be capable of saving us; we come and trust him, we risk our souls with him, believing that there is no risk; we venture on him confident that it is no venture; giving up every other hope or shadow of a hope, we trust in what Jesus did, is doing, and is in himself, and thus he becomes to us our ark, and we are in him.

Rev. C. H. Spurgeon.

JUDGE HALE, one of the greatest ornaments of the English church, and the English bench, in expressing the value he set on the Sabbath as a day, not of business or worldly recreation, but of holy rest, said that he found the work of the week go well according as the Sabbath had been kept well. For as I have seen one stroke of an eagle's wings send her, without further effort, sailing a long way on through the fields of air, the impulse which a well-spent Sabbath gave him was sensibly felt, throughout all the running week.

Thomas Guthrie, D.D.

IF you have received, come and receive again; you have not received the whole of Christ's fulness yet. But all that is in Christ is meant to be received. Jesus Christ is like the sun, — he is a store-house of light, but the light is there to be shed abroad. He is like the clouds, a storehouse of waters, but all that is in him is to descend in showers upon thirsty souls. There is nothing in Christ but what was meant to be distributed. He is like Joseph's granaries in Egypt, full of corn for hungry men. Dost thou read of mercy in Christ? — say, "That mercy was meant for a needy sinner; I will even have it." Little children, when they come to table, seem to know by instinct that everything there is meant to be eaten; so they cry, "Give me this, give me that." Now, in this be ye children. If you see anything in Christ, however rich and rare, however precious and choice, say, "Lord, give me that, and give me that;" for it is all meant to be given away — it is all provided on purpose to meet the needs of the Lord's people.

Rev. C. H. Spurgeon.

THERE was a young man of earnest mind, of sound and promising scholarship, who was among the mourners around the altar night after night and week after week. I talked with him frequently; we prayed for him earnestly; and yet, somehow or other, he seemed to obtain no deliverance, and we had begun almost to despair of him. I remember one night going to him and talking with him. My heart yearned to bring him to Christ, and my soul was in a struggling agony that seemed as though I could not let him go without bringing him to the blessed Saviour. The meeting closed, and I was among the last to leave the church. As I came out to the door, I found him standing, with a lantern in his hand, waiting to accompany me down to the seminary. As we passed out into the yard (it was a dense, foggy night), I asked him to hold his lantern up. He held it up, and I said it was very dark. I had just been in conversation with him, when he said to me, "I feel that I could venture upon Christ; I feel that I have given up everything, yet I do not see my way clearly along. I am afraid that I shall backslide, and that I shall dishonor the cause of Christ." Said I, "Hold up your lantern." He held it up, and as we looked there was blackness ahead. "Your light does not shine very far ahead, George." — "It is a pretty dark night," he replied. "Well," said I, "now, suppose a man was standing here as you are, and held his light up and saw only a little shining around the very spot where he stood, and it did not shine on the road all the way down to the seminary, and he refused to go because, as he held his light up, it did not illuminate his path all along, what would you say of him?" — "I should say," said he, "he was a fool." In a moment more he said, "Oh! I see it," and the big tears gathered in his eyes and rolled down his cheeks. "I see it; that is just what I have been doing." And that moment, there, in the darkness, he believed in Christ, and received the salvation from on high.

Bishop Clark.

IT is in the morning and evening that Nature, who gives her nights to sleep and her days to work, pays, if I may so say, her worship to God. At dewy morn and eve, from their golden and silver censers, the flowers offer the incense of their fragrance, and skies and woods which were mute during the heat of the day and darkness of the night, break out into a melodious burst of song. The bird that, leaving God to care for it, sleeps with its head beneath its wing in the darkness, and spends the busy day gathering its food or catering for its young, drops at even from the skies, singing, into its grassy nest; and mounts thence at rosy dawn, to praise God by the gate of heaven ere it begins the labors of the day. And so, in a way, does every man and woman who has the least pretension to a Christian's character — morning and evening find them on their knees before God. What day closes without many mercies to be grateful for, and many sins to be confessed and pardoned, and what day is entered on that has not burdens to be borne, and battles to be fought to which it behooves us to go forth guided by the counsel, guarded by the power, strengthened by the grace, and defended, like a mail-clad warrior, from head to heel, by the whole armor of God?

Thomas Guthrie, D.D.

THEY loved us: and my proposition is, that if they loved us before they left us, they do not cease to love us now; that they are still our friends, not only still our brothers and sisters by blood, and still our loved friends by memory; not only do we often call them back again to our thoughts and enjoy sweet communion with them, so to speak, in spirit, but that they reciprocate such thoughts and such memories. They have left us, but they have not forgotten us: we have lost them from our bodily vision, but we have not lost them from our affection. How sweetly it links the two worlds together to think that they have just crossed over the undiscernible line that separates time from eternity! Did they lose their personal identity by crossing? They carried that with them, and have only shed their imperfections. Now, it is a beautiful thought, friends, that these loved ones of ours, just as long as we could see them, as they went down toward the swellings of Jordan, loved us. What were their last moments occupied with? With glances of affection.

Their last words were requests, perhaps, to meet them in the kingdom of heaven. A pressure of the hand told of love to us even when they could no longer speak, and the glistening tear-drops that seemed to be the very dew of heaven told us of the love that lived in their hearts. Little children were called in, all the cherished ones were around the bedside, and the last utterance was an expression of the strongest and tenderest love.

Rev. Dr. Nadal.

NOW, suppose you were a beggar. You know what beggars do. If they go to a door and get anything, they make a little mark; you and I do not understand it, but it means "Good house to knock at;" and the next beggar who comes sees that token, and he knocks boldly. If they get nothing, of course they make some scurvy remark or another, after their own fashion, which the next beggar understands. Now, I have already made that mark on Christ's door, and I have told you of it; it is a good house to knock at, for I have tried it. But suppose, being a beggar, you were to meet some fifty or sixty tramps, all coming down the street, and they were to say to you, "Are you in the same trade as we are?" — "Yes, I am a beggar." — "Well," say they, "there's a good house down there; we have all of us been to it, and they have given us all something." — "What! given something to all of you?" — "Yes, to every one of us." — "What, to that man yonder?

why he looks good for nothing!"—"Ah, well, they gave him something."—"What, to the whole of you?"—"Yes."—"Then I shall be as quick as I can to knock and get the next turn." Why, of course, everybody would feel that that is the shop to beg at, where nobody has been rejected. Now, since the world began, there never has been a sinner who sincerely asked for mercy through faith in the precious blood of Jesus, who has been rejected. Since Adam was cast out of the garden, there has never been a sinner, whoever he might have been, that has cast himself by simple trust upon the blood and righteousness of Jesus Christ, whom God has cast out. Well, but if they all received, and all received "of his fulness," why not you?

Rev. C. H. Spurgeon.

ABOVE the anthems of the celestial choir, he hears our feeblest cry; and amid the glories of the upper sanctuary, Christ's eye turns less on the glittering crowns his redeemed ones cast at his feet than on his people here—fighting in this field of battle, weeping in this vale of tears.

Thomas Guthrie, D.D.

EVERY step you have to go from the gate of the City of Destruction up to the pearl-gate of the New Jerusalem, it is all grace. The road to glory is paved with stones of grace. The chariot in which we ride to heaven is all of grace. The strength that draws it, and the axle that bears it up, is all of grace and grace alone. In the whole covenant of grace, from the first letter of the charter down to its last word, there is nothing at all of merit or man's goodness, but it is grace, grace, grace. As grace laid the foundation, so grace brings out every stone, and as we sing —

"It lays in heaven the topmost stone,
And well deserves the praise."

Rev. C. H. Spurgeon.

WE think, then, that the inhabitants of heaven and our loved friends that have gone up yonder, love us as they did before, only better; we think they have carried our faces up to heaven, and that they have carried endearing thoughts with them, and that their memories of us are fresh and verdant as the flowers of the unchanging seasons of Paradise. They love us still.

Rev. Dr. Nadal.

ONE part of the glory of the Christian Church is the glory of a pure, spiritual worship. No matter whether it be the lone worship of the closet, or the domestic worship of the family altar, or the social worship of the prayer-meeting or class-room, or the public worship of the great congregation — no matter; the glowing heart, the swelling bosom, the lighted brow, the joyful song, the happy shout, the melting influence, the thrilling power, oh! these give to pure Christian worship a transcendent glory of which heaven alone is the perfect antitype!

Rev. N. Vansant.

BEAR thy cross cheerfully,
  Brother, the night
Passeth, though tearfully
  Dim is thy sight.
Carry it duteously,
  Looking afar,
Where gleameth beauteously
  The morning star.

Bear it with white hands up,
  Sister in pain,
Drinking life's bitterest cup,
  Know 'tis in vain.
Hopefully, prayerfully,
  Light then 'twill be,
For the Lord carefully
  Thus leadeth thee.

Through surging sorrow-tides,
  Vales dark and lone,
Up rugged mountain sides,
  Making no moan.
Though shrinking wearily
  Beneath the load,
Take it up cheerily,
  'Tis from thy God.

Bear thy cross trustingly
  Whate'er it be,
Then will it tenderly
  Rest upon thee.
Think not to lay it down
  Till life is done;
The cross shall wear the crown
  When heaven is won.

I SHOULD not wonder if our friends sometimes talk about us: if they love us they do. They gather, perchance, around the river of life, and sit under the blessed shadow of the tree of life, and tell the story of their earthly experiences, bringing in the names of those they love. I do not know what language they talk there. "The languages of earth are many, the language of heaven is one." I do not know what words of divine music, what golden strains of divine speech pass between angels and men, but they talk there a sweet and blessed language; and it is a precious thought to me to-day, as, no doubt, it is to you, that your name and my name, unworthy as they are, and not fit to stand on the records of the book of life, are mentioned by the blessed spirits that live yonder by the throne of God. I not only suppose that our blessed friends, made perfect in heaven, talk with one another, but I suppose they talk with the angels, and it seems to me that it is not going too far to say that they may seek to become acquainted with the angels that minister among their own friends. It is nonsense to say that angels are ministering spirits, unless they minister in some place ; they minister as individuals. It seems to me, then, that those who loved me on earth and who love me in heaven would be looking out for the angels who minister about me. The thought is precious, and while I indulge it I seem almost to hear the tread of the blessed angels about me. Your name, I repeat it, may this moment have passed between the spirit of your departed and sainted friend and the blessed angel that has just ascended on Jacob's ladder.

Rev. Dr. Nadal.

CREATION is the work of God alone. It must be so. If any doubt it, let us bid them make the effort to create the smallest object. The potter places his clay upon the wheel, and shapes it after his own pleasure ; he fashions the vase, but he is not the creator of it. The clay was there beforehand : he does but change its shape. Will any man who thinks he can play the creator, produce a single grain of dust? Call now, and see if there be any that will answer thee — call into nothingness, and bid a grain of dust appear at thy bidding. It cannot be. Now, inasmuch as Paul declares the Christian man to be a new creature, it is proven that the Christian man is the work of God, and the work of God alone, "Which were born, not of blood, nor of the will of the flesh, nor of the will of man, but of God."

Rev. C. H. Spurgeon.

"HE knoweth not whither he goeth." The traveller that is lost in the desert may find himself in a perilous and wearisome journey; he may not know whither he is going; but, after all, there is a prospect of recovery. But to see an immortal man going forth to eternity, to the judgment-bar of the final Judge, and yet not knowing whither he is going, is one of the saddest and most fearful spectacles that can touch the human heart.

Bishop Clark.

IN creation, who helped God? who poised the clouds for him? who weighed the hills in scales to aid his skill, or helped him dig the channels of the sea? Who aided in rolling the stars along? who took a torch to light up the lamps of heaven? With whom took the Almighty counsel, and who instructed him? If there be any that can stand with God in the making of the world, then may some pretend to compare with him in the conversion of souls, but until that shall be, the new creation is God's sole domain, and in it his attributes, and his attributes alone, shine resplendent. "It is not of him that willeth, nor of him that runneth, but of God that showeth mercy." The sovereign will of God creates men heirs of grace.

Rev. C. H. Spurgeon.

EXPOSE water to fire, and it dissolves in vapor; wood, and it vanishes in smoke and flame, leaving but gray ashes behind; iron, and it is converted into rust; but fire may play on gold for a thousand years without depriving it of a degree of its lustre or an atom of its weight. Beautiful emblem of the saints of God, gold cannot perish—their trials, like the action of fire on this precious metal, but purifying what they cannot destroy.

Thomas Guthrie, D.D.

LET us never forget that forms are not religion, but only its drapery; and that, as they dress children lightly who wish to brace their frames, as the laborer throws off his coat to work, and, as in the ancient games the candidates stepped into the race-course unencumbered with many, or heavy garments, the fewer forms which religion wears, consistent with decency and order, the more robust she will grow—she will work with greater energy—and, like one of beautiful mould and symmetry, she will walk with more native, queenly grace—when

"Unadorned, adorned the most."

Thomas Guthrie, D.D.

WE may be in Christ also as the stone is in the building. The stone is built into the wall and is a part of it. In some of the old Roman walls you can scarcely tell which is the firmer, the cement or the stone, for their cement was so exceedingly strong, that it held the stones together as though they were one mass of rock; and such is the eternal love which binds the saints to Christ. They become one rock, one palace wall, one temple, to the praise and glory of the God who built the fabric. Thus you see what it is to be in Christ. It is to trust him for salvation as Noah trusted the ark; it is to derive real life from him as the branch does from the stem; it is to lean on him, and to be united to him, as the stone leans on the foundation and becomes an integral part of the structure.

Rev. C. H. Spurgeon.

CHRIST first loved us! Did he do so because we were especially lovable and attractive? Nay, he loved us when we were especially unlovely and ungrateful. It is very easy to grow fond of a sweet, beautiful child, who wins us by its music of voice and witchery of face. But to pick up the filthy waif of the streets, or the poor, diseased orphan of the hospital, and to love that forlorn object, requires *heart*. Christ did and does more than this. He loves the sinner who is in open, obstinate rebellion against him. While we were yet sinners, "Christ died for the ungodly." Not for the godly, observe; but for the ungodly. While we were in the far country of sin, Christ called us. When we opposed him, he strove with us and conquered us. While we were filthy, he pitied us, and "washed us from our sins in his own blood." This is the history of every conversion. The love of Jesus for the sinner goes before the sinner's love for him.

Rev. T. L. Cuyler.

MAN would indeed be a curious spectacle to himself if he could daguerreotype upon his memory a perfect image of his own feelings as they lie scattered here and there along the path of life — an image so perfect as to present the total reality, with all its lights and shades, blending each item with the whole and yet making each so distinct as to be seen by itself. This would be such a picture as art never painted, such a bust as no chisel ever carved. But one being in the universe is adequate to the task; and that being is God. The fact, however, is as real as it would be if we could perfectly represent it. Time writes its name on the feelings. Time gives them their specific coloring. Time explains why it is that men starting with the same native capacities are so differently shaded as the creatures of feeling. Time plays all these tunes, and finally settles the man down into a fixed habit of special tunes.

Rev. S. T. Spear.

IF geologists tell true, there have been several series of creatures in different periods of time, and each race has given place to another race of new creatures fresh from creation's mint, new from God's hand. But it is now six thousand years at least, and some of us think many thousand years more, since the day when this last set of creatures came into this world, and started upon the race of life; all the creatures we now see are old and antiquated. The flower which springs from the soil is the repetition of its like which bloomed five thousand years ago. Yonder meads bedecked with yellow king-cups and fair daisies are the fac-similies of those our sires looked upon three score years ago. As for ourselves, removed by long lines of pedigree from the man whom Jehovah formed in the garden, we by nature show small signs of the undefiled hand and sacred finger. The world is hackneyed and stale and old. Time wearily drags on to its Saturday-night; it draws near to the last of its work-days with heavy footsteps. Any new creature coming fresh into the world would startle and amaze us all. What would men give if the Almighty hand would form a novelty in life, and send it among us; and yet, ye Athenian wits, that are forever seeking after some new thing, the text tells you that there are new creatures upon earth, positive new creations; fruits that have the freshness and bloom of Eden about them, flowers unfaded, life with the dew of its youth upon it; and these new creatures are Christian men; these new creatures, fresh from the divine hand, as though just fashioned between the eternal palms, are the men that weep for sin, the men that confess their iniquity, the men that say, "God be merciful to us, sinners," the men who rest in the blood of the atonement, the men who love Christ Jesus, and live to the glory of the Most High, — these are new creatures. There is a freshness about them; they have just come from the hand of God; they enjoy nearness to God; they get to the fountain-head of life, and drink where the crystal stream is cool and clear, and not mud died by long trickling through earthly channels.

Rev. C. H. Spurgeon.

ON the rocks by the sea-shore I have seen marine creatures living when the tide was out; not in the briny pools it leaves, but on the dry and naked rock, in the withering air — in the burning, broiling sun. They lived because, when twice each day the foaming tide came in, and, rising, covered the rocky shelves they clung to, they opened and shut their shelly mouths to drink water enough to last them when the tide was out, and till the next tide came in. Even so, twice a day at the least, are we to replenish our thirsty souls — fill our emptiness from the ocean of grace and mercy that flows, free and full in Christ, to the least of saints and chief of sinners.

Thomas Guthrie, D.D.

THERE is an abiding fulness of truth in Christ, after you have heard it for fifty years, you see more of its fulness than you did at first. Other truths weary the ear. I will defy any man to hold together a large congregation, year after year, with any other subject but Christ Jesus. He might do it for a time; he might charm the ear with the discoveries of science, or with the beauties of poetry, and his oratory might be of so high an order that he might attract the multitudes who have itching ears, but they would in time turn away and say, "This is no longer to be endured. We know it all." All music becomes wearisome but that of heaven; but oh! if the minstrel doth but strike this celestial harp, though he keepeth his fingers always among its golden strings, and be but poor and unskilled upon an instrument so divine, yet the melody of Jesus' name, and the sweet harmony of all his acts and attributes, will hold his listeners by the ears and thrill their hearts as naught beside can do. The theme of Jesus' love is inexhaustible, though preachers may have dwelt upon it century after century, a freshness and fullness still remain.

Rev. C. H. Spurgeon.

OH! what blessings are afflictions to those who can bless God *for* afflictions! "Oh!" said a bright-hearted young man, who was tortured with a fatal and painful bodily disease; "when I have the most pain in my body I have the most comfort in my soul. When Christ suffered, he had none but enemies about him, and they gave him gall and vinegar to drink. When I thirst, I have beside me the friend that sticketh closer than a brother. The cup that he gives me, shall I not drink it? I do not doubt but that there is love in the bottom of the cup, though it is bitter in the mouth."

Rev. T. L. Cuyler.

IT is God who made this beauteous world of ours; it is God who spread the firmament above us, and scattered there its sun-cloud of shining worlds; and the same power that created now upholds; it is God who hath clothed the fields in this glorious season of verdure; it is God whose hand paints each flower that adorns our fields; it is God who whispers to us in the zephyr and in the murmuring brook; it is God whose voice speaks in the tempest and in tones of Niagara's thunder; it is God in whom, in a literal sense, we move and live and have our being — he, by his own power moving upon us and keeping the vital organs in play, on which our life depends.

Rev. Dr. Cummings.

OH! how true —

"The chamber where the good man meets his fate
Is privileged above the common walks of virtuous life,
Quite on the verge of heaven."

That chamber may not always be the well-furnished apartment, with its soft bed and sympathizing attendants; that chamber may sometimes be the lonely hut, where poverty has left its footprints, and grim want stares out from walls and floor and couch of straw; that chamber may be the block where the martyring axe deals down the sudden, fatal blow; that chamber may be the stake where the fire crackles and crisps and consumes; that chamber may be the amphitheatre where savage beasts prey, revel, and glut, and devour; that chamber may be the rack on which the human frame is tortured and torn asunder. No matter — no matter where, no matter how the Christian dies, he hears a voice that comes down from beyond the stars, and says, "Fear not, fear not: death cannot injure you; the grave cannot hold you; through its chill mansion I will conduct you to glory." That grace which during all his life he has found sufficient, now wraps him in its mantle of beauty for his death-robe and his winding-sheet.

Rev. N. Vansant.

A HOLY life uniformly leads to a safe and happy death. What convincing majesty in the one, what subduing glory in the other — a holy life, a triumphant death! A holy life is a perpetual sun shining in his strength, day after day, and shedding on all around his enlightening and warming beams; a holy life is an ever-flowing river, fertilizing its banks and clothing them with never-fading verdure; a holy life is an unfailing fountain, sending forth its gushing streams to refresh the way-worn and weary; a holy life is an endless telegraph-line, stretching itself all along the devious highways of human existence, and guiding the lonely and the lost to a safe destination. We are told concerning Lord Peterborough, who was more famed for his wit than for his religion, that, having once lodged with Archbishop Fenelon, he was so impressed with his fervent piety and with his beautiful Christian character, that, on parting with him, he said, "I must stay no longer, or I shall become a Christian in spite of myself," thus showing the power of a holy life. Can we wonder that such a life should be crowned with a triumphant death?

Rev. N. Vansant.

WE look over the friends of our youth, and many of us who have come to middle years, or even to riper age, almost feel like some lone tree that once saw its associates around it, but has witnessed their falling trunks and peeled bark; has seen some of them riven by the lightnings, others prostrated by the storm; so we are standing while the generations that rose up by our side are sleeping in the ground; we stand as the remnants of the great multitude that in our younger days with gleeful feet trod our native soil. Why is this? Why are we spared when so many have fallen — the bright, the joyous, the beautiful, the gifted, the glorious? Oh! how many, like opening buds, were blasted by the frost — half-developed flowers! The storm swept them from the earth. Others, in riper age, wilted, hour by hour, and we have seen them pass away.

Even in our own households, the angel of death has entered, and we have seen the dark shadow thrown over our hearthstone. Why is it that we live? Because our times are in the hand of God. We live because it is his good pleasure that we should still have a work to do and responsibilities to fulfil.

Bishop Simpson.

I HAVE noticed that when a church-member grows very profuse in his style of living, and spends extravagantly in self-indulgences, he commonly becomes stingy toward the Lord. A genuine Christ-loving Christian gives the key of his purse or his iron safe to his Master. When a dispute once arose in a company as to which had the finest hand, a lady shrewdly said, "The handsomest hand here is the one that gives the most liberally." I believe that a servant of Christ should systematically bestow in charity at least *one-tenth* of his annual income, and just as much more as he can afford without robbing others. I never knew of a child of God being bankrupted by his benevolence. What you keep you may lose; what you give to Christ you are sure to keep.

Rev. Theo. L. Cuyler.

"GOD loves a cheerful giver," and, like love,
The more we give, the more we still receive;
Our mites at interest in the land above —
We only lend what charities we give.

S. H. Daddon

OUR observation and experience pause with death. Looking beyond it, the eye passes into a dense and solemn shade, overhanging the margins of time, and covering the frontier of the great future. That shade we cannot penetrate; and no voice from beyond it salutes us. There is a fascination in this mystery. The problem which it starts and conceals man never perfectly solves. We are of necessity a world of inquisitive gazers, ever looking up to a sky whose lights and shades excite the soul to the utmost alertness and intensity of thought; ever turning the ear toward that far-off land, that perchance some echo of a spirit gone may reach us on these mortal shores. God has ordained that such should be our mental position in respect to the sequel which awaits us after death. It is not our fault; and we do not know enough to pronounce it our misfortune.

Rev. Samuel T. Spear.

GOD revealed himself in love. Love is infinite; but love is just the same in quality in the mother's breast as it is in God. Love is the same in quality everywhere. It is like the sunshine. We cannot comprehend the stars in all their vast multitude, but we can comprehend the sunshine.

Sunshine is the same, whether striking upon the laborer's hut or upon the prince's palace. It is the same where it strikes upon our little, dim earth, as where it blazes forth in space. It is the same, and we can comprehend it in its essence. So love can be comprehended.

Rev. E. H. Chapin.

OH! how sweet is that idea of heaven that presents it as a Sabbath of eternal rest! During that endless, unclouded day, the glorified believer shall mingle in those celestial activities that shall be so pure, so unfettered, so unwearying, so delightful, that the Word of God pronounces them a perfect "*rest.*" The thought of it has made many a child of Jesus homesick. How oft has his tired soul been ready to exclaim, —

"Rest, weary head!
Lie down to slumber in the peaceful tomb,
Light from above has broken through its gloom;
Here, in the place where once thy Saviour lay,
Where he shall wake thee on a future day,
Like a tired child upon his mother's breast,
Rest, sweetly rest.

"Rest, spirit, free!
In the green pastures of the heavenly shore,
Where sin and sorrow can approach no more,
With all the flock by the Good Shepherd led,
Beside the streams of life eternal led,
Forever with thy God and Saviour blest,
Rest, spirit rest!"

Rev. Theo. L. Cuyler.

YOUNG man, learn to say "No." When you are tempted, utter it with a will, — "NO." When fair hands offer you the wine-cup say it gently, yet with unwavering firmness, — "No." A young companion invites you to the theatre, or to the billiard-room, or the dance-house. Do you think it would be well to go? No. Well, then, how will you answer him? "I—I—I *think* I wont go to-night." He will collar you and say, "Oh, come along now." If you add, with bated breath, "I was brought up not to go to such places," he will say, "Be your own man; I wouldn't always be tied to my mother's apron-string; come on;" and on you go like a dumb ox to the slaughter. A decided and emphatic "*No*," which would have made your tempter feel that your self-respect was touched by his proposal, would have sent him away to return on such an errand no more.

Rev. C. D. Foss.

IF the thoughts have been fixed upon fineries for the hour before service, they will naturally flow on in the same channel after the service begins; and instead of joining in the song, or the prayer, or the study of truth, the worshipper will be making eager observation of the various styles of dress exhibited, and plotting the purchase or the manufacture of new adornments.

Rev. W. Glidden.

IMAGINE a tree expostulating with an orchardist, and saying, "Why is this oft-coming of this knife? Is it not the nature of a tree to grow? I am shooting out branches on every side, and up ward, according to the law of nature; and where fore am I lopped back every now and then?" Symmetry is in the mind of the man that trains the tree, and it must grow for that very sake, and must be cut back for that very sake, though symmetry is not in the thought of the tree. And with symmetry is something higher yet — fruit; though that is not in the thought of the tree, while it is in the thought of the orchardist. And as he nurtures for these ends, blind nature knows nothing about them.

But in human life it would seem as if suffering ought not to have been a part of the earthly course; it would seem as if, God having ordained the body with all its functions and faculties, the natural process of growth would be an easy and progressive evolution by such arrangements as should be devoid of suffering; but actually, human experience shows exactly another thing. If any thing can be shown by the indications and facts of nature, it is that man never grows to a full man's estate without a certain degree of ministration of suffering; and that suffering is a part of nature, or it could not be universal everywhere, always having infallible signs and tokens of universality.

Rev. H. W. Beecher.

I HEAR God speaking in his word to us: "Rejoice evermore; and again I say rejoice." There is enough to make us joyous. Jesus is our Saviour,

God is our Father, heaven is our home; mansions are prepared for us, crowns are burnished for us, and white robes are ready for us. Pure spirits are looking down upon us; sainted mothers and fathers, who bore us in their arms, are looking over the walls for us to come; and little children who dropped out of our arms are waiting like cherubim on the walls of glory for us.

Bishop Simpson.

THE two things that bring business most frequently to disaster are greediness and dishonesty. They are the breasts on which bankruptcy nurses itself. Instead of being a necessary help, dishonesty is the leak, the weight, the immeasurable evil that oppresses business. More labor is exacted, more care of the mind is required, more wear and tear of watching is rendered necessary, more complexity of business arrangements is called for, more money is spent and wasted on society, by dishonesty, than any man can measure or conceive. I think that if it were given us, by a kind of sorcery, to extract the element of dishonesty from the different spheres of life, it would be found that nearly one-half of the forces applied to business were means uselessly employed to watch men and guard against their dishonesties. If men could be believed when they spoke, and trusted when they promised, it would take from business half of its circuity. Our business is rolled up in complexities. It is like an army marching in an enemy's country, and being obliged to explore every step of the way, and to be constantly ready for battle; whereas, if men were honest, it would be like a man going for pleasure over a friend's territory, enjoying the sweet delights that surround him on every hand.

Rev. H. W. Beecher.

THE best thing to do with our past sin, if it be indeed forgiven, is to bury it; yes, and let us bury it as they used to bury suicides,—let us drive a stake through it, in horror and contempt, and never set up a monument to its memory. If you ever do tell anybody about your youthful wrong-doing, let it be with blushes and tears, with shame and confusion of face; and always speak of it to the honor of the infinite mercy which forgave you. Never let the devil stand behind you and pat you on the back and say, "You did me a good turn in those days." Oh, it is a shameful thing to have sinned, a degrading thing to have lived in sin, and it is not to be wrapped up into a telling story and told out as an exploit, as some do. "The old man is crucified with him," who boasts of being related to the crucified felon. If any member of your family had been hanged, you would tremble to hear any one mention the gallows; you would not run about crying, "Do you know a brother of mine was hanged at Newgate?" Your old man of sin is hanged; do not talk about him, but thank God it is so? and as he blots out the remembrance of it, do you the same, except so far as it may make you humble and grateful.

Rev. S. H. Spurgeon.

IT is a very terrible thing to begin to let conscience grow hard, for it soon sears as with a hot iron. It is like the freezing of a pond. The first film of ice is scarcely perceptible: keep the waters stirring, and you will prevent the ice from hardening it; but once let it film over and remain so, it thickens over the surface, and it thickens still, and at last it is so solid that a wagon might be drawn over the solid water. So with conscience, it films over gradually, and at last it becomes hard, unfeeling, and it can bear up with a weight of iniquity.

Bishop Simpson

WE measure men in the affairs of life. Let an officer go out to select materials for organizing an army, let a commercial agent go out to select men for the various departments of trade, and how instantly do they see that there is a great difference between one and another! and how invariably do they seek for those that have forces as well as good qualities—good qualities with forces behind them! There are a great many who would have made magnificent men if they had had any propelling power. They are quietists. Why? Because they have not blood enough to aerate their brains. Why? Because they are built too large in the head, and too small in the trunk. And what has that to do with it? It interprets God's thought. When God made a man, he made it very important that he should have a head. And then he made that head itself to be dependent for its supplies. The head feeds. And where does it feed? At the heart. The heart brings the food to the head. Where does the heart get it? In the lungs, where it is vitalized. The lungs are the kitchen, the heart is the servant, and the head is the master that eats. And how about the stomach? That is the grand digester that supplies the materials which the heart and lungs send to the head.

Rev. H. W. Beecher.

I SEE a strong man suffering the pangs of indigestion, a load upon his stomach, oppression in his head, fever in his pulse. The physician is called, who proceeds at once to administer a nauseous emetic. "No!" says the sick man; "I am sick; give me something to make me well!" — "I can only make you well by making you sicker first." — "Then you are a hard-hearted, cruel man!"

But which would be the greater cruelty, — to humor his inclination and let him die, or administer the dose and drive away the danger? So we are ever ready to charge cruelty, or at least a disregard of our feelings, upon Providence, when, in reality, it is that goodness "which connot be unkind" that doses us with trials for our spiritual healing. Natural theology expatiates with delight upon the evidences of God's wisdom and goodness revealed in the works of creation; and it is well. But the hand of the spoiler is there! Disease has devastated earth! But with a clear foresight of his reckless smitings, Divine Wisdom has harnessed him in the traces of system, and confined his destructions to the domains of law.

Rev. S. H. Platt.

I OBSERVE from my windows that there come down the East River magnificent men-of-war from the Navy Yard, with a bank of guns that fills the imagination with visions of power and terrible efficiency. And lifted up and lying against the sky are spars and rigging. And as they swing at anchor, the banner of our country — our Stars and Stripes, the sweetest flag on which the sun shines — floats out on the breeze. And the morning and the evening gun booms at the appointed hour. I think that next to the things that God made, the fairest is the ship, which man, learning through ages, has at last learned to make, and which, as it moves on the moving element, is the most strong and powerful, and yet the most plastic and yielding thing in the world. I see, soon after, coming up the bay, wing-worn and way-beaten, a bark. She is not a man-of-war. She is a merchantman. Close after her comes a brig, that runs in and anchors under the guns of the ship. And after her comes a square rigged schooner. And after her a fore-and-aft schooner. And after her a sloop. And after her a smack. And after her a lighter. And I say that whether it be a man-of-war, bark, brig, hermaphrodite brig, square-rigged schooner, fore-and-aft schooner, sloop, smack, lighter, or what not, every one of them must fly its country's flag. It must sail according to its own nature, but it must sail in the interests of patriotism, and in obedience to the laws of the country. And it is just as easy to have a patriotic sloop as a patriotic man-of-war. It is just as easy to have a law-abiding schooner, as a law-abiding bark or brig. And yet, does any man say that because they are cut out on different patterns, and built differently, they cannot be alike patriotic, and that only a man-of-war can be devoted to its country service? Men would be fools to talk so about vessels, and men are fools that talk so about men. Men are built differently in hull and rigging; they are built with different capacities and for different things; but they are all built so that they can fly God's flag, and can sail within the laws of morality: and they are all built so as to be amenable to the great decrees of God in respect to the use of human faculties.

Rev. H. W. Beecher

TRUTH will never die: the stars will grow dim, the sun will pale his glory; but truth will be ever young. Integrity, uprightness, honesty, love, goodness — these are all imperishable. No grave can ever entomb these immortal principles. They have been in prison, but they have been freer than before; those who have enshrined them in their hearts have been burned at the stake; but out of their ashes other witnesses have arisen. No sea can drown, no storm can wreck, no abyss can swallow up the ever-living truth of God. You cannot kill goodness, and truth, and integrity, and faith, and holiness; the way that is consistent with these must be a way everlasting.

Rev. C. H. Spurgeon.

WHAT sublimity does this thought of divine guidance give us! The old Mohammedan soldiers had the idea that they never could die until their time came—that they should die just as soon in the bosom of their family as in the army. What soldiers this belief made of them! How fearless! how daring! how unconquerable, as their hosts marched onward! All the difference, they believed, was, that if they died at home they died cowards and traitors, while if they died in the army they died as saints and as martyrs, and went direct to a world of glory. What resistless power it gave them! Oh! if, as Christians, we feel the full force of the thought that God watches over us, and whether we live or die all is well—that a few days earlier or later makes no difference; that we are for heaven, for glory, working while God lets us work, and rejoicing when God gives us to rejoice—how irresistible would be this power, and how happy would we be! Have you this happiness this morning! Do you know "to live is Christ, to die is gain!" Blessed be the God and Father of our Lord Jesus Christ, you may know it — you may know that you are in harmony with God. To be such, come to the foot of the cross. Feel the sprinkled blood — feel the joys of pardoned sin; become a child of God; enter on life with higher aspirations and higher aims; and thus your times shall be in God's hand, and to all eternity you shall be before the throne.

Bishop Simpson.

BEETHOVEN, it is said, after he became deaf, would sit and play on an old worn out harpsichord that had long been unfit for use, and suppose that he was playing matchless harmonies. The instrument was so poor that not one chord in five responded. Here was one that gave forth some sound, and there was another; but even they were out of harmony. And I sometimes think that God plays on a poor old harpsichord when he takes this world to evolve the melodies of divine love, so few chords respond at all, and so utterly inadequate are those that do respond to illustrate this crowning attribute of the divine mind.

Rev. H. W. Beecher.

TAKE the untutored savage to a bed of iron ore, and bid him to fashion an Indian hatchet from it, and he will select a thin, wedge-shaped lump, and endeavor with stones of flint to hammer and grind it to an edge, and then with rude lashings to fasten it to an unturned handle. He may succeed. But now take the man of science there, and as he selects a portion, breaks it as small as may be needful, the savage wonders how that can make a hatchet. Now he throws the fragments into the heated furnace, and as they catch its ruddy glow, and the molten metal runs in a stream of liquid fire into the receiving ladle, the savage yells his wild derision at the attempt. The mould receives it, and soon the cold, heavy bar excites anew his scorn. Again it is thrust into the furnace, then placed under the heavy steam-hammer, and drawn into the lengthened bar, which, packed in charcoal, ashes, and salt, must feel the furnace heat for eight long days, and then swelter fourteen more, before it becomes the steel from which the smith, with many a blow, and many an alternate heat and chill, can fashion the polished weapon. But, now, compare it with the rude hatchet of the savage, and who shall say that the man of science is not the wiser artisan?

So, our untutored minds would work from the heart's native ore, by a direct and speedy process, the implements of our destiny; but God pulverizes, and smelts, and casts, and draws, and bakes, and hammers, and fashions, and tempers as his science dictates; and who shall say, in view of results, that his is not the better plan? Certainly it were as foolish in us to question the wisdom of his proceedings as in the savage to sneer at the well-considered processes of his learned competitor.

Rev. S. H. Platt.

HERE is a man that was once poor, but that has become wealthy. Bankers bow to him, and pat him familiarly on the shoulder; and because he is rich, and because great men look at him, he is proud, and he begins to feel, "It will not do for my children to be brought up like common folks' children. That boy of mine, I mean shall be a lawyer; and I hope one day to see him in Congress." But the little fellow has an appetite for colors and pencils. He does not like books, and he *will* be running after what he calls "the development of his artist tendency." There is still another boy that gives the father yet more trouble. He has an intense love for mechanics, and is determined that he will be a machinist. Nothing pleases him better than to be in foundries, among dirty stithies, looking at the men at they work, and talking with the foreman and the draughtsmen. And the father is perfectly shocked at the idea that the son of such a respectable rich man as he is should be a mechanic. "Why," says he, "it would be a disgrace to my family! it will not do at all!" And so he attempts to make a merchant out of his son.

Now, no man's flesh and blood is too good to work. If your son wants to go to sea, he is not too good to go to sea. If your son wants to be a mechanic, he is not at all too good to be a mechanic. If your son wants to work on a farm, dirt is healthy for your boy.

Rev. H. W. Beecher.

IF you have ever feasted with the Well-Beloved, I am sure you will wish the festival would never break up; you will long for the time when you may eat the bread of heaven in heaven, and drink the wine of the Kingdom new in glory, and go no more out, but abide with the Father, world without end. Happy, thrice happy is the man who entertains the angels' Lord.

Rev. C. H. Spurgeon.

SUPPOSE a bank across the street contained an unlimited amount of worthless shinplasters, besides untold wealth of gold, and you were empowered to check out either. You are in pressing need. Your note is in bank. The three days' grace is nearly past. It is two o'clock, and but a single hour stands between you and dishonor. You seize your pen and check out a thousand dollars in shinplasters! "What a fool!" exclaims your clerk. "You might as well have drawn a thousand rags!" Yet thus we do every day.

We carry our cares for the missionary and the millennium to God; we lay upon him our burdens for his moral government, and the judgment of the world, but our aching heads, and shattered nerves, and dyspeptic stomachs, and laggard livers, and rheumatic joints, and crazy tongues, and fiery tempers; our cross companions, and fretful children, and fault-finding neighbors; our losses and debts and dues, — for all these, and countless more, we check out shinplasters, or, at the best, we lay them aside, as hodmen do their hods when dinner comes, merely to take them up again when dinner is over.

Now, God does not thank you for not bringing things that do not concern you. He wants your little personal annoyances, your petty solicitudes, your trifling perplexities — too unimportant, you may think, for him to notice; but if they are large enough or sharp enough to worry you, he wants them — wants them all! "Casting all your care," etc.

Rev. S. H. Platt.

THOUSANDS of parents govern their children simply and soley for their own luxury and convenience, and take no pains to smooth the tones of their voice, or to measure their action. The thought of courtesy in their dealings with their children is almost dismissed from their mind. I have seen children insulted so grossly by parents that nature in me said, "The parents ought to be severely punished," while grace in me said, "No, no; they only ought to be reproved and taught better." Because God lent a little child to you, he did not lend it to you to be a rug for you to wipe your feet on; he did not lend it to you to be a slave, to run of errands, merely; he did not lend it to you to practise your cruelty and irritableness on. That child was God's before it was yours. It was only placed in your hands for a little time; and if every parent felt, on addressing a child, "There is something of divinity in it as well as in me," I think it would purge our families of much of the ill-government that is in them.

Rev. H. W. Beecher.

I SAW a temple reared by the hands of man standing with his pinnacle in the distant plain. The streams beat about it, the God of nature hurled his thunderbolt against it, yet it stood firm as adamant. Revelry was in the halls; the gay, the happy, the young, the beautiful were there. I returned — and lo! the temple was no more. Its high walls lay in scattered ruin; moss and grass grew rankly there; and at the midnight hour the owl's long cry added to the deep solitude. The young and gay who had revelled there, had passed away.

I saw a child rejoicing in his youth, the idol of his mother and the pride of his father. I returned — and that child had become old. Trembling with the weight of years, he stood, the last of his generation, a stranger amid the desolation around him.

I saw an old oak standing in all its pride upon the mountain; the birds were carolling in its boughs. I returned — and the oak was leafless and sapless; the winds were playing at their pastimes through its branches.

"Who is this destroyer?" said I to my guardian angel.

"It is Time," said he. "When the morning stars sung together for joy over the new-made world, he commenced his course; and when he has destroyed all that is beautiful on the earth, plucked the sun from his sphere, veiled the moon in blood, yea, when he shall have rolled the heavens and earth away as a scroll, then shall an angel from the throne of God come forth, and, with one foot upon the sea and one upon the land, lift up his hand toward heaven, and swear, by Heaven's Eternal, Time is, Time was, but Time shall be no longer!

Paulding.

LET a man try the experiment of introducing the ballot-box into his machinery of self-government with a view to getting a popular vote on all questions of moment; he will quickly find it not only vain, but ruinous. Those faculties which God has put to the top will come to the bottom. A monarch dethroned cannot be a common man; he must pine in prison or bow to the block. God's order concerning us is, that the passions should lie at the bottom of our nature, under the control of the intellect, and that the intellect should be subject to the divinely illuminated will. Attempt to equalize them, and you will find the regal will discrowned, and lying in the dust under the feet of all the other powers, and the passions rampant and riotous on the wreck of your manhood.

Rev. C. D. Foss.

IF I were called to point out the most alarming sins to-day, — those which are most deceitful in their influence, and most soul-destroying in their ultimate effects, — I would not mention drunkenness with all its fearful havoc, nor gambling with its crazed victims, nor harlotry with its hellish orgies; but the love of money on the part of men, and the love of display on the part of women. While open vice sends its thousands, these fashionable and favored indulgences send their ten thousands to perdition. They sear the conscience, incrust the soul with an impenetrable shell of worldliness; debauch the affections from every high and heavenly object; and make man or woman the worshipper of self. While doing all this, the poor victim is allowed by public opinion to think himself or herself a Christian; while the drunkard, the gambler, or the prostitute, is not deceived by such a thought for a moment.

Dr. Crosby.

YOU call at a friend's house; you are riding on horseback; he takes your horse into the stable, and is remarkably attentive to it; the creature is well groomed, well housed, well fed. You are not at all afraid that you will be shut out: there is surely a warm place in the parlor for the rider, where the horse is so well attended to in the stable. Now, your body, which I might liken to the horse, has had its temporal prosperity in abundance, and surely the Lord will take care of your soul if you seek his face! Let your prayer be, "My God, my father, be my guide. Since thou hast dealt so well with me in these external matters, give me grace within my heart; give me the true riches; give me to love thy Son, and trust in him, to be henceforth thy child. Thou hast given me the nether springs: give me to drink of the upper springs. I have the blessings which thou givest to the ungodly, oh, give me the blessings of the godly, the peculiar heritage of thy saints!" O Holy Spirit, constrain many thus to hope and pray.

Rev. C. H. Spurgeon.

I HAVE heard a loving mother ask her willing little boy to bring her a stick of wood from the yard, and directly he came staggering back, both arms piled full, the great blue veins standing out on face and neck, and every fibre quivering with the tension of his heroic endeavor; the instant she caught sight of his over-burdened obedience, she sprang to his relief, snatched his load, and left her kiss. So God longs to take your cares, but you must cast them upon his outstretched arms. "Casting all your care," etc. He wants to relieve you of life's load, that you may engage more heartily and successfully in its conflicts.

Rev. S. H. Platt.

WE may be able to accept or to repeat the dictum of Cicero, that "the universal consent of nations concerning a life to come has almost the validity and force of a law of nature." We may admit that to be true; but how little we know of the life, and how many questions there are starting up within us concerning it! "Will there be a body as well as a soul? Shall we know one another? Will consciousness continue as it was in this world? Will our thought-power and love-power remain, and be only unfolded and renewed; or is there some strange change to come, and a great chasm to be inserted between our life here and our experience hereafter?" How these questions throng upon us as we come to the death-bed of a friend, and follow him down, step by step, until the soul passes out!

Oh! if we could only shout the question and have it answered on the other side. But it never is answered. Christ dies to answer it. He dies that he may rise again; that he may put the resurrection on the bow of the retiring storm, and set in contrast the ascension with the crucifixion.

Rev. R. S. Storrs, Jr.

THE disposition to pry into the privacy of domestic life is, unfortunately, very common, and is always dishonorable. The appetite for such knowledge is to be regarded as morbid, and the indulgence of it as disgraceful.

A family have a sacred right to privacy. In guarding the delicate relations of the household, secrecy becomes a virtue. Even if by chance the private affairs of a household are laid open to a stranger, honor would require him to turn from them; and if a knowledge of them were forced upon him, they should be locked in a sacred silence.

A double obligation of silence and secrecy rests upon one who is a guest in a family. The turpitude of a betrayal of family history by a visitor, is far greater than theft would be. To pocket half a dozen silver spoons would do far less damage, produce far less suffering, and be less immoral than tale-bearing. It is a thing so scandalous that it should degrade a person and put him out of society. To betray the secrets of a household is not only an odious immorality, but it is a shame to be on terms with those who are known to commit such outrages. They are miscreants. They put themselves out of the pale of decent society. They should be treated as moral outlaws.

These hungry-eyed wretches who sit in the unsuspicious circle of parents and children, treasuring their words, spying their weaknesses, misinterpreting the innocent liberties of the household, and then run from house to house with their shameless news, are worse than poisoners of wells or burners of houses. They poison the faith of man in man. If one opens his mouth to tell you such things, with all your might smite him in the face! There are two actions which justify you in instantly knocking a man down: the one is the act of pointing a gun at you in sport, and the other is the attempt to tell you a secret, which it is disgraceful for him to get and for you to hear. Make no terms with such people. Tale-bearers have no rights. They are common enemies of good men. Hunt, harry, and hound them out of good society. They are the worst of pests save one, and that is the listener to the tale-bearer.

There could be no tattling if there was no one to hear. It takes an ear and a tongue to make a scandal. Greedy listening is as dishonorable as nimble tattling. There is the open market where the tongue sells its ill-gotten wares. Some there are who will not repeat again what they hear, but they are willing to listen to it! They will not trade in contraband goods, but they will buy enough of the smuggler for family use!

These respectable listeners are the patrons of tattlers. It is the ready market that keeps tale-bearing brisk. It is a shame to listen to ill of your neighbor. Christian benevolence demands that you do not love ill-news. A clean heart and a true honor rejoice in kindly things. It should be a pain and sorrow to know of any thing that degrades your neighbor in your eyes, even if he is your enemy; how much more if he is your friend?

Rev. H. W. Beecher.

HERE are several threads. That is silk, that is cotton, that is woollen, and that is linen. You cannot change them by any amount of carding, or dyeing, or spinning, or manipulation of any kind; but you can determine that that silk thread shall be a pair of stockings, a dress, or a foolish window-curtain. You can determine what fabric it shall make; but it is going to be silk when it is manufactured.

You cannot change the fundamental nature of faculties, but you can determine what a particular faculty shall do. You can take silk and cotton, and put them together, and determine what they shall be when they are combined; and education simply undertakes to determine what the faculties shall be when brought into partnerships. By their combination it represses some, or limits them to certain degrees of manifestation. It determines not what they are, but what they shall be permitted or inspired to do. The direction of faculties, and not the changing of their nature, is the appropriate business of education.

Rev. H. W. Beecher.

I WAS reading the other day that on the shores of the Adriatic Sea, the wives of fishermen, whose husbands have gone far off upon the deep, are in the habit at even-tide of going down to the sea-shore, and singing, as female voices only can, the first stanza of a beautiful hymn; after they have sung it they listen, till they hear borne by the wind across the desert sea the second stanza, sung by their gallant husbands as they are tossed by the gale upon the waves; and both are happy. Perhaps if we could listen we too might hear on this desert world of ours some sound, some whisper borne from afar, to remind us that there is a heaven and a home; and when we sing the hymn upon the shores of earth, perhaps we shall hear its sweet echo breaking in music upon the sands of time, and cheering the hearts of them that are pilgrims and strangers, and look for a city that hath foundations.

Dr. John Cumming.

THERE are thousands of persons who are kept out of the kingdom of God because they are such enormous eaters. You are gluttons, a great many times, many of you, long before men call you gluttons. Who is a glutton? That man who eats so much that he cannot think clearly; that man who eats so much that his disposition is affected — he is a glutton. If you eat those things and drink those things which lower your power to act as an intelligent moral being; or if you eat so much and drink so much as to incapacitate yourself to act as an intelligent moral being — you are a glutton. Some men are gluttons occasionally; some are gluttons in spots; and some are gluttons at the close of the day. There are some men who will not eat much in the morning, because they know that excessive eating then will unfit them for the duties of the day; but who, at night, swamp down their whole nature with inordinate gormandizing. And what is it that hinders such men from becoming Christians? It is gluttony.

Rev. H. W. Beecher.

JESUS CHRIST DIVINE. — Napoleon, on the rock of St. Helena, said to General Bertrand, "I know man, and I tell you Christ was not a man. Everything about Christ astonishes me. His spirit overwhelms and confounds me. There is no comparison between him and any other being. He stands single and alone. Alexander, Cæsar, Charlemagne, and I, have founded empires; but on what rests the creation of our genius? On force. Jesus alone founded his kingdom on love; and at this hour millions of men would die for him."

NOTHING can be more beautiful than a loving household. There is no garden, there is no beauty in the heaven, nor upon the earth in the fairest days of the most favored seasons, that for one moment can compare with the beauty of a loving household. Parents with their children, interlocked in love, screened from the outward world, housed and harbored and imparadised — few sights are more beautiful, and few experiences are more delightful. We do not know how happy we are while the happiness is passing. With all the cares, the anxieties, the watchings, the labors, the sicknesses, the memory witnesses that there was, — after all, no period of life when there was so much or so various enjoyment as in the early days of the family, while the children where yet young, were entirely under the parental control, and were simple and loving.

Rev. H. W. Beecher.

IT is the material that leads us downward. Our gross instincts join us to earth; it is man's impulses and passions binding him to the outward and the material that have ever proved his ruin. It was the appetite indulged in the garden of Eden that led to sin, and it is always by the visible and the material that man is led astray. If you can break that bond of thought, and divorce man awhile from the material, let him forget the ties that bind him to the earth; let him be free from the impulses that draw him downward; let him feel that he is joined with eternity, and his home is the eternity to come; let him think of kindred dear that have just gone beyond the vale; let him commune with the invisible and the eternal, — and you give to his thoughts elevation and sublimity. Now, it is thus that the Christian Church, by imparting thoughts of this class, is leading man away from the visible, making him a better man.

Bishop Simpson.

LET no man's, at least no believer's, heart fail because of this king of terrors. Though thousands fall beside us, though ten thousand expire at our right hand, and though we ourselves must quickly give up the ghost; yet the word is gone out of our Redeemer's mouth, and it shall not return unfulfilled, — "I will swallow up death in victory." He shall stand at the latter day upon the earth; he shall say to the grave, Give up; and to the sea, Keep not back; release my sons from your dark confinement, and restore my daughters to their everlasting Father's arms. Then shall we lead him captive, whose captives we were, and triumph eternally over this last enemy. In the mean time, let us lay all our help, all our guilt, upon the divine Author of our faith, and Captain of our salvation. So shall we no longer be in bondage through fear of death; but, with the saints of old, overcome through the blood of the Lamb; overcome the dread, even while we sink beneath the stroke, of this our mortal foe.

Hervey.

IT takes two things to make a violet, — the root and the season. The season cannot make a violet without any root, and the root cannot make a violet without any season. These two things must go together, or there can be no violet. If the thread is there, and the spinner is there, working together, they will make the garniture of the summer.

And so it is with the human soul. God makes nothing without the germs in you, and the germs in you make nothing without God; and when these germs are brought under the influence of God's love, and they reach out and accept these things, then comes on the garden of the Lord in the human soul.

Rev. H. W. Beecher.

IT is a common saying of some men in the world that children are not old enough to select their own religion, and that it is not fair to prejudice their minds beforehand. "Wait," they say, "till the child has arrived at years of discretion, and then let him take his choice." That is about as wise as it would be for a man to say in respect to his field, "I am not going to prejudice that field in favor of wheat, or corn, or any other kind of grain, so I will let it remain uncultivated for ten years." And at the end of the ten years Canada thistles, and burdock, and all manner of weeds have got in, and gone to seed, so that for a foot deep it is one complete mass of germinating mischiefs. And that is the result of what he calls letting his ground alone. If you will agree that the devil shall not sow any seeds in the vacant mind of the child till he is twenty-one, then I will consent that no steps shall be taken toward forming his religion till he is twenty-one. But you are to make a distinction between moral training and dogma. It is not necessary that the child should have any particular theory on election, or moral government, as between the Methodists, the Baptists, the Presbyterians, and the Episcopalians. These external questions he need not adjust till he is older. But moral training is a part of education; and you might as well say that you will not train a child's hand till he is twenty-one, as to say that you will not train his conscience, his sense of right and wrong, his power to discriminate between truth and lie, till he is twenty-one. It is your duty to train the child, and you do him no injustice in guiding his morals and leading him into the path of rectitude. You may let his theological training go, but his religious training ought to be a matter of every-day life.

Rev. H. W. Beecher.

A DYING girl said to her mother, " Ma, I don't want to die, for I saw where they put Susy when she died. The grave is a cold, gloomy place. Won't you die and go into the ground with me? I am afraid to go alone." The mother could say nothing. She only looked out of the window and sobbed. At length the father came in, and the dying child said the same thing to him. With broken words he told her about Jesus; that her parents could not die and be buried with her; that she must look to God to be with her. She turned her face to the wall very sadly, and after thinking a long time, roused herself and said, " Papa! mamma! I don't want you to die and go with me. I am not afraid to die now. I have asked Jesus to be with me. He has been in the grave. He promises to take care of us. He will go with me."

Rev. F. G. Clark.

I HAVE read thy record, O mistress of the house! I say, woman, I have read thy record, and it is enough; I need not cross thy threshold; I do not want to see thy magnificent temple; I never wish to sit in thy splendid halls. It is enough; I am satisfied. Rather would I sleep nightly in my shroud, and sit on my coffin, and have my gravestone in the wall of my study, and live in a vault forever, than I would enter that house of feasting. Good God, may I be kept from sinful mirth! May I be kept from the house of sinful feasting! May I never be tempted to cross that threshold! Oh, thou young man, who art enchanted by its gayety, charmed by its music, stay, stay! for every plank in the floor is rotten, every stone that is there is dug from the quarries of hell; and if thou enterest into that mansion, thou shalt find that her steps lead down to hell, and go down to the chambers of everlasting woe.

Rev. C. H. Spurgeon.

IF you get an invitation to a wedding, and an invitation to a funeral, lay the funeral note on the top. Do not disdain to go there, O son of God! for the Holy Ghost will so reveal Jesus, by the bedside of the mourner, that it will be to thee a Bethel.

Rev. C. H. Spurgeon.

MAN was not made to be stagnant. The sails are for the breeze, and for progress. There is no Castle of Indolence in all our goodly land. There is no languid happiness, no lethargic Christianity. He who would steer clear of all excitement may as well bid adieu to the coast of joy, which is the highest excitement.

Rev. J. W. Alexander.

AN idler is a watch that wants both hands;
As useless if it goes as when it stands.

Cowper.

WE have read of a certain youth, in the early days of Christianity — those periods of historic suffering and heroic patience and legendary wonder to which I call your attention — we read of a Christian youth on whom his persecutors put in practice a more than common share of their ingenuity, that by his torments (let those who can or will go through the horrible details) they might compel him to deny his Lord and Saviour.

After a long endurance of those pains they released him, in wonder at his obstinacy. His Christian brethren are said to have wondered, too, and to have asked him by what mighty faith he could stand even fire, as that neither a cry nor a groan escaped him.

"It was indeed most painful," was the noble youth's reply; "but an angel stood by me when my anguish was at the worst, and with his finger pointed to heaven."

O thou, whoever thou art, that art tempted to

commit a sin, do thou think on death, and that thought will be an angel to thee! The hope of heaven will raise thy courage above the fire-cast threatenings of the world; the fear of hell will rob its persuasions of all their enchantment: and the very extremity of their trial may itself contribute to animate thy exertions by the thought that the greater will be thy reward hereafter.

Bishop Heber.

THE way to bliss lies not on beds of down,
And he that had no cross, deserves no crown.

Francis Quarles.

A MAN'S body is his chariot. Some are put into a broken-down, rickety vehicle, and the chief business of their life is taking care of it. Their thought, perpetually, is of health, of taking care of the animal frame that is committed to them.

Nay, a man's physical organization determines a great many things that are known to be vital to one's success in life. Whether your child shall live by brain-work or hand-work depends very much on the organization of his body. If he is so organized at birth that his strength lies in bone and muscle, no fondness on your part, and no wish on his, will alter the fact that he is made to be a manual worker. There is such a thing as a classification of those that work. We may say what we please about the inequalities of society, but one thing is certain — that men who work with the brain rank higher, and always will rank higher, than those who work under the brain's direction, with the mere bone and muscle. In other words, the higher the range of faculties with which you work, the higher is your rank, and the higher is the price of your work. And men may be said to be divided, at birth, into brain-workers and hand-workers; and hand-workers are the subordinates.

And even among these, birth classifies again; for if a man is born clumsy, awkward, not over-bright, and is simply able to do work that is laid out for him, he ranks lower than the man who, though he may not be a thinker, is born, with skill and aptness of finger.

And when our children come into life, it is as clearly marked down that some shall serve others, as it is marked down that a ton's weight shall surpass a pound's weight. The difference of lengths, the difference of numbers, the difference of quantities, the difference of material qualities, is not more absolutely fixed in the decrees of God than are men's futures relatively fixed in the simple fact of physical organization.

Rev. H. W. Beecher.

YOU have seen the story, I presume, about the man who had been gathering remnants for making paper, and who put them through a chemical process by which all the color and stains were removed, so that the paper would become white. After a long experience, he stated that the hardest color to make white was crimson; the most difficult to be bleached out by any possible chemical process was the crimson. And yet, though our sins are like scarlet and crimson, the blood of Christ takes every stain away.

Bishop Simpson.

A MAN'S eyes were given to him to see with; but only a few have found that out. A man's ears were given to him to hear with; but there is little that he does hear except tittle-tattle. There are many things that you should hear, but that you do not hear. There is so much given, that, if a man has curiosity and application he might just as well throw out a net into the sea swarming with fish, and bring it back empty, as to throw out his observation and not bring back full hands. There is not a time that you walk through the street, when, if you employed your senses, you would not learn something worth while. The world is full of lore and knowledge and it comes knocking at the door of observation; but still it is true, "Eyes have they, but they see not; they have ears, but they hear not."

Rev. H. W. Beecher.

IT is the nature of God to draw men toward goodness. That is the thing that he loves best, that he follows himself, and that his influence tends to produce. Men draw men by the nature that they have — some toward one thing, and some toward another; some toward things that are bright and cheerful, and some toward things that are dark and desponding. Some men stir up in you all that which is good: some men seem perpetually to rankle in you by their influence. The difference between one man and another is not to be measured by what they say and by what they do, alone. When some men have been present with me, I know not why, but I am a better man. Yes, I do know why. It is because, although they may not have had a lesson in their mind, although they may not have had an intention of doing anything, the way in which their mind acted was such as to strike those salient feelings in me that are manly and noble. Their look; what they did not say, as much as what they did; their whole bearing, gave life to that part which should live in me; and, without intending it, they left me a legacy, an annuity, and I was a better man. When others have been with me, though no improper sentence has escaped their lips; though they have done nothing wrong; though certainly they have had no intention of evil, — my hope is drugged, my fear is awakened, my suspicions are on the alert, my sweet-mindedness is gone, and sour predominates in me. I do not suppose that vinegar means to be sour, but it is sour. And so with many men there is a nature of things that goes with character.

Now, it is the nature of the divine mind to lift

up, to cheer, to encourage, to sweeten, to help, to strengthen. It is the nature of God to draw men toward that which is right, pure, truthful, equitable, noble, — in short, royal.

Rev. H. W. Beecher.

IT is said of man, as he thinketh in his heart, so is he. A man's thoughts form his character. A man may, to all public appearance, be a pure man, and yet, if he is indulging unclean and unholy thoughts in his mind, he is forming a base character and is becoming a base man. If a man be intending to wrong, though he may not utter it with his lips; though he may not communicate the conception to his dearest friend, — he is destroying his own true character. The world is oftentimes astonished by base actions on the part of men supposed previously to have been good. It is an old saying that no man becomes suddenly base. It is by entertaining wrong conceptions, by indulging wrong thoughts, by familiarizing himself with improper scenes, and by harboring wrong purposes, that the barriers against sin are finally broken down, and he is led to the commission of evil; and wherever there are influences favoring such thoughts, society is unsafe.

Bishop Simpson.

YOUNG people want to begin further along than they are able to. They want to keep house as twenty years of successful and fruitful industry have enabled other men to do it. They measure everything on the pattern of somebody else. There is a want of self-respect founded on one's good breeding and fundamental honesty. And extravagance is ulmost invariably married to dishonesty.

Rev. H. W. Beecher.

WE read that a few months since a balloon ascended on the western edge of the plains of New England. One mile up it encountered a stratum of cloud a thousand feet thick; emerging from this, it ascended to the deep blue; when four miles above the earth, a pigeon was let loose, which dropped like lead into the depths below; higher up profound silence reigned, and five miles above the earth, everything freezes, and the atmosphere is too thin to sustain life. The steerer, as he watches his instruments, finds his eyes grow dim; he puts forth his hand to get a bottle of brandy near by, but the arm obeys not the will; he tries to speak to his comrade who is steering, but no voice issues from his lips. The rope fortunately comes in; his hands are perfectly stiff; he applies his teeth, and the balloon begins to descend. One minute more of inaction on the part of that steersman and the air-ship would have floated where and how long, with its two frozen corpses, into the wide realms of space, God only knows. So it is with these enthusiasts, who, not content with beholding His improvement in the ordinary walks of the world, seek, by suffering of the flesh, by social isolation and mental crucifixion, to construct a balloon by which they may pierce the skies and pluck holiness from them. That scheme fails.

Bishop Thompson.

HAVE you never seen a wingless insect that had fallen into a glazed dish, and watched his efforts to get out? How nimble he is! and how he is forever running round and round and round his little prison! But it is all to no purpose. So it is with the business man. He runs round and round and round the slippery rim and the narrow bottom of a glazed dish, and cannot get out! And is it strange that one finds it difficult to escape from his low and sordid condition, if he cannot fly nor lift himself up? If he shall escape, there must be some way to give him wings to fly with. So long as he says, "My life must be confined within this circle of material things," he will run round and round, insect-like, and die there. There is no help for him. If to gain the world you are willing to lose your own soul, it is a bargain, and it cannot be helped. But what shall it profit you? — that is another question. And if there be men that say to me, "I believe, Mr. Beecher, that I ought to become a Christian, but I am so tied up by my business that I have not time and strength to do it," — very well; I do not know but you are right; probably you are; and all I have to say to you is, "I am sorry in my soul: farewell, and forever!"

Rev. H. W. Beecher.

BLESSED be God that we live in an age of newspapers and books. For books—they never grow old or require spectacles. They never become gray-haired. They never need sleep. Their voice is never harsh. Nor are they ever dull. Wise books, wisely selected, are immortal companions that bloom with eternal youth, and that are our companions and our teachers at one and the same time. Blessed be they that know how to love and to cherish good books.

Rev. H. W. Beecher.

A MAN that loves Christ, loves work. A dyspeptic Christian dreads work. A lazy Christian shirks it. What a hospital is many a church! Here lies one poor man, down with a paralysis of faith. Here is another laid up by a sprain which he got by a sudden fall into temptation. Here is one whom the fever of passion has burnt out; he looks hardly worth the medicine to cure him. Alas! for another—he is under pastoral treatment for the blindness of unbelief; and for another, whose gaping wound reveals the spot where Satan's fiery dart went in! Here too are a whole dozen who skulked into the hospital with bandages on, just to "get rid of the draft," from Sunday-schools and mission labors. A revival commonly clears the church-hospital. But a long period of spiritual declension crams it to the doorway. Oh, what need that he who went through Galilee healing all manner of diseases, should come into some churches whose atmosphere is loaded with the effluvia of incipient putrefaction!

Rev. T. L. Cuyler.

I WAS called, once, to a consultation in reference to a young man belonging to a large establishment, who was detected in some criminal act; and in a confidential interview that I had with him, he told me that it was not because he was in need that he yielded to the temptation, but because he wanted property. His dishonesty was simply the result of avarice. And if a young man abuses his trust and is dishonest, there is not a word to be said in his justification. And how full of horror the employer is, as he may justly be! And yet, that very employer will go into the market, and, in a different way, practise the same thing upon another merchant, and get his goods from him by methods that are dishonest. While he is horror-stricken at his clerk's conduct, he does the same thing without horror, that the clerk has done, and from the same motive that the clerk did it — an excessive greediness — a fierce lust for gain.

Pleasure next comes in as a strong inducement. There are many young men who have enough to support them; but that is not all that they want.

They have bad companions with whom they associate. These companions are not very temperate. They smoke, and so, of course, they drink. I do not mean that among all men that smoke, drinking is a handmaid vice; but I say that smoking leads, or tends to lead, to the other vice. And smoking and drinking are very expensive. And the expense does not stop with these habits. In the city, young men that smoke and drink, wishing to see life, resort to the theatre. And the theatre is never done when it is out. There are other scenes to be witnessed besides those that are presented on the public stage. And all these things cost money. And the young man pays, week in and week out, his bill for what is called *pleasure*. He drinks when he does not care to, because he must do as the other boys do; and he goes to places that do not interest him, for the same reason.

And his expenses are much greater than his allowance. Some men are said to live on a salary of a thousand, and spend five thousand. But when a man receives one thousand, and spends five, he must steal four somewhere.

Rev. H. W. Beecher.

PRIDE has tripped many a soul and kept it back from Christ. Every sinner has his full share of this; some more than their share. Naaman, the Syrian, had like to have lost his life through this snare. He wished to be saved *like a gentleman;*

but he had to give in, and go to the Jordan like a filthy leper. When you undertake to dictate to God just how he shall save you, it is sheer pride that is keeping you back. When you refuse to go down in the dust before Christ's cross, and confess guilt, and cry out, "God be merciful to me a sinner!" pride is the lurking devil that is plucking at your skirts. If you are saved at all, it must be on God's terms, and in God's way, and in his good time. Count it the greatest marvel of Divine generosity that God is willing to save so perverse a sinner at all. But if you are lost, the inscription which truth will write over you will be, "Perished through pride."

Rev. T. L. Cuyler.

OTHER persons are kept out of the kingdom of God by excessive laziness and semi-sleep. Many persons sleep eight or ten hours during the twenty-four, and then are half-asleep six or eight more. That man is substantially asleep who is not sufficiently awake to know the direction he is going, to have a clear discernment of the condition he is in, and to have control of himself. For not that man alone is in darkness who has no lamp, but that man also whose lamp burns so feebly as to be of no service, so that he might as well be without a light. And, in the use of the reason, that man is not awake who is simply not asleep. I believe there are a great many here to-night for whom it is impossible to enter into the kingdom of God, on account of these low physical conditions of life. There are things that it is unusual and improper to state in public which, are destroying men, body and soul. I know that there are many men who are wasting their lives, who are draining out the very life-blood of their being. No parent teaches them; no physician warns them; and no minister dare, out of a respectable pulpit, say the things that they need to have said to them. You are ruining yourselves by indulgence. Some of you know what I mean. And yet, under these very circumstances, men will say, "I wonder if it is not election that keeps me out of the kingdom of God?" Election! You know what it is that keeps you out of the kingdom of God. You know what guilty practice it is. You know what secret it is. You know what that subterranean current is that rolls damnation to damnation. It is sin; it is wrong known and allowed; and if you are to be saved, you must strive. There are many of you who are in the hands of an inexorable tyrant; there are many of you in the hands of a fiery tyrant; there are many of you in the hands of a spider tyrant, whose web, most invisible, is winding about you and entangling you; and if you are to be saved, it is high time that you should strive to enter into the kingdom of God.

Rev. H. W. Beecher.

SIMPLY go on as you have begun — simply "*neglect* the great salvation" — and you will make your everlasting ruin sure. Many foolish, faithless parents have stood by the grave of a child which they dug with their own hands. How? Did they administer slow poison, or strike an assassin-knife through the young heart? No: but they killed their child just as surely, by simple neglect of the first laws of health. Many a father, too, has wrung his hands in agony before the prison-cell which held a ruined son, or over the letter which told him of a son's disgrace, and on those very hands rested the guilt of that boy's ruin. Why? Had they led that son into Sabbath-breaking, or theft, or profligacy? No: but they had let the youth alone, and left him to rush into them unrestrained. *Neglect* was the boy's ruin. There is no need that the man in a skiff amid Niagara's rapids should row toward the cataract; resting on his oars is quite enough to send him over the awful verge.

Rev. T. L. Cuyler.

IMAGINE, if you please, a spider attempting to bring up a bumble-bee according to a spider's nature. What work would be made? Imagine a dove in whose nest had been left a little eaglet attempting to bring it up as though it was a dove, and according to a dove's theory and notion. Imagine a mole attempting to make a mouse or a rat burrow and work under ground, and have no eyes, and only a snout. Imagine any thing attempting to impose its inward nature on any thing that has a different inward nature. We see the folly of this as applied to lower animals and birds; but it is precisely as foolish as applied to men. It is preposterous for a stern man to govern a pliable child according to the law of sternness, or for a sober man to govern a genial child according to the law of sobriety.

Rev. H. W. Beecher.

MEN'S lives should be like the day, more beautiful in the evening; or, like the summer, aglow with promise; and like the autumn, rich with the golden sheaves, where the good works and deeds have ripened on the field.

WE should have a purpose, an aim in life. That vessel is a noble structure, its timbers solid and strong, and put together with the greatest artistic skill, and firmly bolted. In form she is exactly adapted to the sea, beautifully painted, and well rigged with masts, sails, compass, and helm. A joyous company are on board, and they launch out upon the ocean. They have no port in view, but yield themselves to hilarious and joyous amusements, reckless of sun and storm. Shipwreck and destruction will assuredly be the fate of that vessel and crew. There is a bare possibility that they may be drifted to some pleasant and desirable haven, some beautiful golden shore. But no reasonable man would risk life or property on such a voyage. Such is the desperate venture of him who enters on life's journey without a plan. There is no reasonable prospect of other result than lamentable failure. Will the bewildered traveller, at night, entangled in the morass, be likely, by following the will-of-the-wisp that sports before him, to reach solid ground, and some delightful and gorgeous mansion? Even less probable is it that he who has no plan will attain any desirable success in life.

Rev. C. Nutt, D.D.

WHEN men are prosperous, and are making money, and considering themselves rich, I wonder that it so seldom comes home to them that they are liable to reverses, which shall plunge their families into the utmost pecuniary distress. Men know that business is subject to fluctuations, and that nothing is more frequent than that men should in one year have all the comforts and advantages of wealth, and the next year be stripped bare. But a vicious hopefulness prevents them from realizing that *they* shall ever be subject to this fate which befalls others.

Men expect to live; they do not anticipate bankruptcy. When times change, and the pinch comes, it is too late for them to make provision for the family. The wife, the children, the whole household, are suddenly plunged into distress. Indeed, much as the business man suffers for himself, his own pangs are the least part of the suffering.

I have lived long enough to see the overthrow of a great many families because the father, believing that he should live and always keep them in comfortable circumstances, had neglected to make an independent provision for them.

At the man's death, the estate proves either insolvent, or is reduced to a minimum. The wife, not trained to business, is obliged to settle the estate by agents. What with unskilful management, carelessness, or even sometimes deliberate fraud, the residuum melts in her hands, and the widow, with five or six young children to be fed, clothed, and educated, finds herself alone and penniless! Habits cannot be changed in a day. She has not been trained to business. She may have been a good housekeeper, but now she must *earn money*, which is a very different thing from ordering a household skilfully. Some, utterly overmatched, break down under the trial, and the children are scattered like young partridges whose mother the hawk has devoured.

I believe it to be the duty of every man who is prosperous, out of debt, and making money, to settle upon his wife a certain amount of property, which shall not be affected by either his bankruptcy or his death. This may be done by a life insurance — especially if it be a policy which is not forfeited by neglect of payment. But a still better way is to settle upon the wife a good house, and the furniture. Then, if misfortune comes, the man will still have a home. He will be secure at the root, and may begin again with some hope. If death takes away the father, the nest remains. The children do not need to be scattered.

Some persons have questioned whether a scrupulous honesty would allow one to hold back from creditors any part of a husband's property. A settlement of property on another, while debt hangs over it, either for the sake of avoiding payment of debt, or of securing the family, would be fraudulent, dishonest, and wicked. But if, while clear of debt, the husband settles property on his wife for the just maintenance of herself and children, his after debts have no more claim upon that property than if he had sold and transferred it to a neighbor instead of to his own wife. No man has a right to leave a family, whom he has accustomed to affluence, liable to sudden and wasting poverty. A provision made betimes, in property, for the safety of his family in case of his death or bankruptcy, may be accepted and employed by the most sensitive conscience. I write strongly on the subject, because I have seen so much distress arising from the want of such precaution.

Rev. H. W. Beecher, in Ledger.

AND oh! what shall we see of order then! I stand and gaze at the heavens. I see a planet pursuing its course onward, and then it seems to pause and turn back again. And why? I am not standing at the centre. If I were standing at the sun, I would see that movement that now seems so irregular — forward and backward — to be steadily onward. I would see that planet moving in its orbit coming to the time to a moment, for thousands of years, keeping step with the great movement of the universe, joining in the music of the heavenly choirs, and would behold wisdom, regularity, beauty, and glory everywhere displayed. So, when I am out of harmony with God's plans, not seeing his designs, the world is all confusion and darkness: wrong is triumphing; empires are rising and falling without order; there is no clue to history; battles, revolutions, convulsions, are without object or aim.

But let me stand at the centre; let me comprehend the plans of Infinite Wisdom, and I see society in all its movements steadily advancing. Great ideas are being diffused. In every change I recognize the hand of God.

Bishop Simpson.

THE man who walks in the way of God passes through death as through a temporary gloom, but he still pursues the even tenor of his way; what he did on earth he shall do in heaven, only he shall do it better and after a nobler sort. On earth he loved his God, in heaven he shall do the same; on earth he found his joy in a sight of Christ, in heaven he shall enjoy that sight more near and unveiled; on earth he loved the true, and the right, and the good, and in heaven he shall dwell in the midst of the city that is of pure gold, and whose light is brighter than the sun, where only holiness and perfection are admitted. He shall not even change his company, for the church militant in which he fought on earth is also the church triumphant with which he shall reign for ever and ever in heaven.

Rev. C. H. Spurgeon.

THY way, not mine, O Lord!
However dark it be;
Lead me by thine own hand,
Choose out the path for me.

Smooth let it be, or rough,
It will be still the best;
Winding or straight, it leads
Right onward to thy rest.

I dare not choose my lot;
I would not if I might;
Choose thou for me, my God;
So shall I walk aright.

I REMEMBER well being taken one day to see a gorgeous palace at Venice, where every piece of furniture was made with most exquisite taste, and of the richest material, where statues and pictures of enormous price abounded on all hands, and the floor of each room was paved with mosaics of marvellous art and extraordinary value. As I was shown from room to room, and allowed to roam amid the treasures by its courteous owner, I felt a considerable timidity. I was afraid to sit down anywhere, nor did I hardly dare to put down my foot, or rest my hand to lean. Every thing seemed to be too good for ordinary mortals like myself; but when one is introduced into the gorgeous palace of infinite goodness, costlier and fairer far, one gazes wonderingly with reverential awe at the matchless vision. "How excellent is thy loving-kindness, O God!" I am not worthy of the least of all thy benefits. Oh, the depths of the love and goodness of the Lord!

Rev. C. H. Spurgeon.

AN invalid detects the first symptom of returning health in the new relish for the once loathed trencher of bread or rasher of bacon. He craves food. So does a healthy child of God. He enters church on Sabbath morning positively *hungry*—not for an intellectual tickle or a spiced pastry, but for the simple bread of life Christ Jesus, for truth to grow by, for the strong meat of the Word of God. He builds that truth into his soul, as food is built into the physical frame. Nor does he satisfy his soul-hunger with truth alone. He craves the indwelling of the Holy Ghost. He hungers for a sanctified heart. He yearns after a similitude to Christ. And every thing that makes him like Christ he relishes. It is delightful to preach to hungry Christians: you know just what they crave; and the Bible larder is always full, while the pastry-shop of a confectioner in poetry is often full of emptiness.

Rev. T. L. Cuyler.

OH! if I were to gaze on yon heavens, and in some clear, starry night should see some orb, unknown before, shining in those heavens, how I would watch it! Every astronomer would turn his glass toward it, would calculate its magnitude and position, and ask why this new world was created to shine amidst the older constellations. We might not be able perfectly to determine the great purposes of the Creator, but we would hail it with joy. So, young man, young woman, he sends you into society to be as a light. "Ye are the light of the world," to shine amid the stars which have preceded you, and you have your mission that no one can take from you. You are not here for a moment, but for eternity; your times are in God's hand. He leads you as much as if you saw the divine arm encircling you. He directs your pathway as fully as though he sent his angel to show you every step you should take.

Bishop Simpson.

BUT this simple method of preaching, which to the world looks so inadequate and so foolish, is God's chosen method of saving the world. And this with reason. A guide-post may be so wreathed with roses as to conceal from your view the very informa tion which it is to impart. A path may be so covered and overgrown with shrubbery and with flowers as to hide from your vision the very way in which you would walk; and so may Christ be concealed from your vision by the flowers that are wreathed around his cross and the superfluity of forms attached to his service. So it pleased God, and it pleases him still, to save men by the simple, single, yet all-potent method of preaching the word of life

Rev. C. H. Payne.

A MAN who knows how to take his mind with all its sensibilities, and bring it into tune with divine love, and who knows how to carry it harmoniously through all the hours of the day, so that it shall all the time be in tune with other minds, has very little to learn before he goes to heaven.

Rev. H. W. Beecher.

WHEN you choose your associates, you choose on the principle of elective affinity; but when you go on a mission of mercy, you choose on the opposite principle. When you choose companions, you choose those that are of your own class; but when you choose objects of charity, you choose those that are beneath you. When you choose children for your own pleasure, you choose those that had happy parents, that are happily organized, and that are contented and full of merriment; but when you go out in search of children that you may benefit them, if you see a scrawny, uncombed, swearing.

spiteful little brat, you say, "I want him." Why? Because he is so good? A wasp is good just as much. You say, "The child is a poor, wretched creature, and there must be some one to take care of him."

Now, God in heaven administers a realm of perfect character, and there his administration is with reference to perfect character; but on earth, where all men are sinners, and will be sinners, there is a mediatorial administration in which the principle of benevolence administers and takes men in their sin-sickness to help them out of it. And if a man says, "Lord, I am full of corruption," Christ says, "Come to me and I will cure you." And if he says, "Lord, I am so bound up by my passions that I cannot live as I would," Christ says, "Dost thou desire to be made whole?" And if the man says, and says truly, "I do desire it; but, Lord, my strength is not sufficient to secure the realization of that desire," Christ has mercy upon him, and supplies him with the additional strength that he needs.

Rev. H. W. Beecher.

DO not stop to pick flaws in others, when God sees in thee the huge sin of rejecting the blood of Jesus. Do not prate about the "inconsistencie of Christians," when your whole life is one long inconsistency of admitting that religion is the only *one thing needful* and yet making it less than nothing. There is no inconsistency on earth that compares with his who knows that Christ Jesus is willing to save him and yet persists in damning his own soul! Whatever you say now in self-excuse, we warn you that at the judgment-seat you will be ready to confess with bitterness of spirit, *God was right, and I was wrong.* Why not confess that now, and act upon it, before it is too late?

Rev. T. L. Cuyler.

WHAT a glorious fact it is that there is one life that can be held up before the eyes of humanity as a perfect pattern! There were lips that never spake unkindness, that never uttered an untruth; there were eyes that never looked aught but love and purity and bliss; there were arms that never closed against wretchedness or penitence; there was a bosom which never throbbed with sin, nor ever was excited by unholy impulse; there was a man free from all undue selfishness, and whose life was spent in going about doing good. There was One who loved all mankind, and loved them more than himself, and who gave himself to die that they might live; there was One who went into the gates of death, that the gates of death might never hold us in; there was One who laid in the grave to take its damp, its coldness, its chill, and its horror, and taught humanity how it might ascend above the grave; there was One who, though he walked on earth, had his conversation in heaven, and took away the curtain that hid immortality from view, and presented us the

Father God in all his glory and in all his love. Such an One is the standard held up in the Church of Christ; it is a Church that rallies round the cross and that gathers around Jesus; and it is because he is attractive and lovely and glorious that they are coming from the ends of the earth to see the salvation of God.

Bishop Simpson.

A MAN may stand in the midst of summer and harvests, and yet have nothing, because he does not choose to receive that which blesses other men. And so God may fill the world and the ages with a bounty of love, which shall be free to all men, and yet, so far as many are concerned, it may be as a castle locked up. There is many and many a castle in England whose royal owners have gone abroad and left the windows curtained, to shut out the best thing that God has for us, — the light. Within are pictures, and statues, and a multitude of costly and beautiful things; and the sun comes and pours the effulgence of its light on the outside of the structure, but cannot penetrate to where these are. The roof takes its share, and the walls take their share; but inside it is dark as midnight. The windows are closed, and the doors are closed, and April, May, June, July, August, and the whole procession of autumnal months roll over the castle, and no light and no warmth is within. And yet, what an infinite abundance of these things is shed down upon the building!

Now, men can stand in the solar flood of God's love, and be no better for it. As the sunlight may pour on slated roofs, or on brick walls, and nothing may grow on them, so the love of God, which is infinite, measureless, and boundless, may pour upon a man, and he may be a poor wretch.

The fact, then, that God loves, and is so good, should lay no foundation for the plea that men may go on and do as they please, and sin as they list. The fact that God's love is boundless and measureless and infinite, is no evidence that it shall carry benefit to all. Though it is within the reach of all, and is intended for all, there is not a man born who cannot throw it away, and be benefited by it. For the love of God, like the sunlight, must be appropriated to be beneficial.

Rev. H. W. Beecher.

THERE is in the parental example, too frequently, and in the public sentiment of the family a flavor given to smart and ingenious dishonesty that sets aside all preceptive teaching. For although parents, in words tell their children that honesty is the best policy; that dishonesty is wicked, and that if they indulge in it they will have to give an account of it,—yet, in other ways they teach them that it is much to their advantage if they practise it adroitiy, shrewdly, cunningly. A father tells of advantages that he has gained by a turn that was not honest, by some dashing exploit which carried the taint of dishonesty in it. It was unexpected and very ingenious, and was rather a brilliant wickedness; and the father seems to think that it was really charming. His child, from hearing his narration, thinks that the abstract quality of honesty is a virtue much to be admired, but that vulgar dishonesty in practical life is an evil not much to be meddled with by a gentleman. And so, as parents teach their children abstractly to revere honesty, there is all the time coming along a counteracting influence that brings the child out into life, at last, without correct training and a fixed habit in the matter of honesty.

And in this thing there are some children that seem as though they were unspoilable. Some children are born honest, where, according to every hereditary law, they ought to have been thieves. There are children that, if they followed the example of their parents, would be spoiled, but that grow up with sturdy morality and integrity. On the other hand, there are some children that seem to be born to speak lies quicker than anything else. There are children that apparently are born to steal. They are the marvel and horror of their parents.

Now, we are to remember that children are animals before they are men. They are all little beasts of prey; they are monkeys; they are pigs; they are all kinds of creatures endowed with lower instincts, and indulging sometimes in this passion, and sometimes in that. And we are to judge of them from their later developments. When children begin to act they do not manifest much moral sentiment. *That* is of a subsequent growth. They are unripe. And we are not to think that they are coming to the gallows because they falsify and go to the sweetmeat jar in childhood. They will not always lie and steal, if you are faithful. If you take occasion to instruct them and train them aright, you need not be alarmed to think that they will end badly because there seems to be such a perverse bias to their mind in the beginning. Many parents have felt that they were rocking a little pirate, when they rocked their child. Many parents have felt that God had cursed them by giving then a thief with their first-born.

Now, many children have this unregulated action of the lower passions in early childhood; and in the greater number of these cases, if you are faithful to instruct their understanding and develop their conscience, in a few years their moral sense will come up in sufficient strength to put them all right. With proper subordination and obedience, such children will grow into the love of honesty as much as others; but there must be parental faithfulness.

Rev. H. W. Beecher.

A MUDDY stream, flowing into one clear and sparkling, for a time rolls along by itself. A little further down they unite, and the whole is impure. So youth, untouched by sin, may for a short time keep its purity in foul company, but a little later and they mingle.

SOME seem to think that a man, to be a Christian, ought to be able not to suffer when suffering comes; but the ache of suffering is a part of its medicine. You might as well say that manliness requires that a man should drink bitters, and not taste them, and call them sweet, as to say that Christianity requires that a man should bear suffering, and say that it is not suffering. It requires no such thing. It does not even require that we should illumine suffering so that for the present it shall seem joyous. A man is not bound, when his companion is taken from him, to say, "I am so wonderfully strengthened that I have no suffering." A mother is not called upon, when she has given up her child to God, to say, "I suffer none." You have a right to suffer. And God has been pleased to whisper and say, that though no afflictions for the present are joyous, but grievous, nevertheless *afterward* they work the peaceable fruit of righteousness unto them that are exercised thereby.

Rev. H. W. Beecher.

IF I delight but in some garden, or walk, or gallery, I would be much in it; if I love my books, I am much with them, and almost unweariedly poring them. The food which I love, I would often feed on; the clothes that I love, I would often wear;

the recreations which I love, I would often use them; the business which I love, I would be much employed in. And can I love God, and that above all these, and yet have no desires to be with him? Is it not a far likelier sign of hatred than of love, when the thoughts of our appearing before God are our most grievous thoughts, and when we take ourselves as undone because we must die and come unto him.

Baxter.

FRIENDSHIP, founded on the principles of worldly morality, recognized by virtuous heathen, such as that which subsisted between Atticus and Cicero, which the last of these illustrious men has rendered immortal, is fitted to survive through all the vicissitudes of life; but it belongs only to a union founded on religion, to continue through an endless duration. The former of these stood the shock of conflicting opinions and of a revolution that shook the world; the latter is destined to survive when the heavens are no more, and to spring fresh from the ashes of the universe. The former possessed all the stability which is possible to sublunary things; the latter partakes of the eternity of God. Friendship founded on worldly principles is natural, and though composed of the best elements of nature, is not exempt from its mutability and frailty; the latter is spiritual, and, therefore, unchanging and imperishable. The friendship which is founded on kindred tastes and congenial habits, apart from piety, is permitted by the benignity of Providence to embellish a world, which, with all its magnificence and beauty, will shortly pass away; that which has religion for its basis will ere long be transplanted in order to adorn the paradise of God

Robert Hall.

ON the summit of a hill in a Western state is a court-house so situated that the rain-drops that fall on one side of the roof descend into Lake Erie, and thence through the St. Lawrence into the Atlantic; the drops on the other side trickle down from rivulet to river until they reach the Ohio and the Mississippi, and enter the ocean by the Gulf of Mexico. A faint breath of wind determines the destination of these rain-drops for three thousand miles. So a single act determines sometimes a human destiny for all time and for eternity! A fashionable young man, partially reformed from drinking habits, came home to his father's house, rejoicing in his emancipation. His gay, light-hearted sister thoughtlessly proposed a glass of wine "to drink his safe return." He was excited and off his guard; he yielded, and the single glass rekindled a thirst that carried him back again into drunkenness. The hand that should have sustained him laid him low. If all the ruined men who have first received the fatal glass from woman's hand could utter their testimony, how many a drunkard's grave would become vocal with terrible upbraidings! Surely one would think that woman had already suffered enough from the poison of this adder to make her refuse to touch the cup that conceals his serpent fang.

Rev. T. L. Cuyler.

NO one can so well see what that misery springs from which is distilled from every man's life each day. No one sees the care, and trouble, and fret, and anxiety, and things that rasp life and make it hard, so well as he. No one so well as he traces these things back to the nerve of wrong, in one form or another. No one sees the invisible soul-house which we are building, but God. We are like bees in a dark hive, that fly in from their floral banquets, and build, and build, without seeing or knowing what they build. We are perpetually, day by day, gathering material for our soul-house, and building faculty, after faculty, and yet we never see what is growing up under our daily manipulation. But God sees the style and shape of that dwelling which we are erecting, and sees too often that it is a house for the torment of the soul. And because God so loves, and loves so much, he deeply pities men for their sins. He is one that must naturally turn toward sinners the aspect of mildness and gentleness.

Rev. H. W. Beecher.

AS the verdure of the fields wears a brighter green and revels in richer luxuriance when the sunshine of spring frequently alternates with showers, so does Christian faith become brighest and mightiest when it shines amidst the tears of the soul. And as faith won victories which amazed the earth and charmed the heavens, and added higher strains to the songs celestial, amid the storms of the primitive age, so is it the mission of faith still to evidence its divine birth and energy by casting a heavenly beauty over the rough ways of mortal sorrow, and upbearing souls through the waves and storms of earth's tribulations onward to the glory and rest of God.

Rev. J. Atkinson.

WHEN we bring our men-children to manhood, and they are about to part from us, and go out into the world, we too have our anxieties. For it may be said that a man is an iron-clad — only the mail is inside instead of outside, if he is well clad; and you cannot tell what an iron-clad will bear until you have put it under a fort, and exposed it to the enemy's fire. And then sometimes it stands, and sometimes it sinks, like the Keokuk. You cannot tell, however well a vessel is built in the yard, how much battering it will endure. It is experience, after all, that tests your work. And parents know it.

Rev. H. W. Beecher.

BACON asserts that reading makes a full man; but without digestion, fulness is dyspepsia, and creates sleepiness and inert fat, incapable of action.

Hazlitt says you might as well ask the paralytic to leap from his chair and throw away his crutch, or without a miracle to take up his bed and walk, as to expect the learned reader to throw down his book and think for himself. He is a borrower of sense. He has no ideas of his own, and must live on those of others. The habit of supplying our ideas from foreign sources enfeebles all internal strength of thought, as a course of dram-drinking destroys the tone of the stomach. The word of God is pre-eminently a book for direct reading, and is never seen in its glory, if we will persist in wearing the colored spectacles of another man's comment. Pure and cool are its streams, if we drink immediately from the well-head; but when the precious crystal has long stood in earthen vessels, its freshness is gone; the truth is there, perhaps, but not the life. We should let texts lie on our hearts till they melt into them like snow-flakes dissolving into the soil.

Spurgeon.

I'D a dream to-night;
  As I fell asleep.
Oh! the touching sight
  Makes me still to weep;
Of my little lad,
Gone to leave me sad,
Aye, the child I had,
  But was not to keep.

As in heaven high,
I my child did seek,
There, in train, came by
Children fair and meek,
Each in lily white,
With a lamp alight;
Each was clear to sight,
But they did not speak.

Then, a little sad,
Came my child in turn,
But the lamp he had,
Oh! it did not burn;
He, to clear my doubt,
Said, half turned about,
"Your tears put it out;
Mother, never mourn!"

William Barnes.

AT no period, perhaps, in their life, do young men need the inspiration of virtuous love, and the sympathy of a companion in their self-denying toil, as when they enter the battle for their own support.

Early marriages are permanent moralities, and deferred marriages are temptations to wickedness. And yet every year it becomes more and more difficult, concurring with the reigning ideas of society, for young men to enter upon that matrimonial state, which is the proper guard of their virtue, as well as the source of their courage and enterprise. The battle of life is almost always at the beginning. Then it is that man needs wedlock. But a wicked and ridiculous public sentiment puts a man who is in society, or out of society, for that matter, largely on the ground of condition, and not of disposition and character. The man that has means wherewith he can, visibly, live amply, is in good society, as a general rule. The man that has virtue and sterling manliness, but has nothing withal external to show, is not usually considered in good society. Ambitious young men will not, therefore, marry, until they can meet their expenses; but that is deferring for years and years the indispensable virtue. Society is bad where two cannot live cheaper than one! and young men are under bad influences who, when in the very morning of life and better fitted than at any later period to grow together with one who is their equal and mate, are debarred from marrying, through scores of years, from mere prudential considerations, and the heart and the life are sacrificed to the pocket. They are empted to substitute ambition for love, when at last, over the ashes and expiring embers of their early romance, they select their wife. It is said that men who wait till they are forty or forty-five years of age, select prudently. Alas, for the wife who was not *first* a sweetheart! Prudence is good; but is prudence servant or queen? Prudence is good; but what is prudence? Is it the dry calculation of the head leagued with the pocket? Is there no prudence in taste, no prudence in the inspiration of a generous love? Is there no prudence in the faith by which, banded, two young persons go down into the struggle of life, saying, "Come weal, come woe, come storm, come calm, love is a match for circumstances, and we will be all to each other?" Woe be to that society in which the customs and the manners of the times put off, beyond the period of romance and affiancing, the wedding. You have adjourned the most important secular act of a man's life. You have adjourned it out of Eden into the wilderness! The girl, next infected (and even women fall) with the public spirit, too often waits to be wooed by those who can place her again, in the very beginning of her wedded life, where she was when she was broken off as a branch from the parental tree. But a graft should always be willing to be a graft, and wait till it can make its own top by legitimate growing. And woe is the day when every girl says, "I will not marry until my husband, in the beginning, has as much as my father had at the end of his life." Who was it that Jupiter won in a shower of gold? Whoever it was, that is the type. She whose heart is won by abundance; she who is bought into matrimony by house and land; she who marries for genteel wealth — she it is that Jupiter seduced by gold. For all wedlock is adulterous in which it is not the *heart* that inspires marriage. Noble is that young spirit which, seeing and loving, and choosing, silently biding her choice, and giving herself freely, romantically, if you will (God be thanked for the romance!) goes down to the level of her husband's nothingness and poverty, that he and she may, with willing hands, from the bottom build up their estate. Blessed is that woman who sees that in going down she is going up, and that it is the losing of life that saves it. Blessed is that woman who carries with her into married life all that she learned in the refinement of her father's family; who proves that she is a woman in this; that gentleness, and praise, and abundance, and luxury even, ministered to the better parts of her nature, and prepared her to go forth and minister earnestly and permanently in the midst of difficulties. Thousands there are who, when once they are called, and know their master, Love, go cheerfully out with the young man and take part and lot with him. Oh! that young men would trust them more, and prove them better, and see if this is not so. How noble a thing it is to see the cultured, the polished, and the refined go down to the very beginning of things, led by love, fed by love, and at last rewarded by love.

Live together alone, if you have to go into a desert for it, and feed on herbs! Abhor Sodom and Gomorrah—or boarding-houses! Men sometimes speak of pinched fare. These are not worthy of notice. It is not these. It is that men learn self-indulgence there. Men learn there not to be householders. And all the various discipline, all that ministration of care, all that drill of contrivance, all that social independence, all that subtle atmosphere, indescribable and unanalyzable, which belongs to the solitary household, they miss. No men can make husband and wife, father and mother, and householders on the pattern of their fathers, who begin and continue their married life in this hot-bed style of existence. And yet they are unwilling to take a house that they can afford; and they cannot afford to take the house they fain would live in, because furniture is so dear, and virtue is so cheap; because society requires a certain amount of appearance, you know; because it would not do to go to the outskirts of the town! A log cabin is better for young married people than the Fifth Avenue Hotel would be, if they had the whole of it for nothing! What you get for nothing is the least valuable to you of any thing. What you earn is all value. Under these influences, the whole of life is written in the wrong key. Men having started on the false principle, they do not get over it. They are perpetually tempted to over-live their very affections. If there is any thing that an honorable and sensitive man's nature feels and cannot stand, it is the silent comparison on the part of the wife, by a look even, of the way in which she *did* live, and the way in which she *does* live. How does this drive men into dishonesties! How does it drive them out of simplicity and bold willingness to live according to their circumstances! How does it teach them to live for other peoples's eyes, and not for their own actual needs! How does it teach them to be more subject to vanity than to love! Such life is hollow. Ostentation takes the place of sincerity. And so, ere long, a man is educated to be a rogue, and steals. And woman takes on unvirtue, because that pays the bills of extravagance quicker than any thing else.

Rev. Henry Ward Beecher.

I NEVER thought that classifications of society were mischievous. There *must* be classifications. If you were to bring men to an equality by some artificial means, in less than ten years, in less than five years, in less than six months, they would shake themselves out from their false positions, and assume their relative places; and there would be a bottom and a top, with a long scale between. Classification is not bad. It is not bad that some men should be at the bottom. It is our neglect of duty in our relative classes that makes the mischief; for if we understood the Christian doctrine as to the law of strength, to every man below us we should be a friend and a benefactor. God's command is, "Inasmuch as you are superior to the man below you, help him." Man's interpretation of the law of strength, is, "Inasmuch as you are superior to the man below you, use him." God says, "Inasmuch as I have given you more light than those below you, let it shine upon them." Men, in interpreting the fact of relative differences, say, "Inasmuch as you are smarter than that man, use him." God says to men, "If you are better placed in life than others, remember the unfortunate." Men say, "Because you are better placed in life than others, keep aloof from the unfortunate, and take good care of yourself." Man, by the power of selfishness, disintegrates and treads down those that are low already. God, by the power of love, would have men take wisdom, skill, genius, moral endowments, every element of body and soul, and with them become schoolmasters of Christ to those who are less fortunate than themselves.

Rev. H. W. Beecher.

THE apostle bids us present our body as well as our soul to Christ; and oh! what a wretched, worn-out, dyspeptic, lust-eaten carcass is sometimes offered to him! The body of a believer is the "temple of the Holy Ghost." Shall the divine Spirit be invited to dwell in what is sometimes turned into a dram-shop, sometimes into a brothel, and sometimes into a sty? "For if ye live after the flesh, ye shall die; but if ye, through the Spirit, do mortify the deeds of the body, ye shall *live*."

Rev. T. L. Cuyler.

"BUT the father of the family? Ah! for the true father of a family, for the true head of a house, his home is the dream of all his day. For long, long hours, work and business keep him away from it. But in the evening? The day is for labor, the evening is for the family and for God! The star shines not in the sky so sweetly as the rays of the lamp or the reflection of the firelight in the window of that distant house, the place of his joys and his repose, toward which he wends his way in meditation or in prayer. But no! what should he do there? Home has no charm for him: his children are no longer there; his wife is there, no doubt — yes, his wife! — but too often virtual divorce has divided them in heart and mind: they bear the same name, they live in the same house; but there is no near and high communion between the two. They have nothing to say to each other, because there is no love between them — no community of thought and feeling."

A MAN blind from his birth, a man of much intellectual vigor and with many engaging social qualities, found a woman who, appreciating his worth was willing to cast in her lot with him and become his wife. Several bright, beautiful children became theirs, who tenderly and equally loved both their parents. An eminent French surgeon while in this country called upon them, and examining the blind man with much interest and care, said to him, "Your blindness is wholly artificial; your eyes are naturally good, and could I have operated upon them twenty years ago, I think I could have given you sight. It is barely possible that I can do it now, though it will cause you much pain."—"I can bear that," was the reply, "so you but enable me to see." The surgeon operated upon him, and was gradually successful; first there were faint glimmerings of light, then more distinct vision. The blind father was handed a rose; he had smelt one before, but had never seen one; then he looked upon the face of his wife who had been so true and faithful to him; and then his children were brought, whom he had so often fondled and whose charming prattle had so frequently fallen upon his ears, but whose beaming countenances he had never beheld. He then exclaimed, "Oh, why have I seen these things before inquiring for the man by whose skill I have been enabled to behold them! Show me the *doctor!*" and when he was pointed out to him, he embraced him with tears of gratitude and joy. So when we reach heaven, and with unclouded eyes look upon its glories, we shall not be content with a view of these. No, we shall say, Where is Christ? — He to whom I am indebted for what heaven is; show me him, that with all my soul I may adore and praise him through endless ages.

"IN the poorer classes, there was a time when woman was called wife, mother; they have baptized her, nowadays, by a name that does not belong in our language — the *workwoman!* The workman I know and honor; but I do not know the workwoman. I am astounded, I am alarmed, whenever I hear this word. What? This young woman — is toil, unpitying, unintelligent toil, to come bursting in her door in the early morning, to seize her in its two iron fists, and drag her from what ought to be her home and sanctuary to the factory that is withering and consuming her day by day? What? Is toil — brutal, murderous toil — to kill her children or at least to snatch them screaming from their cradles and give them over into stranger hands? And all the time a false philosophy will be lifting its head and shouting: 'Equality! equality for man and woman! equality for the workwoman by the side of the workman!"

WHAT a wonderful adaptation there is in this to human wants! We feel it difficult to exhibit that close sympathy toward a stranger which we feel toward persons of our own nation, having been brought up differently, with different habits, different scenery, and the whole surroundings different; we cannot feel the beatings of their hearts against our heart, as we can where we have been brought under similar circumstances, and had every thing alike. But with Jesus it is different. Wherever his character can be understood, there is a felt adaptation. The poor Esquimau in his hut of snow and ice, the African upon the burning sand, the jealous Chinaman, and the proud, conceited Greek, whenever the name of Jesus is fully before him (as he is the Son of man), and the soul is awake to his wants, he sees that he is life from the dead. "We have known Christ after the flesh," says an apostle; "yet henceforth know we him so no more." We do not know him as a Jew any more; we know him as the Son of man, as the Saviour, as the great representative of the human race; we know him as having something in common with every thing that is human; we know him as being more nearly related to human beings than any human being is to another, feeling every throb — shall I say, every motion — and every anxiety of every human creature, with an interest, a depth, and a nearness of sympathy that no mother ever felt for her child. He is our Head; he is our life; the Church is his body.

Bishop Kingsley.

WHAT does the grave say to you, to me, and to every one that looks into it? What hail has it as we stand by its side and look down into its narrow passage? What cheer breathes forth from it? What does the grave say to us but "corruption and decay"? What does it say but that "I am the end of all glory"? Ah! we go from the clasp and the caress and the kiss to the grave, that has neither kiss nor caress nor clasping.

We leave behind us the heart as we go to bury our dead; we cling to them, we look wistfully after them; and as the sad soil beats upon the drumming coffin with horror in the sound, what says the grave to us but "Go back again, earth to earth; all is over and ended"? And yet what may it say to us if we were but wise to interpret it? "Here thine eye shall see nothing more, but look up, and look through, and look beyond; for to thine heart there is immortality beyond." The grave is but the shutting of the hand — the angel hand that keeps the treasure and conveys it safely to the other side. As they that sail over the sea go down into the cabin, and are hid, so the grave is but the resting-place of the dead for a little time — not decayed, not lost, not final separation, not darkness. No: instructed by those words the voice should sound out to every one of us that go to the grave-side, "All hail!" and, as we look again, "Be not afraid."

Rev. H. W. Beecher.

MAN is a complex being. He has a body and he has a soul. He is capable of labor and of rest. He is susceptible of hope and fear, of pleasure and pain; rapture thrills him and anguish wastes him; he can love and hate, blaspheme and adore. Now a being that has so many points to his character as man has must evidently require a variety of processes to develop him, and bring him up to a state of perfection. An artist cannot make a statue by the use of one instrument; he requires a variety, each one adapted to its specific purpose; a physician cannot relieve every patient by the same treatment: neither can men be trained in the Christian life by one method, which is to be applied to all, and to each one, at all times.

Men often think that God deals most strangely and mysteriously with them, because he treats them just as they treat their own children. A judicious parent sends his child to school at a proper age, to sit in a quiet posture, with eyes fastened upon the page of a book. But that is not all a parent does. He also tells him to run and leap and bound and exercise himself vigorously out of doors. Now these two things are very diverse in their character; yet they are both absolutely essential to the child, and the parent knows it. If he sits over his book all the time, his mental energies will be developed at the expense of the physical; and if he play, and exercise his limbs and muscles all the time, the body will be developed at the expense of the mind. As it is important, therefore, that every man should have a strong mind and strong body both, so it is necessary that boys should sit and quietly study their lessons in study hours, and leap and enjoy themselves in play hours. The discipline of the school is for the development of the mind, and the discipline of the playground for the development of the body.

Now, in the case of the Christian, there are many virtues to be brought out and put into exercise; there are many excrescences to be removed; there are many errors and faults to be corrected. God does not, therefore, put a book into his hand and say, "Sit down and learn that, and then you will be perfect;" but he gives him a variety of lessons, and leads him into a variety of exercises, and drills him in a variety of ways; by which means he touches all the points of his character, and develops all in harmonious pro portion, so that in the end he is not on one side a giant and on the other a pigmy, but a *man*, perfect in Christ Jesus.

The child sometimes thinks it is very hard that it cannot play all the time, and is sometimes disposed to feel that its parent is unkind in wishing to interrupt its diversions by summoning it to its school-task; but the parent knows he would be untrue to the child's interests were he not to do so. Now all of us would like to have God deal with us in just the same manner as the child would have its parent do. We would have God use one method of training us, and one only, and that would be by prosperity. We would none of us have him interrupt our ease and our pleasure. But this method would only develop one side of our character, and that generally the very worst side, while the other would be entirely neglected. Prosperity is a good means for developing pride, strengthening vanity and earthly-mindedness, while it is not often remarked for its tendency to bring forth the opposite qualities of humility and spirituality of temper. So true is this, that if a case is known where an individual has floated uninterruptedly upon a tide of prosperity, and grown in humility and spirituality at the same time, he is likely to be considered as a marvel; while no one thinks it strange that a man who has always been prosperous should be proud and arrogant and selfish.

A piano has many keys, every one of which strikes a different note. How foolish would it be, then, to expect to draw perfect music from the instrument by using but one key. And it is so with the soul. It might well be called "a harp of a thousand strings." Now God designs that it shall pour forth full tides of harmonious melody. He designs that the plaintive note of submission shall blend with the lofty carol of triumph, and that the soft vibrations of humility shall join in accord with the bolders wellings of hope, gratitude, and love. But in order to this, all these points or keys of the soul must be touched, otherwise they will be silent, just as the piano with all its keys breathes forth no sound until the skilful fingers wake its slumbering chords into melody.

Here is a man who loves God and serves him, but whose bark has always gayly sailed on smooth, sparkling waters. Ever since he has been a Christian every thing has gone with him much as he desired. Of him it might be said, in the language of inspired poetry, "God, thy God, hath anointed thee with the oil of gladness above thy fellows. All thy garments smell of myrrh and aloes and cassia, out of the ivory palaces, whereby they have made thee glad." It would be strange if such a man, with even a little grace, were not thankful and hopeful and joyous. It would also be strange if, having things go according to his own way, he should not become self-willed and unduly attached to earth, so as to be inclined to say, "This is my rest forever; here will I dwell, for I have desired it." The virtue of submission in that man's soul has not yet been called into exercise, because he has never had any thing come upon him from the Lord, to which it was any trial to submit. So now God says, "I will make that man submissive: and in order to show submission he must have trial; so I will lay the rod upon him." And so God scourges him, it may be sorely, that the music of resignation may gush from the chords of his soul, even while they tremble and bleed with anguish.

And so in regard to the undue love of earthly things. We are affected by sensible objects, and unseen realities are liable to be overlooked amid the overpowering influences of the visible around us. It is often the case that the world holds the heart as by the spell of an enchantment, and that spell must be broken or heaven will not be gained; and so God sends trials to break our attachment to earth, and lead the affections heavenward. And it is not, perhaps, too much to say that it is impossible to realize fully the worthlessness of the world, as the portion of the soul, except through the agency of trial. I have heard a Christian minister say that he always shunned those verses that spoke of this world as a howling wilderness. Well, that will do very well for a man who has always softly glided down a placid and shining current of worldly prosperity, bordered on either side with gorgeous and fragrant flowers; but the time will come when darkness shall settle upon the waters, and when the calm surface will be supplanted by whirling eddies and roaring breakers, and the flowers shall droop and wither, and their perfume vanish from the air; then, instead of shunning such a truthful representation of the world, he will be glad to sing, if faith triumphs amid his adversities, —

"This world's a wilderness of woe,
This world is not my home;"

and looking upward through dimming tears, while his enfranchised affections soar far above to the cloudless regions of immortality, his soul will still warble,—

"O heaven, sweet heaven, O heaven of the blest!
How I long to be there,
In its glories to share,
And lean on Jesus's breast!"

One of the most common things among religious circles is to hear language expressive of the vanity and emptiness of earth; but how many that utter such language have no adequate realization of its truthfulness! It is hard to gather up our furniture and move out of a palace that we have found delightful to dwell in, because the architect says the foundation is rickety, and it is likely to tumble into ruins; and though we assent to his declaration, and tell our friends that our dwelling is insecure, yet still it is our beautiful abode, and its charms are potent over us, until we see the walls cracking, and the ceiling loosening, and the timbers shaking and sagging, and then we feel what we before had only a sort of semi-belief in — the building is worthless; it will be best to forsake it. And so, though we assent to the truth that "this world is all a fleeting show," and are accustomed to repeat it, it is not, after all, until sad experiences have revealed to our inmost soul, its vanity and illusiveness, that we actually realize the fact.

Now, prosperity and ease and pleasure will not, at least, ordinarily they do not, have the effect to make us feel "how vain are all things here below!" and to lead us to set our affections on things above, and not on things on the earth, and therefore it is necessary that God should vary his dealings according to our requirements; and so he causes the desolating gales of adversity to sweep over our earthly prospects, that the love of the world in us may be repressed, and the attractions of heaven become more potent over our hearts. And in thus subjecting us to trial, God deals more lovingly with us than if he were to allow our prosperity to flow on uninterruptedly, for —

"Each care, each ill of mortal birth,
Is sent in pitying love,
To lift the lingering heart from earth,
And speed its flight above.
And every pang that wrings the breast,
And every joy that dies,
Tell us to seek a purer rest,
And trust to holier ties."

All the divine dealings with us have for their end, therefore, our sanctification, our perfection, and, as a sequence, out everlasting enthronement in glory. Every providence, every event of life, is designed to produce in us the peaceable fruits of righteousness.

A green apple holds most tenaciously to the bough, but as it approaches perfection it loosens its hold, and when fully ripe a touch will cause it to fall to the ground. And it is so with us. While our affections are unsanctified by grace, we cling to earth; but as God fashions our soul into his image, and ripens us for heaven, our hearts let go of earth and fall sweetly upon the bosom of Jesus.

And have you ever thought of the variety of agencies that are requisite to mature a single apple? There is necessary to its production a depth and subtleness of operation in nature more wonderful than we can conceive. There is the agency of the tree itself sacrificing its woody growth, and by mysterious and silent alchemies co-operating with the elements and ministries of nature, such as sun and soil, vapors and winds, torrid heats and northern blasts, all of which are necessary to the development and perfection of the fruit. And so all the toils and conflicts, all the successes and disappointments, all the losses and sufferings of the man that fears God, are but the forces which, co-operating with the Spirit within him, are, under the divine adminstration, elevating him to a fulness and maturity of saintly character, and so working for him a far more exceeding and eternal weight of glory.

THINK what you will of it, I never stand in a summer's morning before the sun dawns, long before waked by birds to look out upon the yet dim and dusky landscape, that I do not think that this is the hour of resurrection. As the night held the day, but could not long hold it, but unclasped its dark arms to let forth the morning again, so every day is, to them that have an imagination therefor, a resurrection-day, and sets forth by these most notable and beauteous features in earth, and symbolizes forever and forever the resurrection of our Master. Why do we need robes, and why do we need church symbols, when every feature of nature is itself one divinely constituted symbolization, not simply of spiritual truths, but, if well used, of almost every event that occurred in the life of our Lord Jesus Christ? And no other one thing more beautifully symbolizes the resurrection than the silent coming of the bright day every morning from out of the darkness of the night, saying to those that have ears to hear, "All hail!"

Rev. H. W. Beecher.

IT is impossible for us here to begin to conceive what we shall be. The life, the capacity of the mightiest oak was once all contained in the acorn. Time is but the planting period, or at most the brief germinating hour of the soul. The memory, the reason, the love of the soul in this life are as nothing compared with what they will be. Here and there is found a soul with rapid, premature development in a certain direction which startles us. Now a mere child rushes through the longest and most intricate mathematical calculation with the aim and speed of lightning. Then a memory develops which seems capable of retaining absolutely indefinitely. All the words and letters of a volume are daguerreotyped and held on the tablets as by a beam of light from the Omnipotent. The capacity of Seneca's memory seems inconceivable. He could repeat two thousand words upon once hearing them, each in its order, though they had no connection in meaning. Cyrus knew every soldier in his army by name. Carneades, when asked, would repeat any volume found in the libraries as if he were reading. Dr. Wallis was able, by mere force of memory, to perform the extraction of roots to forty places of figures. And there are similar instances of amazing development in all the other mental faculties.

These cases in our probationary state furnish us with faint glimpses of what the human soul will yet be. The memory in the other life is to go on growing, and having more and more to retain as new scenes and new worlds open before the soul eternally, until it will yet gather in and hold at command more facts and theories than are to be found in all the writings of men. It has been said that the visions of one day on the Isle of Patmos made the Apostle John a poet. What, then, may not eighteen hundred years of heavenly vision have made him; and what may he or any of us not become a million years hence! Shall the soul not be forever accumulating new images of beauty, new treasuries of suggestion, contrast, and comparison, under the quickening, stimulating, and health-bringing influences of the spiritual life?

What a difference in capacity may be seen between the mind of the child and the mind of the full grown and educated man! What a difference of soul is everywhere seen between the uneducated and the educated! If such is the growth of the soul under the education of half a century in this dark, material, and sluggish state, what will it be in thousands of centuries in the other life?

See what the soul accomplishes even in this short, wearying, painful, and cloudy life! What discoveries in science, what improvements in art, what development and application of the powers hidden in Nature! "Iron is taken out of the earth, and brass is molten out of the stone. He setteth an end to darkness, and searcheth out all perfection. He putteth forth his hand upon the rock; he overturneth the mountains by the roots. He cutteth out rivers among the rocks; and his eye seeth every precious thing. He bindeth the floods from overflowing; and the thing that is hid bringeth he forth to light." What, then, shall limit the discoveries and the progress of man in the active, favoring, eternal life and growth of the soul!

Who of us value the soul as we should! How little we realize the vastness of the capacities with which we are endowed? We have little sense of what we are, because "it doth not yet appear what we shall be." But God knows what we are, and in his word sets a value upon us which often astonishes us and staggers our belief. His solicitude that we should be wise, that we should make the right choice for time and for eternity, reveals the high estimation which he puts on an immortal soul. The soul that is lost in sin and given over to perpetual ruin, may be impelled onward by its vital forces, growing in capacity to reap the bitter results of sin. What a treasury of guilt it may accumulate ! What poignant memories will it retain ! What growing capacity to feel pangs of conscience will it acquire !

In the light of such thoughts of the soul, how precious must redemption appear! The greatness of redemption is manifested by the greatness of the soul's endowment. It was such souls — souls that are to grow forever — that were lost in sin, and that were redeemed with a great price, even the death of the eternal Son of God. It is not extravagant that Jesus is very God, coming upon such a mission to earth. It is not wonderful that all the heavenly inhabitants are deeply interested in the race of man, and in the process of its salvation.

OVER the river they beckon to me —
Loved ones who've crossed to the farther side ;
The gleam of their snowy robes I see,
But their voices are drowned in the rushing tide.
There's one with ringlets of sunny gold,
And eyes, the reflection of heaven's own blue ,

He crossed in the twilight, gray and cold,
  And the pale mist hid him from mortal view.
We saw not the angels that met him there,
  The gates of the city we could not see;
Over the river, over the river,
  My brother stands waiting to welcome me.

Over the river the boatman pale
  Carried another — the household pet;
Her brown curls waved in the gentle gale —
  Darling Minnie! I see her yet!
She crossed on her bosom her dimpled hands,
  And fearlessly entered the phantom bark;
We watched it glide from the silver sands,
  And all our sunshine grew strangely dark.
We know she is safe on the farther side,
  Where all the ransomed and angels be;
Over the river, the mystic river,
  My childhood's idol is waiting for me!

For none return from those quiet shores,
  Who cross with the boatman cold and pale;
We hear the dip of the golden oars,
  And catch a gleam of the snowy sail;
And lo! they have passed from our yearning hearts;
  They cross the stream and are gone for aye;
We may not sunder the veil apart
  That hides from our vision the gates of day;
We only know that their bark no more
  May sail with us o'er life's stormy sea;

Yet somewhere, I know, on the unseen shore
They watch and wait, and beckon for me!

And I sit and think, when the sunset's gold
Is flushing river and hill and shore,
I shall one day stand by the water cold,
And list for the sound of the boatman's oar;
I shall watch for a gleam of the flapping sail;
I shall hear the boat as it gains the strand;
I shall pass from sight, with the boatman pale,
To the better shore of the spirit land;
I shall know the loved who have gone before,
And joyfully sweet shall the meeting be,
When over the river, the peaceful river,
The Angel of Death shall carry me!

I DO object to a young man's having companions merely for the sake of passing the time away in frivolity. I do not object to hilarity; and laugh I would with the loudest — there is a time for laughing as well as for crying. But it is a shame or a misfortune unutterable for a man to have at no time a companion that he selects for instruction. It is a shame for a man to be so destitute of an appetite for knowing that he never feels any attraction toward men that know more than he does. And it is a greater shame for a man to have that kind of vanity which makes him prefer to shine on with his little rush-light, rather than to go among those who know more than he does, because when he is in their presence he feels rebuked for his ignorance. And yet, many men do not pick out superiors to associate with, because they are made conscious of their own inferiority when among those superiors. But a man should begin on the ground of his unknowingness, and there should be nothing that he should be so grateful for as the privilege of associating with some one that knows more than he. You are willing to borrow money: be more willing to borrow knowledge, which you are never obliged to return, and which increases in your hands with compound interest. There is scarcely a person that may not climb higher in knowledge than he does, by a discreet use of companionship.

Rev. H. W. Beecher.

THE roseate hues of early dawn,
  The brightness of the day,
The crimson of the sunset sky —
  How fast they fade away!
Oh, for the pearly gates of heaven!
  Oh, for the golden floor!
Oh, for the Sun of Righteousness,
  That setteth nevermore!

The highest hopes we cherish here —
  How fast they tire and faint!
How many a spot defiles the robe
  That wraps an earthly saint!

Oh, for a heart that never sins!
Oh, for a soul washed white!
Oh, for a voice to praise our King,
Nor weary day or night!

Here faith is ours, and heavenly hope,
And grace to lead us higher;
But there are perfectness and peace
Beyond our best desire.
Oh, by thy love and anguish, Lord!
Oh, by Thy life laid down!
Oh, that we fall not from Thy grace,
Nor cast away our crown!

Cecil Frances Alexander.

THERE are times when God's dealings with his people are perplexing, his thoughts very deep, his ways past finding out; when the present is full of anxiety, the future full of difficulty. Their condition is that of blind men groping at noontide; the whole of life a mazy labyrinth, of which they have lost the guiding thread. Their path seems shut up. Pharaoh is behind, and the raging Red Sea in front: their feeling is, "We are entangled; the wilderness hath shut us in." Or they may be embarrassed in solving some question of duty. The employment and destiny of a lifetime may depend on a moment's choice. They may feel the responsibility of deciding between rival and competing claims; trembling and fearful lest some selfish, carnal, unworthy motive may mingle in the decision, and yet experiencing a painful inability to decide what is best.

Perplexed or desponding one! amid these thine anxious, wavering, undecided thoughts, be this thy comfort — *God's* thoughts are upon thee. He is the leader of the blind. "Speak," says he, "to the children of Israel, that they go forward." At the crisis-hour of difficulty or trial, he will appear to all his seeking, trusting people, and vouchsafe guidance or deliverance; not, perhaps, what they expect, but what he knows to be best for them. At the fourth watch of the night Jesus came to his disciples, walking upon the sea. "They wandered in the wilderness in a solitary way: they found no city to dwell in. Hungry and thirsty, their soul fainted in them. Then they cried unto the Lord in their trouble, and he delivered them out of their distresses. And he led them forth by the right way, that they might go to a city of habitation" (Psa. cvii. 4–7). Rely on the God of the pillar-cloud. He will bring thee, as he did his Israel, "through the flood on foot." "Be still!" is his tender rebuke to the distrustful soul, "and know that I am God."

How it would disarm life of many of its anxieties, and take the sting from many perplexities, if we were careful to listen to his voice: "*This* is the way: walk ye in it." A wondrous way — a tender way — but with all its humiliations, THE right way. Yes, believe it — "*all* the paths of the Lord (and this present dark and perplexing path of yours, whatever it be, is one of them) are mercy and truth to such as keep his covenant and his testimonies." Confide in no fallible guidance. Be this your lofty resolve, — "In the *Lord* put I my trust; how say ye to my soul, Flee as a bird to your mountain?" Regard every new turn in existence as a wise, provident "thought" of your heavenly Father. Make it your earnest prayer in the words of Nehemiah, "*Think upon me*, my God *for good*" (Neh. v. 19). Thus, putting your case in his hands, and leaving it there, "he shall bring forth thy righteousness as the light, and thy judgment as the noonday." Yours may be a mingled, checkered past; yet too how bright with blessings! how full of remembrances of God's loving thoughts, his gracious interventions, his signal deliverances! Make these an argument, and reason for implicit trust in the future: "Thou hast *been* my help; leave me not, neither forsake me, O God of my salvation!"

"Whoso is wise, and will observe these things, even they shall understand the loving-kindness of the Lord."

Rev. I. R. Macduff.

THE great mission of life is to prepare for death; and if we fail in this mission our fortunes are irretrievably lost. And what constitutes this personal calling, this work of a human lifetime? First of all, in the stately language of Calvin, we are to be impressed with this primal fact, that "this is life everlasting, to know our only true God, and him whom he hath sent, Jesus Christ, in whom he hath appointed the beginning and end of our salvation." "This Isaac, the beloved son; this Jacob, the vigilant shepherd; this good and merciful brother Joseph; this high-priest and bishop Melchizedek; this excellant law-maker, Moses; this faithful captain and guide, Joshua; this noble and victorious king, David; this magnificent and triumphing king, Solomon; this strong and valiant Samson;" this man and God, concentrating and absorbing all the graces of patriarchs and prophets, and all the sinless perfections of angels and seraphs.

And how are we to know this adorable and soul-saving personage, so that the foundations of our mission may be securely and permanently laid? We are to discern him in the pardon of our sins; in faith in his bloody sacrifice, which can wash away the stains of all our past transgressions; in a hearty repentance toward God, and a total amendment of life, putting away the works of the flesh, and adopting all the graces of the Holy Spirit.

When these sacred foundations shall have been laid and cemented, what will be the superstructure reared on its solid spiritual walls? It will be this, —

"Eternal God, what peace of mind has he —
What light, what love, what joy of various kind,
When to the world and self no more inclined,
His heart with full desire is turned to thee!"

How peaceful all the voyage of life, when the soul

is brought under the mild and merciful discipline of the gospel! Kindness takes the room of bitterness, long-suffering the place of unquiet. The evening of existence, cold and dark in its natural features, becomes light and warm with the expectant joys of a blessed hereafter. Death itself, the most formidable of all foes, when we consider the sublime truth, that "the kingdom of God is not coeval with our earthly mansions," sinks into comparative insignificance, and the soul, reposing fully in God, passes serenely to its rest. This, then, is the great mission of life, — to prepare for death. If the work be performed, when we come to die, all the vapors and thick clouds will roll away, and we shall die in the sunlight. But if this mission be not performed, if we fail to estimate its transcendent magnitude,—what is the fearful destiny that awaits us? Words can scarcely convey the deep import of the thought; nothing is left but the fearful looking-for of "wrath and fiery indignation."

Hobart Berrian.

"HOW can I believe on Christ? My Bible tells me that I must believe on the Lord Jesus in order to be saved. What is saving faith, and how must I believe?" If one reader propounds these questions, there must be others who are perplexed with the same difficulty. In replying briefly to one, we may reach the others likewise.

Friend! have you *tried* to believe? As to the

theory of faith, you have been informed, probably, very often; you may know already that faith in Jesus Christ comprises three things, —*knowing* about Christ, *assenting* to the claims of Christ, and *trusting* in Christ for salvation. So much for theory; but let us assure you that you will never fully understand faith till you practise it. Would your child ever learn how to walk in ten years if you were to keep him in a cradle, and talk to him about the laws of equilibrium, and the "centre of gravity"? No; you set the timid creature on the carpet and let him practise. He will catch a few hard falls, but you pick him up and let him try again; presently he can make a tour from the sofa to the door without a tumble. So Christ bids the weak, trembling sinner come to him. Your first attempts may bring spiritual falls and failures; but there is a more than motherly pity for your moral weakness, and an everlasting arm to help you up. Christ blesses and rewards immediate obedience. "Stretch forth thy hand," said he to the man whose arm was withered from the shoulder. He did not lecture the poor invalid on the nature of paralysis. He demanded obedience: the man obeyed, and his arm was restored whole as the other. One day of faith practised is worth a lifetime of faith explained and expounded.

If a Norwegian were to visit the island of Cuba, a friend there might attempt to describe to him a delicious fruit that grows on that island. He mihgt tell his northern visitor that the fruit was globular, of a deep yellow tint; that it belonged to the genus *citrus;* that it grew on a tree of glossy green, etc., etc.; and we question if the Norwegian would get a very definite idea of an orange. But let his Cuban host only lead him out to an orange-grove, and bid him "lay hold" of the fruit for himself, and one moment of seeing and tasting would teach him more about an orange that an hour's botanical lecture. You must *lay hold* of Christ, and taste the sweetness of forgiving love, and receive the blessings of his grace, if you would find out the nature of true aith. If your heart is stubborn and obstinate, cry unto God for his subduing grace. From him cometh a power that can crush the most stubborn unbelief.

You inquire, "Can an unconverted person pray an acceptable prayer?" We answer that an unconverted man is one who has never *turned to God*, and, while he *refuses* to turn, his prayer is a mockery. If you honestly admit the wickedness of your present heart, and, coming to Christ in sincere penitence, ask for a new heart, you will be answered. But if you continue to live on in admitted sin, and refuse to give your heart to God, you will never be regenerated through prayer, though you were on your knees for a century. Remember that *conversion* is your own act of turning from sin to God, and *regeneration* is the implanting of a new principle within you by the Holy Spirit after you have turned. What does God say? "Give *me* thy heart." He does not change your heart until you give it to him. "Let the wicked forsake his way, and the unrighteous man his thoughts, and *return* unto the Lord, and he will have mercy upon him." It is when you *return* that you find mercy; not before. The prayer that you offer while on your way toward God, he heareth; but the prayer of him who is deliberately pushing away from God in the path of sin is a mockery. You will "pray acceptably" when you give your heart to God; we dare not tell you that you can do so before.

"Oh! but," you cry out, "if you make me stop praying, you cut off all hope." Not so, friend. We only ask you to stop *praying for impossibilities.* We ask you to cease praying for a new heart while you hold fast to your old one — to cease praying to be made a Christian while you are living as a sinner; we ask you to stop praying for faith while you refuse to believe. God never promises to save the man's life who swallows strychnine. Nor does he promise to save the sick soul that swallows Satan's anodynes, instead of accepting the spiritual remedies which the Saviour offers.

Finally, my troubled friend, if you are in earnest for the salvation of your soul; if you do, indeed, admit your personal guilt before God, and long for a better life, then take faith out of the cold regions of the head, and put into the vital region of the heart. Cease to speculate, and begin to *practise.* You have lost time enough already. Every hour spent without abandoning sin and believing on Jesus is an hour wasted; worse still, it is an hour's additional guilt incurred. Those who tell you that the soul is wholly "passive" in the work of conversion, mislead you. Bartimeus was active in coming to Christ, active in praying to him for restoration to sight, voluntary in submitting to be cured; but in *receiving* the miraculous gift of sight, he was indeed "passive," for he could not be otherwise. When you do for your blind and depraved heart what Bartimeus did for his blind eyes, you will soon be found, like him, rejoicing and "following Jesus in the way."

Rev. T. L. Cuyler.

THE wisdom of God in thousands of adaptations to a thoughtful man, is a matter of great wonder. When our war commenced, in our patriotism, we at first thought it was only necessary to pick up a musket and start for Washington; but men after a little found out they had stomachs, and that a commissary department was a larger affair than they had calculated upon. There was not a man known in the country at first who could provide for a hundred thousand men, because the nation never had such a thing to do before. God even in this planet is providing all the time for twelve or fourteen hundred millions of human mouths, with all others that are looking to him, — the young lions, the ravens, and the innumerable beasts, birds, fishes, and insects. When you think of it a little, you will see that the commissary department of God's universe is a wonder. His wisdom in governing the world is wonderful, in controlling the myriads of counter forces and opposing influences, and bringing out results just the contrary from those intended by the parties. That is amazing wisdom.

Bishop Kingsley.

ASK my family physician to cure my child who has been shivering and burning, shivering and burning, and he gives him quinine, and breaks up the disease; but he says: "I want to look into your cellar." And he goes down cellar, and there he finds potatoes, and cabbages, and all sorts of vegatables decaying; and while he gives my child medicine, he urges upon me the necessity of keeping my cellar clean; and I at once have it cleansed. In looking about the premises, he examines the well, and finds that in a foul condition, and says to me: "Do you know that your barn-yard drains right into your well, and that you are drinking excrement? You must have pure water or you will not have good health." And I instantly take care of my well. And after looking further about the premises, he says: "Do you know that you have a swamp here, that is all the while generating a foul atmosphere? It would be a very simple matter to purify it. It would not require more than five days' work to cut through the neck of land and thoroughly drain it. Do not you see that there is no use of your sending for me while you are living in such a malarious re gion?" And I go to work and drain my swamp. And the doctor says: "Now, your child will get well, and you need not send for me any more."

He has not merely given my child quinine — he has cleaned out my house and well and swamp. He has put me in circumstances where nature has a chance to work. And what a broad gift he has given me in answering my prayer in that way!

Now, in the morning you go to God, and say, "Lord, I am as fiery as John;" — he, you know, was so fiery that he called fire down on the villagers because they could not take Christ; — "give me patience." And you do not get out of the house before you find that the servant has left the slop-pail at the foot of the stairs, and you step right into it. Your mouth is hardly wiped from that prayer, and here is a chance for you to exercise the patience that you ask for. But no; you give the pail a kick, and would like to give the servant one, too; and you go away scolding. It never occurs to you that your prayer was answered almost before you got down-stairs. How is a man going to be patient unless there is something to try him? "But I do not want that kind of a trial," you say. You must take that kind which God chooses to give you. He is not going to take away from you trouble. He is going to work out in you to will and to do of his good pleasure. If you are desirous of being patient, and you ask the Lord to make you patient, to some of you he will say: "If you will quit drinking stimulants, you will be more patient." To others he will say, "I will make you more patient, but you must drill for it;" and he will drill you, and you may be sure that he will know just where you are sensitive; just where, touching you, you will be likely to fail; just where you will be obliged to summon resolution, conscience, and grace to your aid if you are successful. But it is in vain for you to go to God and ask him to make you humble, and then, when you are put in circumstances that are trying to your pride, straighten up and say: "I will not yield to this thing." You have just been asking God to teach you how to be humble, and the first thing he sends to you, you refuse to take. It is like a man's going to the dentist to have out a tooth that aches so that he cannot stand it, and then, when he gets there, saying that it does not ache any more, and refusing to have it out. You go two or three times to a dentist, frequently, before you can make up your mind to have your aching tooth out. Men go to God to have him extract this trouble or that, and then, when he offers to do it, you refuse to have it done. You ask him to make you humble, and he persecutes your pride, and you are angry and prouder than before. You ask him to make you patient, and you become more impatient. You ask him to make you gentle, and you manifest a spirit which shows that you are not willing to be made gentle.

In short, what you want is, that God should do the

work for you. You want he should take these qualities and put them into you, as a Frenchman would put the works of a clock into a marble stand all ready made, and set them running and striking without any thought or care on your part. You do not want the Lord to work out in you to will and to do of his good pleasure.

If you will work, I think you will find that all prayers for things right God will answer; and that, wherever it is practicable, he will answer them — not instantaneously, but by working in you the things that you ask for.

Rev. H. W. Beecher.

I NEVER can forget that word which was once whispered to me in an inquiry-meeting." — "What word was it?" — "It was the word *eternity*. A young Christian friend, who was yearning for my salvation, came up to me as I sat in my pew, and simply whispered 'eternity' in my ear, with great solemnity and tenderness, and then left me. That word *made me think*, and I found no peace till I came to the cross of Christ for salvation."

It is enough to make any one think. My friend, have you ever taken the measure of that word? Have you ever weighed it? You are wearing out life, perhaps, in the desperate endeavor to grow rich: have you ever asked yourself how much you will be worth in eternity. Some men will be millionnaires in heaven; men like Paul, and Oberlin, and Luther, and

Wilbefore: how rich will you be when death has reduced your form to a house of six feet by two? You are anxious, perhaps, about your society on earth; have you thought, With whom shall I spend my eternity? and where?

Eternity! Dwell on that portentous word. Revolve it. Study it. Hang over its infinite depths; *fathom* it, if you can. Gaze upward and scale its heights, if you can. Stretch away over its illimitable breadth; *measure* it, if you can. Give wings to your imagination and speed onward; *find its end*, if you can.

Think of as many centuries as there are drops in yonder Atlantic. When these have all passed away, begin a new series of as many centuries as there are sands on the Atlantic shores. Multiply all these centuries by the number of the stars in the sky, and then remember that eternity has but *begun!* The music of heaven just opened! The remorseful agonies of the pit, still in their first pangs of wretchedness; the death of the lost soul ever undying! Let but the lost soul be left to itself—let it only grow worse and worse by the natural law of growth in iniquity—let all grace be totally withdrawn, and the soul be given up to upbraid itself, and torture itself, and sting itself with hateful memories forever, and you need to conceive of no material hell. You need no accessories. We are not obliged to conceive of a sulphurous lake foaming in crests of fire, nor of undying worms shooting their fangs into writhing forms; the simple withdrawal of God's love forever from a wicked soul, and the imprisonment of that soul forever in a dungeon of depravity without a ray of hope, this will be a "death everlasting" too fearful to think of without a shudder.

At the end of myriads of centuries, these pangs will have just begun! The worm yet undying—the fires of remorse yet unquenched! The damnation unslumbering! On every wall of this vast prison-house of despair the self-tortured soul will read as in letters of fire, "*Ye knew your duty, and ye did it not.*"

Heaven will be as endless in its joys as hell is endless in its remorseful agonies of soul. So I read, for one, the revelations of God's word, In heaven new joys must open every moment; new recognitions of the Lord; new discoveries of God's uuexhausted truth. New strains of rapture will fill the ear; new banquets of God's beauty and glory fill the soul. And yet never fresher, sublimer, more magnificent revelations ever bursting upon the glorified spirit!

> "How long art thou, Eternity?
> As long as God is God—so long
> Endure the pangs of sin and wrong;
> So long the joys of Heaven remain:
> Oh! endless joy! oh! endless pain!
> Ponder, oh man! Eternity!"

This eternity is just at the door. You and I may be launched into it before to-morow's sun goes down. What is time to us, but the brief hour for preparing to meet the destinies of that eternal state? What have we to do but to save our souls, and to save others, too, with the utmost alacrity of Christian love? Every moment spent for God and our fellow-men now will yield its centuries of bliss. Let us live — as earth's best and holiest have lived — in the light of eternity.

"Here, take this watch, my friend," said the noble Lord Russell, when he mounted the scaffold to die as a patriot-martyr,— "take this watch; I have no more to do with *time*. My thoughts are now about eternity."

So would I say to many a reader with whom I have grown intimate in these pages, Take your Bible, my friend; learn from it how to live, and how to die. You will soon have done with time. Let your thoughts be about ETERNITY.

Rev. T. L. Cuyler.

I WAS alive," the apostle says, "without the law once; but when the commandment came, sin revived, and I died." So long as he was measured only by the worldly rules which obtained in society, he was well enough off, he thought; but when God's law came down, and he was measured by that, he detected sin everywhere in himself.

Let a man take a barrel of iron filings and put his hand through them, and not a particle of the filings will stick to his hand; but if he takes a magnet and puts that through, how quick it is covered with the filings! for that is a thing which measures metallic substances.

Just so, let a man take the average goodness in the community, and measure his life by it, and it seems all right; but if he takes the law of God, and measures his life by that, he finds every single one of his feelings to be crooked in the extreme.

Let a boy who is unskilled in the use of tools take a board and try to plane it straight, and then let him take a straight edge and lay it on. A rat could run between that edge and the board in a dozen places.

A man seems all right to himself while he measures himself by conceit and self-love; but let him take God's straight-edge, and lay it alongside of his faculties, and according to that test every one of them is crooked—not one of them is straight.

Rev. H. W. Beecher.

CAN any thing be more sad than the wreck of a man? We mourn over the destruction of many noble things that have existed in the world. Men, when they hear of the old Phidian Jupiter—that sat forty feet high, carved of ivory and gold, and that was so magnificent, so transcendent, that all the ancient world counted him unhappy who died without having seen this most memorable statue that ever existed in the world—often mourn to think that its exceeding value led to its destruction, and that it perished. It was a great loss to art that such a thing should perish. Can any man look upon the Acropolis — shattered with balls, crumbled by the various influences of the elements, and utterly destroyed — and not mourn to think that such a stately temple, a temple so unparalleled in its exquisite symmetry and beauty, should be desolate and scattered? Can there be any thing more melancholy than the destruction, not only of such temples as the Acropolis and the Parthenon, but of a whole city of temples and statues? More melancholy than the destruction of a statue, or a temple, or a city, or a nation, in its physical aspects, is the destruction of a man, the wreck of the understanding, the ruin of the moral feelings, the scattering all abroad of those elements of power that, united together, make man fitly the noblest creature that walks on the earth. Thousands and thousands of men make foreign pilgrimages to visit and mourn over fallen and destroyed cities of former grandeur and beauty; and yet, all around about every one of us, in every street, and in almost every neighborhood, there are ruins more stupendous, more pitiful, and more heart touching than that of any city. And how strange would be the wonder if, as men wandered in the Orient, there should come some one that should call from the mounds all the scattered ruins of Babylon, or build again Tadmor of the desert! How strange it would be to see a city, that at night was a waste heap, so restored that in the morning the light of the sun should flash from pinnacle, and tower, and wall, and roof! How marvellous would be that creative miracle, but more marvellous, ten thousand times, is that divine touch by which a man, broken down and scattered, is raised up in his right mind, and made to sit, clothed at the feet of Jesus.

Rev. H. W. Beecher.

THE tongue is called in the Bible "an unruly member." Our own experience accords perfectly with the statement, and observations on the tongues of others have satisfied us of the fact. We think the following rules, if carefully followed, will be found of great use in taming that which has not yet been perfectly tamed:

1. Never use your tongue in speaking any thing but truth. The God of truth, who made the tongue, did not intend it for any other use. It will not work well in falsehood; it will run in such inconsistencies as to detect itself. To use the organ for publishing falsehood, is as incongruous as the use of the eye for hearing, or the ear for smelling.

2. Do not use your tongue too much. It is a kind of waste-gate to let off the thoughts as they collect and expand the mind; but if the waste-gate is always open, the water will soon run shallow. Many people use their tongues too much. Shut the gate, and let streams of thought flow in till the mind is full, and then you may let off with some effect.

3. Never let the stream of passion move the tongue. Some people, when they are about to put this member in motion, hoist the wrong gate — they

let out passion instead of reason. The tongue then makes a great noise — disturbs the quiet of the neighbors, exhausts the person's strength, but does no good. The whirlwind has ceased, but what is the benefit?

4. Look into the pond and see if there is water enough to move the wheel to any purpose before you open the gate; or, plainly, think before you speak.

5. Never put your tongue in motion while your respondent has his in motion. The two streams will meet, and the reaction will be so great the words of neither will reach the other, but come back in a blinding sprinkle upon himself.

6. See that your tongue is hung true before using it. Some tongues we have observed are so hung that they sometimes equivocate considerably. Let the owners of such turn the screw of conscience until the tongue moves true.

7. Expect that others will use their tongues for what you do yours. Some claim the privilege of reporting all the news, and charge others not to do so. Your neighbor will not allow you to monopolize the business. If you have any thing to be kept secret, keep it to yourself.

"HE has made his bed, now let him lie in it!" We confess, this sounds, at first thought, very rough indeed; but, after all, isn't society entitled to some vindication just here?

The young man who has run riot over every better instinct; recklessly wasted his strength and his means; frittered away his influence; kicked at his best opportunities; who is in a fever till he gets out of every good situation; who swings out into crazy license, calling that liberty, till, finally, he worries out the patience, and tires to utter exhaustion, the help of his best friends — we confess to some sympathy for that view of the case — "he has compounded his draught, now let him have his fill of it." If he has "stuffed his pillow with thistles, let him have them."

There is something ominous in that silence which encircles a young man's career — when his best friends cease to suggest, criticize, plead, and protest — when acquaintances look in at the shop windows at the time he passes, and others cross over on the other side of the street. All this interpreted, means that they are determined to give him a wide berth in his wilfulness. He shall now have plenty of room and no favors more. He his *bound* for his own proper place.

He needn't say that the "world owes him a living." It owes him a halter, and he is twisting it for himself.

We sympathize with Talleyrand somewhat in this matter, who, when having detected his private secretary at pilfering and charging him with the offence, met the reply — "I have a small salary, and you know, monsieur, I must live!" — by the prompt answer — "Indeed! I don't see the necessity."

You and I can afford to *die*, but we can't afford to follow any such example as this.

But the expression applies equally well to what is better. Society generally does not move very far wide of the mark. Men are generally set down (and sometimes very hard) pretty near where they belong — just as players at chess do not often mistake the squares appropriate to the several pieces.

A man is pretty sure finally, if not long before, to settle down in just that place for which his qualifications prepare him.

If he studies to polish his manners and refine his tastes, carrying himself with due regard to the interests and opinions of others, he will gravitate, inevitably, toward the society of true gentlemen.

If he takes pride in "bluffing people off," as he calls it, and thinks this manner a mark of independent superiority, he will drift toward the society of boors.

If he makes a "good hand" by dealing in the tricks of the trade, and is amused at his own cleverness, he will make a bed for himself among the rogues; for certain it is, that when honest people find him out, which they are sure to do, they will leave him with plenty of room to himself.

The law here in the statics and dynamics of society, is as the law of the Medes and Persians. A fish may feel very much at home in water, but so long as I have not fins and scales, so long that elements is no home for me.

The lout in the parlor, the booby in the drawing-room, and the clown among the literati, are not in their own places; because there must be correspondence between the surroundings and a man's own fittings. The two edges of paper on the wall determine whether the figures can match; and it takes both the man and the place to produce a propriety.

One man, hunter-clad, and gun in hand, is in his own place buried in the wilderness; another, quill in hand, finds his own in the quiet study; and to reverse these you make both men miserable.

The eagle in his eyry, and the cock on the dunghill, are each at home; force the one into the place of the other, and the cock is dashed to pieces and the eagle pines away and dies.

The law is just this: the place is not for the man, but the man for the place—yet men forget it.

"I'll tell you," said a young Pecksniff, talking to a sweet, modest, sensible girl, "what sort of a prize I mean to work my cards for. She must be young and beautiful, she must be rich and accomplished, every way very good and very nice; in short, she must have all the modern improvements."

"And what," replied the sensible young lady, "have *you*, sir, to offer on your part for all this wealth of possession?"

And he said—nothing.

When you want a place—what have *you got for* the place?

Life is a pair of balances.

Rev. A. M'Elroy Wylie.

ALAS for him who never sees
The stars shine through his cypress-trees!
Who, hopeless, lays his dead away,
Nor looks to see the breaking day
Across the mournful marbles play;
Who hath not learned, in hours of faith,
The truth, to flesh and sense unknown,
That life is ever lord of death,
And love can never lose its own.

Whittier.

LIKE snow that falls where waters glide,
Earth's pleasures fade away;
They melt in time's destroying tide,
And cold are while they stay;
But joys that from religion flow,
Like stars that gild the night,
Amid the darkest gloom of woe,
Shine forth with sweetest light.

Religion's ray no clouds obscure;
But o'er the Christian's soul
It sheds a radiance calm and pure,
Though tempests round him roll;
His heart may break 'neath sorrow's stroke;
But to its latest thrill,
Like diamonds shining when they're broke,
Religion lights it still.

William Leggett.

IT would be very difficult to take statistics of men's opinions of themselves, but, after all, it would be a thing profoundly instructive if it could be done. I wish I could find out by looking at a man just where that man puts the most value on himself. You know how it is with muscle. You know there are moral athletes, whose value consists in their ingenuity; they think themselves so acute, such admirable wrestlers, such fine logicians, they have such tact, such skill, they know how by indirection to do so much. I know men who never are so proud of direct victories as of stolen ones. If they can make a good reply, or turn a man's flank unexpectedly; if in any thing they can show tact rather than power, — they are exceedingly proud of that. I know some men who are more proud of earning money than of any thing else. They may be proud, as perhaps they are, they may be selfish, as perhaps they are; but oh! it is the thing that goes to bed with them, and that rises up with them in the morning, —"You are a great man to make money." There is where their strength lies, and their glory. Another man is proud of himself on account of, it may be, his great enduring energies; another man on account of his quiet but complex administrative energies. Go over and look at men, and see what it is they are proud of in themselves, and you shall find that, in the vast majority of instances, if you trace men back to the place where they put their little throne, where they sit thinking themselves to be sovereigns, it is their lower faculties that they glory over themselves. How many there are that, being skilful, energetic, all-accomplishing, say to themselves, "After all, because I am patient with the poor, with the weak, I am prouder of myself than I am of all the rest of my life. Because I will not hate those that hate me, of that I feel proud. I may be wise; I may be strong, and accomplishing; but, after all, I am weak, and I really feel more proud of that than of every other thing." Many a man is proud of himself because he has that fiery flash of cruel honor. No man shall look upon him with contempt, or a questioning meaning of the eye of no man shall dare put insult upon him. Quicker than powder resents the fire, will they resent a wrong. Christians they are; frequently officers; and ministers sometimes, too, they are. But yet, proud, resentful honor, avenging honor. You are not half so good as the lion. You don't need to be a man to be that. They found that out in the brute creation before God got half-way up to you. Did God go on and put story upon story on you that you might look out of your higher windows, and can you not look above that? These men have the direction of spiritual matters, but they never for a moment value themselves upon these traits; it is upon the lower traits that tney value themselves. So it comes to pass men are clothed with supernal faculties, true aristocrats of soul, with these higher instincts, and they care nothing for them. A man dies and leaves his son as his heir.

There is the library stored with all the lore of antiquity as well as of modern days, and the booby-faced boy don't care for them. There are his galleries of Raphael and Michael Angelo. Here are the representative schools that show what those noble men have thought who were honored in color and by form; there are the *repertoires* of music-thought, giving to us those prophet sounds of all utterances: not one of these things does he care any thing about. The first thing he does is to call the butler, "Come here, my jolly boy, and tell me what is in the cellar." Ah! it is the wine; it is riot and wassail; it is the brutal, vulgar element he is proud of. His stable, his dog-kennel, his wine, will constitute the glory of the young spendthrift, while in the same mansion are all the treasures of science and of art, all the lore and wealth of history, that he cares nothing for. It is that which causes men to glory in the lower part of their nature, quite unconscious and inconsiderate of that which is highest and best.

Rev. H. W. Beecher.

DEATH OF THE LOVELY.—When the good and the lovely die, the memory of their good deeds, like the moonbeams on the stormy sea, lights up our darkened hearts and lends to the surrounding gloom a beauty so sad, so sweet, that we would not, if we could, dispel the darkness that environs it.

Geo. D. Prentice.

AND upon the other side, when these eyes shall open again, and these hearts, chilled with death, begin once more to beat, then the first words of greeting upon the other side, O mother! will not be from your child — O husband! not from your wife; but Jesus shall meet us and say in the early morning of the eternal world, "All hail!" And trembling, lost, uncertain, he shall clasp us in his arms and shall say, "Be not afraid."

Then, as if the seas had broke forth, and as if all the heavens were but one mighty music-band, the angels of God shall acclaim us ransomed, and bring us where death shall have no more dominion over us forever and forever. To the faith and to the love of this ascended Saviour, I commend your souls!

Rev. H. W. Beecher.

IT was pointed out by Lord Macaulay that in an English cathedral there is an exquisite stained window, which was made by an apprentice out of the pieces of glass rejected by his master, and it was so far superior to every other in the church, that, according to tradition, the envious artist killed himself with vexation.

All the builders of society had rejected the "sinners," and made the painted window of the "righteous." A new builder came; his plan was original, startling, revolutionary; his eye was upon the condemned material; he made the first last and the last first, and the stone which the builders rejected he made the head stone of the corner. He always specially cared for the rejected stone. Men had always cared for the beautiful, the righteous; it was left to Christ to care for sinners.

THE old adage that a girl is worth a thousand dollars, and a boy worth fifteen hundred, is a depreciation of values. I warrant that the man who invented the theory was a bachelor, or he would not have set down the youngsters so far below cost. When the poorest child is born, a star of joy points down to the manger.

We are tired of hearing of the duty that children owe to their parents. Let some one write a disquisition on what parents owe to their children. What though they do upset things, and chase the cats, and eat themselves into colic with green apples, and empty the castor of sweet oil into the gravy, and bedaub their hands with tar. Grown people have the privilege of larger difficulties, and will you not let the children have a few smaller predicaments? How can we ever pay them for the prattle that drives our cares away, and the shower of soft flaxen curls on our hot cheek, and the flowers with which they have strewn our way, plucking them from the margin of their cradles, and the opening with little hands of doors into new dispensations of love?

A well-regulated home is a millennium on a small scale — the lion and leopard nature by infantile stroke subdued — and "a little child shall lead them." Blessed the pillow of the trundle-bed on which rests the young head that never ached! Blessed the day whose morning is wakened by the patter of little feet! Blessed the heart from which all the soreness is drawn out by the soft hand of a babe!

But there are children which have been so thoroughly spoiled, they are a terror to the community. As you are about to enter your neighbor's door, his turbulent boy will come at you with the plunge of a buffalo, pitching his head into your diaphragm. He will in the night stretch a rope from tree to tree to dislocate your hat, or give some passing citizen a sudden halt as the rope catches at the throat, and he is hung before his time. They can, in a day, break more toys, slit more kites, lose more marbles than all the fathers and mothers of the neighborhood could restore in a week. They talk roughly, make old people stop to let them pass, upset the little girl's school-basket, and make themselves universally disagreeable. You feel as if you would like to get hold of them just once, or in their behalf call on the firm of Birch & Spank.

It is easy enough to spoil a child. No great art is demanded. Only three or four things are requisite to complete the work. Make all the nurses wait on him and fly at his bidding. Let him learn to never go for a drink, but always have it brought to him. At ten years of age have Bridget tie his shoe-strings. Let him strike auntie because she will not get him a sugar-plum. He will soon learn that the house is his realm, and he is to rule it. He will come up into manhood one of those precious spirits that demand obeisance and service, and with the theory that the world is his oyster, which with knife he will proceed to open.

If that does not spoil him, buy him a horse. It is exhilarating and enlarging for a man to own such an animal. A good horseback ride shakes up the liver and helps the man to be virtuous, for it is almost impossible to be good with too much bile, an enlarged spleen, or a stomach off duty. We congratulate any man who can afford to own a horse; but if a boy own one, he will probably ride on it to destruction. He will stop at the tavern for drinks. He will bet at the races. There will be room enough in the same saddle for idleness and dissipation to ride, one of them before and one of them behind. The bit will not be strong enough to rein in at the right place. There are men who all their lives have been going down hill, and the reason is, that in boyhood they sprang astride a horse, and got going so fast that they have never been able to stop.

But if the child be insensible to all such efforts to spoil him, try the plan of never saying any thing encouraging to him. If he do wrong, thrash him soundly; but if he do well, keep on reading the newspaper, pretending not to see him. There are excellent people, who, through fear of producing childish vanity, are unresponsive to the very best endeavor

When a child earns parental applause, he ought to have it. If he get up head at school, give him a book or an apple. If he saw a bully on the play-ground trampling on a sickly boy, and your son took the bully by the throat so tightly that he became a little variegated in color, praise your boy, and let him know that you love to have him the champion of the weak. Perhaps *you* would not do right a day, if you had no more prospect of reward than that which you have given him. If on commencement day he make the best speech, or read the best essay, tell him of it. Truth is always harmless, and the more you use of it the better. If your daughter at the conservatory take the palm, give her a new piece of music, a ring, a kiss, or a blessing.

But if you have a child invulnerable to all other influences, and he cannot be spoiled by any means already recommended, give him plenty of money without any questions as to what he does with it. The fare is cheap on the road between here and Smashupton. I have known boys with five dollars to pay their way clear through, and make all the connections on the "Grand Trunk" route to perdition. We know not why loose cash in a boy's pocket is called *pin* money, unless because it often sticks a hole into his habits. First, he will buy raisins, then almonds, then a whisk cane, then a breast-pin, then cigars, then a keg of "lager," then a ticket for a drunken excursion, and there may possibly be money enough left for the father to buy for his boy a coffin.

Let a child know something of the worth of money by earning it. Over pay them if you will, but let them get some idea of equivalents. If he get distorted notions of values at the start, he never will be righted. Daniel Webster knew every thing except how to use money. From boyhood he had things mixed up. His mother gave him and Ezekiel money for Fourth of July. As the boys came back from the village, the mother said, "Daniel, what did you buy with your money?" and he answered, "I bought a cake, and a candy, and some beer, and some fire-crackers." Then, turning to Ezekiel, she said, "What did you buy with *your* money?" "Oh," said Ezekiel, "*Daniel* borrowed mine."

On the other hand it is a ruinous policy to be parsimonious with children. If a boy find that a parent has plenty of money, and he, the boy, has none, the temptation will be to steal the first cent he can lay his hand on. Oh! the joy that five pennies can buy for a boy! They seem to open before him a Paradise of liquorice-drops and cream candy. You cannot in after life buy so much superb satisfaction with five thousand dollars as you bought with your first five cents. Children need *enough* money, but not a superfluity. Freshets wash away more cornfields than they culture.

Boys and girls are often spoiled by parental gloom. The father never unbends. The mother's rheumatism hurts so, she does not see how little Maggie can ever laugh. Childish curiosity is denounced as impertinence. The parlor is a Parliament, and every thing in everlasting order. Balls and tops in that house are a nuisance, and the pap that the boy is expected most to relish is Geometry, a little sweetened with the chalk of black-boards. For cheerful reading the father would recommend "Young's Night Thoughts," and Harvey's "Meditations among the Tombs."

At the first chance the boy will break loose. With one grand leap he will clear the catechisms. He will burst away into all riotous living. He will be so glad to get out of Egypt, that he will jump into the Red Sea. The hardest colts to catch are those that have a long while been locked up. Restraints are necessary, but there must be some outlet. Too high a dam will overflow all the meadows.

A sure way of spoiling children is by surfeiting them with food. Many of them have been stuffed to death. The mother spoke of it as a grand achievement that her boy ate ten eggs at Easter. He waddles across the room under burdens of porter-house steak and plum-pudding enough to swamp a day-laborer. He runs his arm up to the elbow in the jar of blackberry jam, and pulls it out amid the roar of the whole household thrown into hysterics with the witticism. After a while he has a pain, then he gets "the dumps," soon he will be troubled with indigestion, occasionally he will have a fit, and last of all he gets a fever and dies. The parents have no idea that they are to blame. Beautiful verses are cut on the tombstone, when if the truth had been told the epitaph would have read, KILLED BY APPLE DUMPLINGS.

Rev. T. De Witt Talmage.

SUPPOSE we were very much troubled and disposed to go to ever so kind a friend and begin to tell him our troubles. He hears us for a season, sympathizes with us, and takes an interest in us, but he cannot devote all his time to us. He has other engagements, and if we stay too long, he will show signs of uneasiness, because he thinks it time for us to retire; and if we do not take the hint, he will say to us: "You must excuse me; I have an engagement now. I shall be glad to give you more time if you will call again, and then I'll see what I can do for you." This has to be said by the very best of friends. Oh! what if it were so with Jesus, the sinner's Friend, just at the time when we needed him the most — just at the time when our wants were most imperative! What if he were to say: "I have an engagement this afternoon; some persons from Africa, from Asia, and the islands of the sea are to call upon me; I have agreed to have a conference with them to help them, and you must excuse me now." But death will not release the inexorable grasp of his icy fingers upon your heart-strings, and you must have help now or never. I have seen the poor soldier all shot to pieces, who had only time to look up and ask Jesus for salvation, and receive it before his soul left the body; there was no time for any thing else. A Saviour who was not there then would be unavailing. Is there nothing in this consideration adapted to human want? Is there nothing in this that should fill us with adoring wonder? Oh! I wonder that men who want to ridicule a provision so infinitely precious do not hide their heads in shame!

Bishop Kingsley.

THERE is a stream whose narrow tide
The known and unknown worlds divide,
Where all must go;
Its waveless waters, dark and deep,
'Mid sullen silence downward sweep
With moanless flow.

I saw where at the dreary flood
A smiling infant prattling stood,
Whose hour was come;
Untaught of all, it neared the tide —
Sunk as to cradled rest, and died
Like going home.

Followed with languid eye anon,
A youth diseased, and pale and wan;
And there alone
He gazed upon the leaden stream,
And feared to plunge — I heard a scream! —
And he was gone!

And then a form of manhood's strength
Came bustling on, till there at length
He saw life's bound;
He shrunk, and raised the bitter prayer —
Too late! His shriek of wild despair
The waters drowned!

Next stood upon that surgeless shore,
A being bowed with many a score
Of toilsome years.
Earth-bound and sad, he left the bank,
Backturned his dimming eye, and sank,
Ah! full of fears!

How bitter must thy waters be,
O death! How hard a thing, ah me!
It is to die!
I mused — when to that stream again,
Another child of mortal mien,
With smiles drew nigh

'Tis the last pang — he calmly said —
"To me, O death! thou hast no dread! —
Saviour, I come!
Spread but thine arms on yonder shore
I see — ye waters bear me o'er —
There is my home!"

IN the dim recess of thy spirit's chamber,
  Is there some hidden grief thou mayst not tell?
Let not thine heart forsake thee, but remember
  His pitying eye who sees and knows it well:
                God knows it all.

And art thou tossed on billows of temptation,
  And wouldst do good, but evil oft prevails?
Oh, think, amid the waves of tribulation,
  When earthly hopes, when earthly refuge fails, —
                He knows it all.

Art thou oppressed and poor and heavy-hearted,
  The heavens above thee in thick clouds arrayed,
And well-nigh crushed, no earthly strength imparted,
  No friendly voice to say, "Be not afraid"?
                He knows it all.

Art thou a mourner? Are thy tear-drops flowing
  For one too early lost to earth and thee?
The depths of grief no human spirit knowing —
  Which moan in secret, like the moaning sea?
                He knows it all.

Dost thou look back upon a life of sinning?
  Forward, and tremble for thy future lot?
By Him who sees the end from the beginning,
  Thy tear of penitence is not forgot:
                He knows it all.

Then go to God; pour out your heart before Him;
  There is no grief your Father cannot feel:
And let your grateful song of praise adore Him, —
  To save, forgive, and every wound to heal:
                God knows it all.

"SHOW me families worthy the name — true domestic commonwealths, father and mother, king and minister, enthroned together in the midst of the circle of their children, talking to them of ancestors, of honor, of duty, and being hearkened to — commanding in respect, and still more in love, and being obeyed; show me a father, king in his own house, and so much the more free in the world without, as he is authoritative in the world within; show me homes like these, and I will show you republics! The genuine free citizen is the father, respected and obeyed at home. It is out of such sturdy materials as this that lasting social order can be built."

"COME this way, father!"
  'Twas my little boy's voice
Which guided my way,
When on the wide sea
In the fog my boat lay.
'Twas the voice of my child
As he stood on the shore;
It sounded out clear
O'er the dark billows' roar,

"Come this way, my father,
And steer straight for me:
Here, safe on the shore,
I am waiting for thee."

I knew that sweet voice
'Midst rocks and rough breakers
And high dashing spray:
How sweet to my heart
Did it sound from the shore,
As it came out so clear
O'er the dark billows' roar!
"Come this way, my father,
And steer straight for me:
Here, safe on the shore,
I am waiting for thee."

How great was my joy
When I held to my breast
The form of that dear one,
And soothed it to rest!
For the tones of my child,
"I call'd you, dear father,
And knew you would hear
The voice of your darling
Far o'er the dark sea,
While, safe on the shore,
I was waiting for thee."

That voice is now hushed
Which then guided my way;
The form I then pressed
Is now mingled with clay:
But the tones of my child
Still sound in my ear,
"I am calling you, father.
Oh! can you not hear
The voice of your darling,
As you toss on Life's sea?
For on a bright shore
I am waiting for thee."

I think of that voice
In many a lone hour;
It speaks to my heart
With fresh beauty and power;
And still echoes far out
Over Life's troubled wave,
And sounds from loved lips
That lie in the grave, —
"Come this way, my father;
Oh! steer straight for me:
Here, safely in heaven,
I am waiting for thee."

AS the morning comes, still it is "All hail!" to those who know how to listen; and in the great and hot noons of summer, when all the air in the great ball above our head trembles as wine in the cup, it is still from out of the air above us: "All hail!" And when evening, coming forth, trembles with tenderness, it is still "All hail!" And every day and every year the voice still sounds, to those that have an ear to hear, and shall to the very end of life, "All hail!" and when death itself shall come to us, still the greeting will be: "All hail!" As we leave things dear and venture into things uncertain, still the voice will be, "Be not afraid;" for these first words with which Christ came back to his disciples are words that now sit high in the heavens, singing forever and forever the notes of the world's joy and of the world's deliverance.

Rev. H. W. Beecher.

NEWSPAPERS don't praise men who ought to be praised; they praise men the people want praised, or who want to be praised themselves. Praising and blaming is a matter of bargain and sale; rank is a matter of selling as much as offices are in Washington or Albany. All these things are bought and sold; the classifications of society are various; therefore the word of the Saviour, "The last shall be first, and the first last; the highest shall be lowest, and the lowest highest," because in society the best men are frequently the most obscure; not the less influential, but they are obscure. There are thousands of cases in which the magistrate who sits highest, and really has most extraordinary power, is no match even for one lordly mother, dwelling in a house of poverty, it may be, but, after all, sending out her example, her moral influence into every family in the neighborhood. Here is actual power, although there are no bells on her horses as there are on his, and people don't know it. So, when thunder-storms come up in summer, what a racket the thunder does make! You would think the thunder was Lord of every thing. A drop of rain comes down with a swift hissing, and smites the ground; it is lost in it. Well, the thunder goes roaring past and bellowing by, but after all it doesn't do any thing; it is the most useless of any part of the storm. But the raindrop falls and tugs at the roots. There is more power in one drop of rain than there is in all the thunders that roll over the mountains, filling them with their echoes. So it is with life. Not the highest, not the most conspicuous, not what are called the most influential are the most powerful. It is they that shed upon society the commonest light of reason, it is they that shed upon society the purest light of justice; it is they that fill the veins of society with the poorest blood of life — it is they that develop the highest moral possibilities, and teach man what can be done by patience, by forbearance, by weakness, by humility. These, after all, are society's best ornaments. We say, "Oh, these are very good people, very good people, but they have no great influence." The more shame for society. We say of people, "They are very admirable people, if they are Christians, and

I think they are Christians; but after all they don't do very much." But don't the light do much be cause it don't hiss?

Doesn't the warmth of the sun do much because it doesn't sound a trumpet before it? They are doing most that seem to be doing the least, that is the salvation of society, who perform their duty as it is given to them to do, and that are good in the essentially noble.

Rev. H. W. Beehcer.

I AM going; yes, I am going;
And oh, hows weet 'twill be to die;
To end this weary, toilsome journey,
And to live beyond the bright blue sky.
The earthly friends I love surround me,
And vainly wish for me to stay,
Yet though I love them, oh, so fondly,
My longing soul would haste away.

I do not like these earthly fetters
That clog the soul's aspiring thought,
I'd rather haste to see my Saviour,
Who long ago its pardon bought.
Oh, who would feed on worldly pleasure,
That soon must perish and decay,
While heaven gives overflowing measure,
Of joys that can not fade away.

The angels now are sweetly singing
  Of perfect love which casts out fear,
E'en while my soul in faith is clinging,
  Fast to the cross of him so dear.
I will not fear death's gloomy portal,
  Since Jesus has before me gone,
To light the way to lands immortal,
  And I shall never feel alone.

For Christ the Son of God will guide me,
  Safe o'er the river dark and chill,
And not a wave shall overflow me,
  For he can yet say "Peace, be still!"
I am going, yes, I am going,
  And Oh, what rapture fills my breast
To know that when this journey endeth,
  My weary soul shall be at rest.

Mrs. H. W. Francis.

IT is not inconsistent with true modesty for a man to know that he is superior to others. There is a distinction to be drawn between self-conceit, which is blind, undiscriminating impulse, and the calm judgment of a superior nature of moral faculties. Indeed, it is for the want of this self-consciousness and self-assertion that good is enfeebled, and that wickedness often is so impudent. Good men are not willing to take it for granted that the truth-speaking man is the natural Lord of the liar. He is. Standing at a corner, I see a man whose business it is to foment the appetites of men. Like a big-bellied spider, he has made himself fat on his victims. He has rather more money than I have; vastly more mouth than I have. He looks upon me with contempt as I go past him, as if I was a venomous insect; he has his tail behind him that join in the ribaldry. I look upon that man; I know that I am infinitely his superior; and it makes no difference whether you elect him to Washington, or to Albany, or anywhere else; I am still his superior. Why? I love large manhood, he loves animalhood; I love the things that make society strong and pure, he loves disorganized society for the sake of sucking its blood. I know I am that man's peer because I am a more true Christian than he. Can any man say that modesty requires him to say that all men are on a level? Is that democracy? Does democracy require you to say that a man six feet six inches high is on precisely the same scale as a man five feet high? I won't say so. If a man weighs one hundred and fifty pounds, and another man weighs two hundred pounds, I say the man who weighs two hundred pounds is superior in avoirdupois to the man who weighs one hundred and fifty pounds. If a man is six feet high he has certainly a foot the advantage of a man five feet high. As in arithmetic there are rules for measuring the values of material objects, so there is a rule for measuring the moral qualities of men. If we say that a man next the brute is the lowest, then the man the highest toward God *is* the highest. If I find in myself traces divine, it is no conceit in me to say I am the natural superior of a man who has no such qualities. Do you think it is conceit to say you are superior to your children? Why is it, then, with other children, who are grown up, conceit to say you are their superior? Ah! that is not the way men measure. A man lives in an obscure street, in a two-story house; another lives in the court part of the town in a magnificent palace, and we, therefore, think he is greatfy superior to the other. He lives in a bigger place. But a very mean man can live in a very big place. That don't make you superior. That makes a man more than another that makes him bigger in his heart. He that has the telescopic eye of faith and can explore the widest celestial range — that is greater. He that has that sympathy which comes from love of truth, from love of justice, from love of rectitude, from love of knowledge, from love of good, from love of man — that is the greatest. Don't measure your magnitude by your pocket, nor by your order, nor by your house, nor by your surroundings. Measure with the rules of judgment. What has God made you, and what have you made yourself in respect to higher moral range? No; I hold that it is the want of this self-assertion that has been the cause of great mischief in society. When a lord's son comes over, if he walks largely, we say he has the blood of his ancestors in him. I do not say whether this is a just judgment, or an unjust judgment. We tolerate it.

Had Washington had a son, we should have said he carried himself as though he knew he was the son of Washington. If the sons of a great man of the earth have a right to be proud of their father, have we not a right to be proud of our father? Am I the object of Christ's thought and sorrowing Gethsemane? was it around me that He wove the anguishful feeling that His nature has suffered? has He thought of me? has He carried me in the arms of His Providence all the way up? for me is there a name written above, and is there waiting for me a crown and a sceptre, and a welcome? and do I know it; and shall I walk all unconscious of these things, and demean myself as if I was fatherless, an orphan, an outcast, a wanderer in the universe? I am a son of God; I know it. I look down on every man who assumes to be my superior by virtue of things infernal or inferior, and I remember my birthright. Young man, you are ashamed to tell the truth because your employer, your partner, an old man with a name in the market, in the whole community, a man of large wealth — he quibbles and makes truth a mere commercial element to be bought and sold according to his interest. He sneers at you, he laughs at you because you are so green as to come down with your farmer notions in your head, and talk of truth. Let me tell you if you know how to tell the truth, you are the natural superior of every man who knows how to tell a lie. Will you assert it? You are ashamed, and are silent among your jeering companions. "Oh, oh! [mockingly] Our "boy's not free from his mother's apron-strings yet! And where is your sister! Good little boy; won't do wrong!" Stand up! [with strong emphasis] let your head shine bright. If you won't do wrong, you are his natural superior. You are the prince of every man who will do wrong. Be proud of your superiority. Would you let a ribald mob put you to shame? If you bore the consequences, and it brought you an honored name in history, you would be proud of it, it would be a shield of glory. I once lived in a community where they called me "Yankee." I told them I gloried in the name, and it meant much to me, although a different thing to them. Ah! That man who casts down his crown in the dust, and lets men trample it under foot! Oh! that man should take his conscience, that man should take his purity, and that he should let these things pay obeisance to animal lust and appetite. You won't drink, and you are ashamed of temperance! It is your glory. You won't run unholy with salacious lust, therefore you are laughed at and jeered at. The disciples were jeered at, too; angelic natures have been jeered at, and will be forever and ever. Be higher than the miserable passions of the men around about you. It is because men don't stand up to their principles, because they are afraid to declare the things truly their glory and honor, that men support so much in society. I say to every maiden, to every young man, and to every man grown, remember the purity of your nature, that which is supreme and noblest and most divine. Be proud of that wherever you go. Lift up your head.

Rev. H. W. Beecher.

NOW, when Christianity makes a gift to the poor, it cannot afford to pick off the meanest products of the tree, and say to them: "You are poor, and you can eat this worm-eaten fruit. When Christianity gives to the poor, it is bound to give them the best it has. Therefore, when you build missions for the poor, build them better than your own churches. When you open reading-rooms for the poor, make them more sumptuous then the reading-rooms which you open for yourselves and your children. Be more generous to the poor than you are to yourselves. That is the spirit of Christianity. Be more kind to them than you are to yourselves. That is the true inspiration of Christianity. And when men shall understand this, and begin to endow missions and reading-rooms for the poor — magnificently endow them, so that they will go on working hundreds and hundreds of years — they can afford to rest from their labor and go to heaven; for being dead, they shall speak in the things they have done, and carry comfort and encouragement and relaxation and knowledge to those who most need them. A man might well place before him in life this single ambition: "I will make myself so well off that I shall have enough to build a kind of home for the poor, so that when my family shall be scattered there shall be gathered a larger family whom I have blessed." Oh! how poor the vision of a life of pleasure seems in comparison and contrast with these munificent and noble ways of life!

Rev. H. W. Beecher.

WHEN, 'midst the strife of earthly life,
  We're sad and weary grown;
By care oppressed we long to rest,
  Where sorrows are unknown;
'Tis sweet to know, though life below
  Is but a fleeting day
Of smiles and tears and hopes and fears,
  "This, too, shall pass away."

Sad mourner here, does life seem drear?
  Have loved ones gone before?
Though life is gloom, beyond the tomb
  Friends meet to part no more;
Here partings come, but in that home
  There comes no parting day,
Though life below is full of wo,
  "This, too, shall pass away."

Aged pilgrim lone, thou'rt journeying on
  Toward a home on high,
Where fairest flowers in Eden bowers
  Shall never fade and die;

In that fair clime, no touch of time
  Takes youthful joys away —
Though sad and lone, and weary grown,
  "This, too, shall pass away."

When life is past, we hope at last
  To reach that heavenly shore,
And free from care, in mansions fair
  We'll dwell forever more —
In that blest home no sorrows come,
  And we shall never say
While with the blest we sweetly rest,
  "This, too, shall pass away."

W. H. H. Pearson.

AS a ship held by an anchor looks as though it were going out with the tide, yet never goes, so some souls that seem constantly to be getting nearer to Christ never come, because they are anchored and held by some secret sin.

ASK the father and the mother, weeping over the coffin of their first-born and only child, whether they regret that the child was born. Ask them the same question in after years, when that little life has come to be a thread of gold running through all their experiences. If they give an affirmative answer, I will be silent. No, my married friends — you who will shrink from accepting the choicest privileges bestowed upon you — you are wrong; and if you live, you will arrive at a period where you will see that there are rewards and punishments attached to this thing. What is to sustain you when in old age — the charms of youth all past, desire extinguished, and the grasshopper a burden — you sit at your lonely board, and think of the strangers who are to enjoy the fruit of your most fruitless life? Who are to feed the deadening affections of your heart, and keep life bright and desirable to its close, but the little ones whom you rear to manhood and womanhood? What is to reward you for the toils of life, if you do not feel that you — your thoughts, your blood, your influence — are to be continued in the future? Do you like the idea of having hirelings, or those who are anxious to get rid of you, about your dying bed? Is it not worth something to have a family of children whom you have reared, lingering about your grave, with tears on their cheeks and blessings on their lips — tears for a great loss, and blessings on the hallowed influence which has trained them in the path of duty, and directed them to life's noblest ends?

BAD thoughts are worse enemies than lions and tigers; for we keep out of the way of wild beasts, but bad thoughts win their way everywhere. The cup that is full will hold no more; keep your hearts full of good thoughts, that bad thoughts may find no room to enter.

"THOSE who have lost an infant are never, as it were, without an infant child. They are the only persons who, in one sense, retain it always, and they furnish other parents with the same idea. The other children grow up to manhood and womanhood, and suffer all the changes of mortality. This alone is rendered an immortal child."

WHEN our Lord sent out his disciples, he gave them what might be called a charge, the most striking sentence of which was: "Behold, I send you forth as sheep in the midst of wolves: be ye wise as serpents, and harmless as doves." We have an impression at times that our Master was one of those simple and transparent persons who are without tact in the adaptation of truth to times and seasons, but the prudence of our Lord was one of his most conspicuous traits.

When he first visited Jerusalem, he found that the Pharisees would persecute him to the death, so he went away. All through life, no one feature is more conspicuous than his nice foresight and wise discretion. He did not say to the disciples, "You have God's everlasting truth to declare, and you may speak without regard to consequences;" but, "I send you as sheep among wolves; under such circumstances, be ye wise as serpents." In our time, the serpent is the emblem of malignity, but with the ancients it was the emblem of wisdom. Christ says to his disciples, "In preaching, be wise, be closely wise, shrewdly wise, think, judge." The servant of the Lord is not at liberty to speak the truth under all circumstances. He is so to speak that men who will not hear on one side will hear on the other. Men call that worldly policy. It may become so, it may degenerate into that; but it is the duty of every man to employ his utmost sagacity, foresight, and prudence to nicely adapt himself to places, times, and circumstances. But you say: "May a man take advantage of the weakness of another?" "May a Christian do so?" Don't a mother take advantage of the weakness of her baby? Don't a teacher take advantage of the weakness of the boy to make him eager, right-minded, noble? You may not play upon a man's weakness to make him worse, but you may to make him better. We are to be all things to all men, if by any means we may save some. This is the law of nature and of conscience. There are some harum-scarum people, who go blundering splash dash, and think it means largeness. They think if they only speak the truth, they may go slam-bang into men.

A true man never employs another's weakness to serve himself. But for the sake of helping men, he may be ignorant with the ignorant, poor with the poor, under the law with those under the law. Those men have always done the most good who have been wise as serpents and harmless as doves.

You are not to be self-seeking. Goodness combined with tact, in the character of a person who is in places of trust, enables him to work in a wide field. What a chance for endeavor is given to such a man! What large conquests he can make, and, in the great harvest, what sheaves he can bring home!

MR. HALLIDAY asked: "If we may take advantage of others to benefit them, then may we not take advantage of others to benefit ourselves, if we do not injure them?"

MR. BEECHER.— That is dangerous; it is more manly to use one's own power. A man will be apt to blunt his sensibilities, and use them in ways that blunt them. If I want to carry a point in which I am very much interested, through a man whom I know to be sensible to praise, I go to him and pat him, and gradually begin to play upon his approbativeness till he feels praise without knowing it is praise; then if I go away, saying, "Poor fool! but I got what I went for," that is detestable. But suppose I know a man in danger of breaking his neck by a certain course. I have an instance in mind of a farmer in Marion County, Ind., who emigrated from Massachusetts. No man made butter and cheese that had a better repute than his. He was a good Presbyterian as I was, but he had refused to pay his subscription on account of some dissatisfaction. The minister had to leave, and the church was broken down. At last there was a revival, and the only stumbling-block in the way was my friend Adams. They came to me to see if I could not persuade him. When he came to see me, he said he did take his knife and cut his name out of the church-list because the minister did not prove as good as he pretended to be. I said to him: "There is a cheese-maker in the next town. Suppose he should make a contract with Harrison to bring him five hundred-weight of cheese. When he comes with his five-hundred weight of cheese, Harrison refuses to fulfil the contract, because his cheese is not as good as Adams's. Who does make as good cheese as yours in this country?"

"Wall, wall, I guess you're right."

He paid his subscription, became a good member of the church, and from it went into the kingdom of heaven. There is a case where I employed his weakness to excite his benevolence, and turned his vanity into a minister of righteousness. It is not the best way to work, but it is better than none. We are to use lower ranges of motive, and then go a step higher. It is better to do the best things through the best motives, but by any means we may win the man to God. For all the farms in the country, I would not have done as I did for my own advantage, but to save that man I would.

Rev. H. W. Beecher.

EDUCATION does not commence with the alphabet; it begins with a mother's look; a father's nod of approbation, or his sign of reproof; with a sister's gentle pressure of the hand, or a brother's noble act of forbearance; with a handful of flowers in green and daisy meadows; with a bird's nest admired, but not touched; with pleasant walks in shady lanes; and with thoughts directed, in sweet and kindly tones and words, to nature, to beauty, to acts of benevolence, to deeds of virtue, and to the source of all good — to God himself!

MEN'S lives should be like the day, more beautiful in the evening; or like the summer, aglow with promise; and the autumn, rich with the golden sheaves, where good works and deeds have ripened on the field.

THE less we expect from this world, the better for us. The less we expect from our fellow-men, whether of spiritual help or of inspiring example, the smaller will be our disappointment. He that leans on his own strength leans on a broken reed. We are always going to be something stronger, purer, and holier. Somewhere in the future there always hangs in the air golden ideal of a higher life that we are going to reach; but as we move on, the dream of better things moves on before us also. It is like the child's running over behind the hill to catch the rainbow. When he gets on the hill-top, the rainbow is as far off as ever. Thus does our day-dream of a higher Christian life keep floating away from us; and we are left to realize what frail, unreliable creatures we are when we rest our expectations of growth and of victory over evil in ourselves. "My soul, wait thou only upon God! My expectation is only from Him."

God never deceives us and never disappoints us. I do not say that God never allows us to be disappointed in our darling plans of life, in our children, or in our most cherished projects. What I mean is, that we are never disappointed in God. When we study the Almighty, whether in his glorious word or in nature, we find our utmost expectation overtopped by the stupendous and magnificent reality. Read such a book as *Ecce Cœlum*, and see if you are disappointed in your Creator. When, too, we obey God, we always find our reward, either sooner or later — just as surely as light comes with sunrise. When we trust God, he never deceives us. When we pray to him aright — that is with faith, with perseverance, with submissiveness, and with a single eye to God's will — he answers us. He always returns the best answer possible. Our heavenly Father makes no mistakes in his dealings with suppliants. He is a sovereign, but not a despot. If it pleases him to keep us waiting for the trial of our faith, then we must wait.

Rev. T. L. Cuyler.

www.ingramcontent.com/pod-product-compliance
Lightning Source LLC
LaVergne TN
LVHW010202110826
845151LV00002B/587

* 9 7 8 1 4 2 5 5 3 6 1 1 4 *